AUSTRIA, GERMANY, AND THE ANSCHLUSS

1931–1938

AUSTRIA, GERMANY, AND THE ANSCHLUSS
1931-1938

JÜRGEN GEHL

Foreword by
ALAN BULLOCK

London
OXFORD UNIVERSITY PRESS
NEW YORK TORONTO
1963

Oxford University Press, Amen House, London E.C.4

GLASGOW NEW YORK TORONTO MELBOURNE WELLINGTON
BOMBAY CALCUTTA MADRAS KARACHI LAHORE DACCA
CAPE TOWN SALISBURY NAIROBI IBADAN ACCRA
KUALA LUMPUR HONG KONG

*Printed in Great Britain
by Richard Clay & Co. Ltd.
Bungay, Suffolk*

PREFACE

This study is based on a doctoral dissertation which I wrote at St. Antony's College, Oxford. I wish to express my gratitude to the Warden, Mr. F. W. D. Deakin, and Fellows of St. Antony's, to Dr. Mandt and the University Society of Hamburg. I owe to them the opportunity of three years' study at Oxford. I am indebted to them not only for their generous assistance but also for making this period the most enjoyable of my career. I owe particular thanks to Mr. James Joll of St. Antony's for his valuable advice and encouragement while this book was being written.

I would like to acknowledge my debt to the staff of the Foreign Office Library in London; I am especially indebted to the Hon. Margaret Lambert and her staff in the German Documents section for their consideration and help. I want to thank Mr. Philip Windsor and Mr. Tony Nicholls, Merton and St. Antony's; Mr. John Whittam, Worcester and St. Antony's; and Mrs. Susan Alliston Moore for their help with the translation of the German documents, the checking of the typescript, and the editing.

The manuscript was completed in the summer of 1960. As far as I could I have taken later publications into consideration; but since this study is mainly based on the German, Austrian, and British documents it did not seem necessary to alter any conclusions which go beyond the available evidence.

JÜRGEN GEHL

FOREWORD

Hitler owed his success to his ability to combine complete opportunism in method and timing with remarkable consistency in his objectives. His annexation of Austria proves one of the best illustrations of the truth of this proposition. The opening paragraph of *Mein Kampf* begins:

It has turned out fortunate for me today that Destiny appointed Braunau on the Inn to be my birthplace. For that little town is situated just on the frontier between those two States the reunion of which seems, at least to us of the younger generation, a task to which we should devote our lives, and in the pursuit of which every possible means should be employed.

German Austria must be restored to the great German Motherland.

This was written in 1924 and Hitler, whose view of politics was formed by his upbringing and experiences in Austria, never altered his opinion. Fourteen years later, in March 1938, he put his words into effect, returning to Vienna in triumph to proclaim the incorporation of Austria in Greater Germany. His voice swelling with pride, he declared:

I believe that it was God's will to send a youth from here into the Reich . . . to raise him to be the leader of the nation so as to enable him to lead back his homeland into the Reich.

Yet, as Dr. Gehl conclusively shows, the decision to march German troops into Austria and annex it was a last minute improvisation.

At the beginning of February 1938 Hitler, who had only just emerged from the domestic crisis of the Fritsch affair, had no plan to bring German relations with Austria to a head. It was Papen who suggested the meeting with Schuschnigg, and as late as 26 February, a fortnight after the famous interview at Berchtesgaden, Hitler insisted to the Austrian Nazi leaders that the Austrian question must be solved by the political methods of pressure and penetration without the open use of force. Up to the last moment he was undecided whether to take the risk of sending his troops across the frontier.

The objective was never in doubt; Hitler meant to secure

control of Austria and make it part of Germany. But the timing
and the methods to be used were improvised on the spur of the
moment.

  In the pages that follow, Dr. Gehl has drawn upon the German
and Austrian records to provide the fullest and clearest account
yet published of the events of 1938 and he has linked these con-
vincingly to the earlier development of Nazi policy from the time
of the unsuccessful *putsch* of 1934. He brings out particularly well
the complex relationship between the part played by the Austrian
Nazi Party and German foreign policy, a classic case of one of
the most characteristic features of the politics of the last thirty
years, the use of a Fifth Column to undermine the resistance of a
state from within.

  But Dr. Gehl rightly takes his account of the Anschluss farther
back than Hitler's advent to power in 1933. For the idea of such a
union was not invented by the Nazis. As the sense of a common
German nationality grew in the nineteenth century and the
demand for political unification gained support, the question
was inevitably raised, whether the Germans living in Austria under
Habsburg rule were to be included or not. The decision between
those who sought to bring them into a *Grossdeutschland* and those
who would be content with a *Kleindeutsch* solution, excluding
them, was a major theme in the political debates of 1848–9.

  Bismarck would have nothing to do with a *Grossdeutschland*:
he saw too clearly its radical implications, the break up of the
multi-national Habsburg monarchy and the danger to the Prussian hegemony which he fastened on Germany. So the Germans
of Austria were excluded from Bismarck's unification. But the
idea of union persisted: among its advocates was Schoenerer
whom Hitler acknowledged as one of his political masters and
who was prepared to see the Habsburg empire broken up to
achieve it.

  By the end of 1918 the Habsburg empire was gone and the
greatest obstacle of the Anschluss of Austria with Germany removed. Post-war Austria was no more than the rump left when
the succession states had secured their independence. Vienna,
once the capital of an empire, now contained a third of the population of the whole country, and many Austrians saw their only

hope in throwing in their lot with Germany. But now there was a new obstacle: the determination of the French and their allies in central Europe to prevent Germany restoring her strength by the absorption of Austria. In the nineteen-twenties no German Government dared take the risk of closer links with Austria and Seipel, the dominant figure in Vienna, was strongly opposed to the whole idea of an Anschluss. It was only in 1931, with Seipel out of office and a German government anxious to assert itself in foreign policy – not least with an eye to the rising nationalist agitation marked by Hitler's success in the 1930 elections – that the two foreign ministers, Curtius and Schober, projected the plan of a customs union between their two countries.

It is at this point that Dr. Gehl begins his narrative. By doing so two years before the Nazis came to power he underlines the fact that Hitler's action in 1938 marked the end of a long historical chapter. The Austria which he annexed was only a part of the German speaking lands which had once been part of the Habsburg empire. When and how he would secure the rest, no one – including Hitler himself – could say. But the portents were clear: the *Grossdeutschland* programme, with Bohemia as the next stage, had found its executor.

ALAN BULLOCK

CONTENTS

ABBREVIATIONS

BrD   *Documents on British Foreign Policy* (London 1946 and fol-
      lowing).

GD   *German Documents,* unpublished; or published as *Documents
      on German Foreign Policy, 1918–1945* (London, 1949 and
      following).

IMT   *Trial of the Major War Criminals before the International
      Military Tribunal* (Nuremberg).

NCA *Nazi Conspiracy and Aggression* (Washington).

US   Papers Relating to the Foreign Relations of the United States
      (Washington, 1946 and following).

MAPS

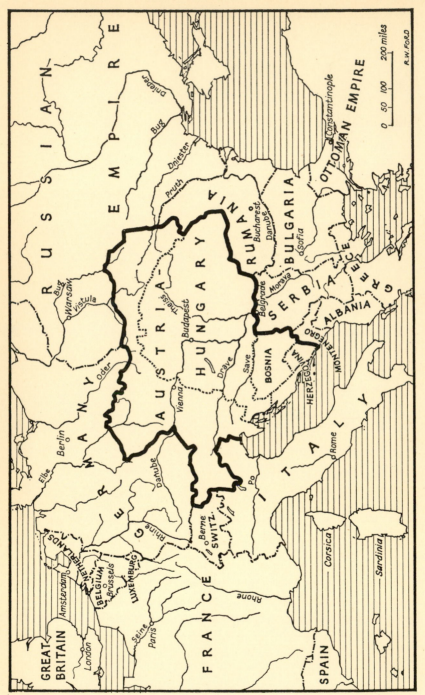

I. Austria–Hungary before the First World War

CHAPTER I

IMPACT OF THE PROJECTED AUSTRO-GERMAN CUSTOMS UNION ON EUROPEAN POLITICS, 1931

Nous n'avons pas perdu la guerre, car nous gagnerons l'Autriche.
Roger Peyrefitte, *Les Ambassades*

THE GENESIS OF THE CUSTOMS UNION PROPOSAL

On 14 October 1918, about a fortnight before the German High Command demanded an armistice, Ludendorff wrote to the German Foreign Ministry concerning Austria that 'the question is increasingly being discussed whether the time has not come to prepare the Anschluss with the German Reich'. Faced with military defeat and its consequences, the idea of a union between Germany and Austria might seem presumptuous. But Ludendorff's reasoning was partly right. The collapse and disintegration of the Austro-Hungarian Empire resulting from the First World War removed the major obstacle to an Anschluss: the different nationalities of which the Habsburg monarchy had been composed. 'There can be hardly any doubt,' pursued Ludendorff in his letter, 'that an Anschluss of the areas of German nationality will come about sooner or later. This development would be, after all, a valuable compensation, which we must not neglect, for the disappointments which the war brings us in other fields.'[1]

The German Foreign Ministry was too realistic to share this sort of optimism. 'The problem is not yet ripe for the adoption of a definite position,' State Secretary Solf replied evasively, whereas in his directives to the German ambassador in Vienna he was more outspoken. Thinking of the Anschluss as a consequence of the impending loss of the war meant, in the last analysis, the

[1] Ludendorff to State Secretary Solf, 14 October 1918, GD 7479/H187450–452; quoted in Arthur G. Kogan, 'Genesis of the Anschluss Problem: Germany and the Germans of the Hapsburg Monarchy in the Autumn of 1918,' *Journal of Central European Affairs*, Vol. XX, 1960, p. 29.

vivisection of Germany's ally. To State Secretary Solf the forth-coming peace conference seemed far more important. Germany's position should not be prejudiced by the policy for an Anschluss. A union with German Austria, he feared, 'would provide the Entente with justification for demanding territorial compensations'.[1]

The Allies, however, were far from having a common policy on the fate of the German part of the Austro-Hungarian Empire. Most articulate was the French desire for security. As French Foreign Minister Pichon reasoned, the Allies 'must see that Germany is not given an opportunity to rebuild her strength by utilizing the Austrian populations which remain outside of Czechoslovakia, Poland, and Jugoslavia'.[2] During the deliberations of the Allies on the Peace Settlement in Paris, Clemenceau demanded not only the prohibition of the Anschluss, but went a step further: Germany had to agree that Austria's independence would be inalienable. French demands for security clashed with President Wilson's principle of self-determination which should be applied in defining the new frontiers.[3] Clemenceau's and Wilson's principles merged in a compromise. Austria could unite with Germany provided the Council of the League of Nations gave its consent. Consequently, Article 80 of the Treaty of Versailles read:

Germany acknowledges and will respect strictly the independence of Austria, within the frontiers which may be fixed in a Treaty between that State and the Principal Allied and Associated Powers; she agrees that this independence shall be inalienable, except with consent of the Council of the League of Nations.

The Austria resulting from the Peace Settlement was not so much a newly created country as the remnant left after the frontiers of the adjacent states had been defined. The post-war population was about six and a half millions, nearly two millions of which were domiciled in Vienna. The capital, with its concentration of population, depended upon a system of banking, trade, and industry originally adapted to the requirements not of a small country but a great empire. The Germans, who had supplied

[1] Solf to Ludendorff, 14 October 1918, *Journal of Central European Affairs*, Vol. XX, 1960, pp. 31–34.
[2] Quoted by Margaret Ball, *Post-War German-Austrian Relations*, 1937, p. 20.
[3] *Les Délibérations du Conseil des Quatre*; Notes de l'Officier Interprête Paul Mantoux, Paris 1955, pp. 461–462.

the services of the middle class and dominated industry and banking, as well as diplomacy, the army, and administrations, had lost
their functions. With the creation of the successor states and their
high tariff barriers, Austrian industry lost the possibility of
exporting to her former provinces.

In 1922 Austria's financial situation had become desperate and
her inability to restore her economic equilibrium was generally
recognized. At this moment the League of Nations came to her
aid. A loan of 650 million gold crowns was raised and guaranteed
by the governments of Great Britain, France, Italy, and Czechoslovakia. The Protocol No. 1 of Geneva, which regulated the
terms of the loan, reflects the political situation of Austria.[1] The
guaranteeing powers, anxious to prevent any one of them from
exploiting Austria's weak position, promised to respect her
political independence and territorial integrity. United in their
desire that Austria should not be allowed to associate with Germany, Austria again had to undertake not to alienate her independence and to 'abstain from any negotiations or from any
economic or financial engagement calculated directly or indirectly
to compromise this independence'. This obligation revealed her
inability to be self-sufficient. Her financial need had furnished the
Powers with a further opportunity to veto the Anschluss. Thus
Austria's independence was based on her weakness rather than on
her strength.

However strong the feeling for an Anschluss in Austria was,
the German governments of the early post-war period were em-
barrassed by it. The primary task was to settle the reparations
question and to lead Germany back into the community of equal
nations. This aim had as a precondition good relations with
France. The prospects of a union could only arouse French suspicion and reinforce her search for security. Postponement of all
attempts for an Anschluss, combined with consideration for
public feelings therefore dictated the conduct of German policy.
Foreign Minister Stresemann explained in a private letter to
Reichstagspräsident Loebe, an ardent supporter of the Anschluss,
that being united in their ultimate aims in the Anschluss problem,
the question was which means were the most practical. 'We are

---

[1] League of Nations. *Restoration of Austria*. Agreements arranged by the
League of Nations and signed at Geneva on 4 October 1922, with the Relevant
Documents and Public Statements, pp. 39–40.

surrounded today by opponents of an Anschluss in a circle which extends from Warsaw through the Little Entente to Rome, Paris, and London,' Stresemann expounded. 'Without the consent of these countries, who play the leading role in the League of Nations, the Anschluss is impossible. The first consideration seems to me to avoid everything in the Anschluss question which could irritate these countries and increase their hostility to the project.'[1]

The popular movement in Germany and Austria for an Anschluss nevertheless made the French government determined to protect the status quo and to reopen the question of French security. It saw two ways of sidestepping the danger of an Anschluss. The first one pointed to Vienna and consisted in incorporating Austria into a Danubian Confederation of all successor states of the Habsburg Empire; the second pointed to Berlin, demanding from Germany the maintenance of the status quo. The French governments tried both means.

In 1927 Paris attempted to initiate a Danubian Confederation. Stresemann regarded this attempt as the first step towards the restoration of the Habsburg Empire, which he was at all costs determined to prevent. Convinced of the impossibility of an Anschluss at this time, Stresemann considered a customs union with Austria as the only immediate alternative to an Anschluss, and as the best countermeasure to the French initiative. When he visited Vienna in November 1927 he told Seipel, the Austrian Chancellor, that Austria should not be forced for economic reasons into a union with the successor states of the Habsburg monarchy. The creation of closer economic ties, he stated plainly, and as a result a customs union between Germany and Austria, could no longer be delayed.[2] But Seipel, during these years the decisive voice in Austrian politics, rejected the proposal. In contrast to Stresemann he opposed the Anschluss for fundamental and not only tactical reasons. Stresemann left Vienna disappointed.

---

[1] Stresemann to Loebe, GD, 3086/614131.

[2] Minutes of the Austro-German meeting, GD, 3086/D614239–260. This leaves no doubt as to the authorship of the projected Austro-German customs union, which had been a subject of controversy, see Craig, *From Bismark to Adenauer*, 1958, p. 96. Stambrook in 'The German–Austrian Customs Union Project of 1931; A Study of German Methods and Motives': *Journal of Central European Affairs*, 21: pp. 15–44 (1961), gives a very valuable account of the diplomatic preparations for the projected customs union. He seems to ignore, however, that the first initiative was taken by Stresemann.

The second way of obtaining from Berlin a final renunciation of the Anschluss was explored soon after the question of the Western frontiers had been settled at Locarno. French policy aimed at a ruling on the Eastern frontiers and the Anschluss similar to that already obtained for the Western. Paris was the more concerned about this in that the limitation of a settlement of the Western frontiers implied the possibility of a revision of the Eastern. The German government might well interpret it in this fashion.

Therefore the plan of the French Foreign Minister, Briand, of 5 September 1929, for European federal union, should be seen as an expression of the French government's concern to stabilize the actual international situation. While France's allies, Poland and the Little Entente, welcomed the plan without hesitation, it was received by the other European powers with reserve. Italy feared that Briand's scheme would perpetuate the status quo and establish a federation, not of free sovereign states, but of satellites under French domination. The Italian Government was determined to reject it.[1] In English circles, too, it was suspected that 'Briand's European Association would set a further seal on the sanctity of the present territorial and political organisation of Europe'.[2] The German government, with its principal aim of a revision of the Versailles settlement, had even stronger reasons for objection. Assuming that the political idea underlying Briand's memorandum was the recognition of the national frontiers as at present drawn, Berlin emphasized that no German government could consider Germany's frontiers as fixed for all time. The German government welcomed the aspect of closer economic co-operation, but saw no need to subordinate the economic to political considerations as proposed in the French memorandum.

The German government pursued its own independent schemes. Seipel's resistance to a customs union did not make Berlin forget the project. It waited for a change of policies in Vienna. This was brought about when Schober was made Austrian Chancellor in September 1929. Supported by the moderate groups of the bourgeois parties, he decided to pursue a more pro-German foreign policy. He lent a sympathetic ear to the

---

[1] Report of the British Ambassador in Rome, 30 May 1930. BrD, 2nd Ser. Vol. I, No. 190.
[2] Memorandum on Briand's proposal, ibid., No. 189.

B

former Austrian Minister in Berlin, Riedl, who had already inspired Stresemann's idea and who now brought Schober round to the view that the only way to defend the Austrian economy was a customs union with Germany. There was much evidence to support this view. In 1930 Germany had six years of economic recovery behind her. Austria on the other hand had been plagued by permanent unemployment and continuous economic crisis. The idea of sharing her neighbour's growing prosperity was tempting to Austria.

When Schober, during his visit to Berlin in February 1930, proposed to go ahead with a customs union he found an immediate response.[1] As for the first time since the war the internal situation in Austria favoured such a union, Berlin was determined to make the most of the chance. This conviction was reinforced by incoming reports that if Schober's advance failed Austria would be forced to turn to other countries, and that Czechoslovakia was ready to step into the breach.[2] Curtius, now in charge of the German Foreign Ministry, regarded himself as the executor of Stresemann's policy, which corresponded with his own. In 1927, as *Reichswirtschaftsminister*, he had actively helped to prepare a customs union with Austria and, as he later emphasized, he would have taken the initiative had Schober not done so himself.[3]

The governmental crisis in Vienna in autumn 1930 interrupted these attempts at a rapprochement. The newly formed government with Seipel as Foreign Minister dropped the plan. It was only after Ender had become Austrian Chancellor in November 1930, with Schober as his Foreign Minister, that contact with Berlin was re-established.

In the meantime Franco-German relations had considerably deteriorated. Both governments found themselves under strong pressure from the right-wing parties. The Young plan, which should have brought a final settlement of the reparation problem, had met with severe criticism from the nationalist parties. A decisive change in French policy was caused by the German Reichstag elections in September 1930 and the success of the National

[1] Minutes of the Austro-German meetings on 22 and 24 February 1930 in Berlin, GD, 3086/D614750–776.

[2] Report from the German Embassy in Vienna, 20 February 1930, GD, K49/4863.

[3] Curtius, *Sechs Jahre Minister*, pp. 107, 119; *Bemühung um Österreich*, p. 24.

Socialists. The conciliatory spirit of Locarno was exhausted. It had nourished two complementary illusions. In Paris it seemed to imply the confirmation of the Peace Treaty. For Berlin it was the first step towards the end of Versailles. 'French public opinion,' reported the German Ambassador from Paris, 'is realizing that we are now on the threshold of a new stage in Franco-German relations, and that the period, which started in spring 1924, has come to an end.'[1]

Thus the German government found itself under pressure from two sources. Paris demanded a renunciation of revisionism, and the nationalist opposition stressed the dictatorial nature of Versailles. The parties advocating a fulfilment of the peace treaty obligations regarded the elections of September 1930 as a sharp vote of censure on their policy. The success of the National Socialists was calculated to stimulate the government to a forward foreign policy. In these straits Curtius decided to withdraw from the policy of Locarno. 'New ways had to be explored.'[2]

In fact Curtius decided that the projected Austro-German customs union should be carried through even against French resistance. When he went to Vienna for the final negotiations from 3 to 5 March 1931 his attitude had completely changed. Whereas in February 1930 he had still intended to wait for a favourable opportunity to act, the projected customs union now became the first consideration in German policy. It would reveal whether a German policy independent of Paris was possible or not, and consequently became the vehicle of German revisionism.

After Berlin and Vienna had reached basic agreement, the German cabinet met on 16 and 18 March 1931 to discuss the plan. Curtius underlined that the Austrian government, having been hesitant until now, had finally accepted the idea of a customs union and overcome the difficulties within Austrian official circles. Austria had at last abandoned all thoughts of a Danubian Confederation. The situation was to be exploited. Politically it was not yet the moment for an Anschluss; economically it was favourable for a decisive advance.[3] The German cabinet followed

---

[1] von Hoesch's report, 11 October 1930, GD, 2406/D58848.
[2] Curtius, *Sechs Jahre Minister*, pp. 108, 109.
[3] Minutes of the German cabinet meetings on 16 and 18 March 1931, GD, K49/K5266–72.

Curtius's reasoning and on 18 March it unanimously accepted his proposal.

As with the customs union Germany was going to assert herself for the first time since the war in the field of foreign affairs independently of the Allies, the most important question was how they could overcome French objections based on the Treaties. In Article 88 of the Treaty of St. Germain Austria had engaged herself to abstain 'from any act which might directly or indirectly or by any means whatever compromise her independence'. In the Geneva protocol of 1922 the Austrian government agreed 'to abstain from any negotiations or from any economic or financial engagement calculated directly or indirectly to compromise Austrian independence', and also to refrain from 'granting to any State a special régime or exclusive advantages which could threaten Austrian economic independence'.

Since on the other hand Austria's obligations should 'not prevent her from maintaining her freedom in all matters relating to her economic régime or her commercial relations', Austria regarded herself entitled to conclude a customs union with Germany, provided that her independence was safeguarded. Every precaution was taken to preserve that freedom. (1) In the guiding principles of the Austro-German customs union project it was laid down that there were to be no common bodies; the Customs Administration in each country was to be independent of that of the other. (2) Both countries were prepared to conclude an agreement on the same basis with any other European state. (3) Provision was made that the treaty could be denounced at any time upon one year's notice, except during the first three years.[1]

It was certain that according to French opinion a customs union was incompatible with Austria's obligations, the argument being that her independence was endangered. The different interpretations of the Geneva Protocol of 1922 and Article 88 of the Treaty of St. Germain masked the underlying political controversy. With the attempt to circumvent French arguments by the inclusion of certain clauses which secured Austria's independence, the German government tried to fight a political battle on a legal field. Curtius, himself a lawyer, might well feel at home on this ground.

[1] For the working out of the details of the draft between Ritter and Schueller see Ritter's note on the negotiations, 7 January 1931, GD, K49/K5109–15.

Politically Berlin and Vienna hoped to overcome French resistance by bringing forward their project within the framework of Pan-European schemes as the only way of turning Briand's plan of European Federation to their advantage. The proclamation of their project in the name of Europe, they hoped, would remove French fears that the customs union served only to extend German influence. As the first principle, therefore, Curtius and Schober laid down that the treaty was destined to mark 'the beginning of a new order of European economic conditions on lines of regional agreements'.

Through the German adoption of Briand's initiative in the form of a customs union the proposal for European union lost for the French whatever attraction it may have once possessed. The customs union constituted in fact a counterplan. Hauser's argument that the customs union was a test-case for the French European spirit and that France could have taken advantage of the Austro-German action, by accepting the offer of participation,[1] seems somewhat academic. Briand's memorandum of May 1930 was strictly opposed to regional agreements. It says:

The policy of European union implies in fact a conception absolutely contrary to that which may have determined formerly, in Europe, the formation of customs unions tending to abolish internal customs houses in order to erect on the boundaries a more rigorous barrier, that is to say, to constitute in fact an instrument of struggle against States situated outside of those unions.[2]

The customs union embodies Berlin's primary objections to Briand's plan, its unwillingness to subordinate the economic to political consideration. The Germans and the Austrians tried to obviate the French initiative. They hoped to initiate European economic union without the corresponding political implications of Briand's proposal. Though their offer of participation was made in good faith they could hardly, for the same reason, expect the French to co-operate. They had no illusions on this score. During their final negotiations Schueller asked Ritter if he seriously considered the inclusion of other countries, and Ritter

[1] Hauser, 'Der Plan einer deutsch-österreichischen Zollunion von 1931 und die europäische Föderation', *Historische Zeitschrift* 1955 (179), p. 59.
[2] League of Nations. *Documents relating to the Organization of a System of European Federal Union*, pp. 7–14.

replied that the participation of other countries was mainly envisaged to get round the objection that Austria's independence
was not safeguarded.[1] State Secretary von Bülow was even more
outspoken, when he mentioned the forthcoming project. 'It is
possible,' he conceded, 'that it may lead to political conflicts,
although we will dress the whole matter up in a Pan-European
cloak.'[2]

France, with her military and financial superiority in question,
thought it absolutely essential to raise the political problem before
entering on economic co-operation. The name of Europe, in
which Briand's plan and the Austro-German customs union were
proclaimed, could not disguise that ultimately the schemes were
directed against each other: European union step by step in the
form of regional agreements on one side, and European union by
a single act with the implied French hegemony on the other.

THE REACTION OF THE EUROPEAN POWERS

As far as the diplomatic procedure was concerned, Curtius and
Schober decided not to consult other governments beforehand.[3]
They feared immediate French resistance when their plan became
known and thought it best to keep it secret.[4] Berlin informed its
embassies about the forthcoming project[5] for the first time on 12
March 1931. Only the British ambassador was allowed to know,
on 13 March, that Curtius had discussed the creation of a customs
union with the Austrian government during his visit to Vienna on
3 March.[6] Curtius and Schober agreed not to surprise the other
countries with a *fait accompli*, but to announce only principles of
a customs union, leaving the details of the treaty subject to later
negotiations. They thought it best to publish the project at the

[1] Ritter's note, 7 January 1931, GD, K49/K5110.
[2] Bülow to Prittwitz, 20 January 1931, GD, 4620/E199138–44, quoted by
Stambrook, op. cit., p. 33.
[3] Edward W. Bennet, *Germany and the Diplomacy of the Financial Crisis, 1931*.
Harvard University Press, Cambridge, 1962, gives a detailed and very valuable
study of the 1931 period. The book appeared after the completion of this study
but the author seems to arrive at the same conclusions where the major events
are concerned.
[4] Curtius's report, 16 January 1931, GD, 3086H/D614924.
[5] Telegram to the German embassies, 12 March 1931, GD, 3086H/D614971.
[6] Rumbold's report, 13 March 1931, BrD, 2nd Ser., Vol. II, No. 358. The
British government did not, however, react. Von Bülow's note on the conversation, GD, 3086H/D614972.

session of the commission for European union at the beginning of May as a 'contribution towards the economic federation of Europe'.

A leakage in Vienna destroyed this plan. As early as 6 March the Pester Lloyd in Budapest wrote that it was no secret in well-informed circles that the question of a customs union had been discussed between Curtius and Schober. This article seems to have attracted little attention at the time. Beneš, however, got secret information direct from Vienna on 13 March about the Austrian and German intentions and forwarded it instantly to Briand and there seems little doubt that this information came from Austrian officials who were opposed to the project.[1] On 17 March, before the German and Austrian cabinets had accepted the project, the *Neue Freie Presse* in Vienna declared that an Austro-German customs union was certain to be announced in the immediate future. These leakages were the first blow to the project.

Berlin and Vienna were forced into the open. They could not wait for the session of the commission for European union in May as they had intended. They had to take immediate steps for an announcement on 21 March. But the initiative had passed to Paris. The French government acted swiftly. On 14 March Briand approached the German ambassador, von Hoesch, and offered instantaneous financial help in return for recognition of the status quo.[2] When the German government indicated that it could not make any concessions of this kind, Berthelot became more concrete and urged strongly the acceptance of the French offer. He proposed that Germany should renounce, in return for the proposed French credits, all categorical demands, especially her rights arising from the Young plan. As this proposal coincided with the information in Paris about the customs union – and in view of Berthelot's insistence – it can be assumed that this was already the first French counteraction, though we do not have conclusive evidence. In the meantime the Czechoslovakian Ambassador in Vienna made a last attempt on 18 March to forestall the consent of the Austrian cabinet by declaring that strong

[1] Beneš to Regendanz, 2 April 1931, Regendanz letter to von Bülow, 4 April 1931, GD, K50/K5752. The date when Beneš obtained the information is not absolutely certain. Beneš said only that he was informed 'eight days before the publication'.

[2] von Hoesch's report, 14 March 1931, GD, 5881H/E430341.

pressure would be brought to bear on Austria if it accepted the project.[1]

Before Berlin and Vienna could approach the other governments, Paris had already informed them of the Austro-German initiative. The Italian government complained bitterly that it found itself under French pressure without having information from the Germans.[2] The French government had also obtained information to the effect that the project was going to be announced on 21 March. It tried to counteract this move by a united *démarche* of the four powers, France, England, Italy, and Czechoslovakia, which had signed the protocol of Geneva in 1922. But this attempt to suppress the plan in its first phase failed.

Italian relations with Germany had gradually improved since Locarno. French hegemony in central Europe presented a greater danger than German. Mussolini refused therefore to take part in the French counteraction. He welcomed the Austro-German project 'as a hopeful sign for the European economy'.[3] He instructed his Foreign Minister, Grandi, to arrive at a direct agreement with the Germans and informed Schober that the Italian government would review the case objectively.[4] At this early stage he was more inclined to favour than to oppose the project.

The German government could hope that the economic union with Austria, far less ambitious than the Anschluss, would meet with no obstacles from the British. The British government was aware of the danger in which the German government found itself, being under pressure from right and left extremists. The British ambassador Rumbold had repeatedly stressed the fact that the political and economic state of affairs was more serious than at any time since the war, and that the German government needed success in its foreign policy.[5] The British government considered it, therefore, its policy to give the German government such support as it properly could, in order to fortify Brüning's position.[6] To increase his position and to bring him,

[1] Ritter's note on a telephone conversation with Vienna, 18 March 1931, GD, 3086H/D614976.
[2] von Schober's report, 23 March 1931, ibid., D615062.
[3] Quoted in Salvemini, *Mussolini Diplomatico*, p. 344.
[4] Stockton's report, 26 March 1931, US, 1931, vol. I, p. 573; Stimson's memorandum, 26 March 1931, ibid., p. 570.
[5] BrD, 2nd Ser., Vol. I, No. 332, 344, 346, 353.
[6] Henderson to Rumbold, 19 February 1931, ibid., No. 350.

as Rumbold put it, 'out of the cold' the British government, early in March 1931, invited Brüning and Curtius for a private visit to Chequers on 1 May 1931. Henderson informed Briand of this invitation and Briand agreed that the visit would be advantageous.

The immediate reaction of the Labour government to the projected customs union corresponded with its policy hitherto. As Labour was strictly opposed to secret diplomacy, the British government criticized the privacy with which the Austro-German negotiations had been conducted over a year. The British Foreign Office did not think, however, that the German and Austrian governments intended to raise the Anschluss question in the near future, nor that a violation of the Treaties was involved. Lord Tyrrel, British ambassador in Paris, reported that the French protest seemed 'to have been somewhat hastily made on the basis of inadequate information'.[1] In the British Foreign Office it was argued that a defeat of the project would embarrass German feeling and be grist to the mill of the National Socialists.[2] Henderson declared, before he left on 23 March for a meeting of the Preparatory European Commission in Paris, that he personally welcomed the assimilation of customs and economic conditions.[3] France had lost the first round.

She could not submit to this failure. With Germany establishing herself for the first time in foreign policy, more was at stake than an economic union between Germany and Austria. French predominance in Europe had been challenged and French security depended upon the status quo. Both Briand and Curtius had personally taken positions from which retreat was impossible without personal defeat. In public opinion their names had become identified with the plan. Briand was the more susceptible to criticism, since only three weeks before the publication of the customs union he had dismissed publicly the danger of an Anschluss. Briand's opponents were not slow to point the lesson. 'Everybody is allowed to let himself be deceived,' wrote *Le Journal des Débats*, 'but not on this point, especially if he is in charge of the foreign policy.' The economic Anschluss was

[1] 27 March 1931, BrD, 2nd Ser., Vol. II, No. 16.

[2] von Neurath's report, 25 March, GD, 3086H/D615120; Vansittart's and Rumbold's reports, 24/26 March 1931, BrD, 2nd Ser., Vol. II, No. 14 and footnote 2.

[3] Henderson to von Neurath, report, 23 March 1931, GD, K49/K5472.

regarded in French nationalist circles as the final result of Briand's Pan-European fancies.[1]

The question was which lever France should apply in order to bring the British and Italian governments into line. The negotiations for a Franco-Italian naval agreement provided an ideal opportunity. In early March 1931 these discussions had been taking place for nearly a year and were approaching a conclusion. The British Foreign Secretary, Henderson, acting as an ardent mediator, had been travelling between Paris and Rome and had made the terms of the agreement acceptable to Briand. On 1 March the terms of the 'bases of agreement' arrived at between the three powers were made public. An early meeting of the drafting committee to elaborate the final text of the naval agreement was planned.

Thus, by using the disarmament situation, Briand could establish a firmer grip upon the foreign policies of London and Rome, which were not directly interested in the Franco-German clash. When, on 19 March, the drafting committee for the naval agreement met, the British and Italian experts found their French colleagues unusually reserved. The French suddenly found fault with the interpretation of the clauses in the 'bases of agreement'. And on 21 March, the same day as the French and Czechoslovakian governments delivered their *démarches* in Vienna against the customs union without British and Italian co-operation, the drafting committee in London had to suspend its sittings because agreement could not be reached.[2]

This unforeseen setback put the Italian Foreign Minister Grandi into a difficult position. Having fought against great odds for the agreement, he thought it impossible to explain to the Italian Senate that the settlement had again been altered to the detriment of Italy. In this situation Mussolini had the alternative of either striking a bargain with the Germans, thus antagonizing the French, or regaining French co-operation in the naval discussions by opposing the customs union. Following Mussolini's instructions Grandi explored the first alternative. In his negotiations with Berlin he insisted on Austria's role as a necessary

[1] Berthelot to von Hoesch, von Hoesch's report, 21 March 1931, GD, K49/K5355.
[2] Claudel and Grandi mentioned, independently of each other, to Stimson that the projected Austro-German customs union had caused the failure of the naval conference. Memoranda of Stimson, 28 May and 9 July 1931, US 1931, Vol. I, pp. 500, 540.

buffer-state between Italy and Germany. The Italian press, he told Curtius, regarded the projected Austro-German customs union as a deliberate action against the incipient Franco-Italian understanding in London.[1] But Grandi's protest was only meant to raise the price. For suitable German concessions, Grandi intimated, Italy would give up her non-committal attitude and come down on the German side.

The Germans had neither political nor economic gifts to offer and tried to avoid the impression that they were wooing Italian patronage. Grandi thereupon succeeded in persuading Mussolini to change his mind and to lend his support to the French counter-action. As a result of Rome's new policy the French attitude in the naval negotiations became more conciliatory and a positive result appeared likely.

On the other hand, by torpedoeing the naval agreement the French had struck British policy, and especially Foreign Secretary Henderson, at the most vulnerable point. Henderson was regarded as 'the most earnest advocate of disarmament in Europe'. Moreover, he had according to the British ambassador in Washington, Lindsay, 'a simple mind but when he took hold of an idea he hung to it with great determination'.[2] Germany's desire for revision could not deflect Henderson from his path. Disarmament and, as a logical consequence, the French demand for security had to precede any alteration in the status quo. Already in December 1930 Henderson had warned the German government that the new, more active policy in the question of revision would force the British government on to the side of the French. Its policy was to fortify Briand's position, which depended largely upon a continuation of the German course hitherto followed.[3] Henderson stressed that if the Germans sincerely desired the maximum reduction of armaments, they would do everything in their power to dissipate the distrust which would inevitably react on the negotiations for disarmament.[4]

When on 23 March, Henderson went to Paris to attend the meeting of the organization committee of the commission for European union, Briand had the chance to play the trump of

---

[1] Memoranda of Curtius, 15/22 May 1931, GD, 3147/662062/662181.
[2] Stimson's memoranda, 28 May 1931, U.S. 1931, Vol. I, p. 500.
[3] Rumbold to Curtius, 11 December 1930, GD, 3086H/D509074.
[4] Henderson to Rumbold, 12 February 1931, BrD, 2nd Ser., Vol. I, No. 348.

disarmament. Henderson was much impressed by the reaction which the customs union had caused in Paris. He did not share Briand's opinion that the customs union was identical with the Anschluss. Nor had he any objections against the customs union as such. But he thought that the political considerations involved dominated the whole problem. The manner of the announcement was in his opinion most unfortunate and the moment inopportune.[1] The success of the Franco-Italian naval discussions meant more to him as he saw in them a welcome precedent for the general disarmament conference which was planned for February 1932 and for which Henderson was to be chosen as president in May 1931. Briand had no difficulty in persuading Henderson to lend his full support to the French against the customs union. Henderson lost no time in sending the necessary instructions to the British Ambassador in Berlin:

The German government should be under no misapprehension as to the serious misgivings which have been aroused by their action in many countries and in France in particular. In this connexion the position of M. Briand has become one of great difficulty, and the influence which he has only at great trouble been able to exercise for many years past in controlling more extreme tendencies among his own countrymen will be unquestionably affected. I should regard this as contrary to the consolidation of peace which I, in concert with the German government, am anxious to preserve.[2]

France had reaffirmed the premise upon which Austrian independence was based; the unity of France, Great Britain, and Italy in face of Germany.

THE CUSTOMS UNION BEFORE THE LEAGUE

Henderson's immediate intention was to prevent a *fait accompli*; ultimately he hoped to scotch the whole project. In order to achieve the first purpose he proposed, on 25 March, to refer the whole question to the League of Nations and suggested that the Germans and Austrians should not advance further with their negotiations before the League Council could form its opinion. Berlin objected to this procedure. It refused to admit an

---

[1] Atherton's report, 11 June 1931, US, 1931, Vol. I, p. 423. Henderson to von Neurath, 16 April, BrD, 2nd Ser., Vol. II, No. 27.
[2] BrD, 2nd Ser., Vol. II, No. 5.

examination of the project by the League from a political stand-point as it was in its opinion of a purely economic character. It was determined to continue the struggle on a judicial and not on a political ground. This gave Henderson the chance for a com-promise. He replied, on 26 March, that the German govern-ment did not seem to have understood his proposal rightly. In fact an examination by the League Council would only involve the legal question. As the Council would be reluctant to pro-nounce on such a question, the procedure would result in the de-mand for an advisory opinion from the Permanent Court of International Justice. To this the Germans tacitly agreed. And on 10 April Henderson requested the Secretary-General of the League to insert the Austro-German customs union in the agenda of the session on 18 May for an examination by the League Council itself.

The second more important demand, to refrain from any negotiations on the project, was rejected by Berlin. Chancellor Brüning replied that the negotiations must naturally take their course. Germany had only few rights. If she were going to be checked at every turn the position of his government would be-come untenable. If he were to give way, he would be accused by all parties of yielding to foreign pressure in a legitimate question.[1]

Similar pressure on Austria had better results. Schober wished to have it both ways. He wanted to obtain the advantages of co-operation with Germany, but he was anxious not to estrange France and Great Britain, from the former of whom he hoped before long to obtain the second part of the Austrian loan. As he wanted to retain the goodwill of the two countries the hostile reception accorded to the Austro-German project shook his determination.[2] Accordingly Schober searched for a way out without offending either side. He tried to label Berlin as the main initiator by pointing out that no Austrian government could have resisted the German offer, thus minimizing the part he had played in the preparation. The demand not to proceed further with the project provided the Austrian government with the solution it needed in this situation. It could still remain faithful to the

[1] Rumbold's reports, 25 and 27 March, BrD, 2nd Ser., Vol. II, No. 7, 8, 17.
[2] von Hoesch's report, 26 April 1931, GD, 5881H/E430353. Henderson to Rumbold, 31 March 1931, ibid., No. 15.

Austro-German plan. On the other side it was able to satisfy, at least partly, the French and English wishes.[1]

In accordance with this policy Schober declared that he could not understand Germany's unwillingness to allow the matter to be discussed by the League Council in May. He refused to follow the German lead. When the Germans urged that the discussions about the details of the agreement should be continued the Austrian government replied that it did not want to expose itself to more criticism.[2] Schober promised the French and British governments definitely not to begin with negotiations before the meeting of the League Council on 17 May. As it takes two to make a bargain the Austrian concession was sufficient to stop a further German advance.

In the meantime Henderson pursued his ultimate aim. He hoped to persuade the Germans to drop their plan. As the British lawyers expected that the court's decision would be in favour of the Germans, Henderson intimated that the Germans should not 'insist upon their pound of flesh'. The British government tried to devise a scheme which would satisfy everybody. This plan on a more general pattern should offer Austria and Germany a substitute. On 1 May Henderson defined in seven points his future policy, which amounted to the request that Germany and Austria should put forward alternative proposals.[3]

But nothing came of this. Henderson's initiative for an alternative raised the old difficulties. A broader scheme demanded French co-operation and would lead to the former setback. Berlin refused to comply with Henderson's proposal as it saw no point in giving up the present plan in exchange for a vague hope. The German reply was uncompromising:

They had no alternative plan; consequently they could not put forward any other proposals; the attitude of the German government all through would be one of rigid adherence to the legal aspect of the case, whether the final verdict went in their favour or not.[4]

But Henderson's action accorded with French tactics. As Paris could not suppress the project in its first stage, all it wanted was

[1] Sir Eric Phipps's reports, BrD, 2nd Ser., Vol. II, No. 6, 9, 10, 23, 24, 25.

[2] Ritter's note about his conversation with Schueller, 15 April 1931, GD, K49/K5522.

[3] Henderson to Rumbold, 1 May 1931, BrD, 2nd Ser., Vol. II, No. 29; enclosure in No. 36.

[4] Thelwall's memorandum, 6 May 1931, ibid., enclosure in No. 34.

an opportunity to bring efficient pressure to bear on Austria and Germany. The reference of the customs union to the League Council was not an end in itself, but a pretext to win the necessary time for a counteraction. The French government was determined, whether or not the customs union violated the letter of Austria's existing obligations, to secure the abandonment of the project.[1]

The secondary French object was to keep the British policy in conformity with its own. The visit of Brüning and Curtius to Chequers, planned for 1 May, was a thorn in the French side. Paris was afraid the Germans could influence the British government in their favour. On 4 April Briand suggested postponing the meeting at Chequers until after the session of the League Council, in view of the controversies about the Austro-German scheme. The British Foreign Office had already been frightened lest the visit would make trouble with France and was therefore willing to comply with Briand's wish. The new date for the German visit was fixed for 5–9 June.

Coinciding with Henderson's intiative for a German alternative scheme, the French government brought forward its own counterplan on 27 April. It could not remain content with a purely negative approach. The main argument in favour of the Austro-German project being an economic one, the French government developed a *plan constructif* to give them the relief they claimed to obtain from the customs union. The main purpose of the *plan constructif* was, however, to check the influence which the customs union was going to have on the Little Entente, and which was one of the declared aims of the Austro-German project. It put the solidarity of the Little Entente on trial. The danger for it derived from its very character. Czechoslovakia, Yugoslavia, and Rumania had formed the Little Entente to preserve the existing order in Central Europe. Czechoslovakia had the strongest interest in its function. Surrounded on three sides by the formerly hostile states of Germany, Austria, and Hungary, it was placed in a more critical position than the others.

Though the countries of the Little Entente were united in their intention to maintain the status quo and to prevent a restoration of the Habsburg monarchy, their emphasis on these aims differed according to their geographical position. While they had a

[1] Lord Tyrrel's report (Paris), 27 March 1931, BrD, 2nd Ser., Vol. II, No. 16.

common interest in resisting the demands of the Hungarian revisionists the Anschluss played a minor role for Yugoslavia and was still less important for Rumania. Nor was there a marked unity of policy towards the great neighbouring states, France, Italy, and Germany. Only after considerable effort and through the persuasion of Beneš did France succeed in extending her treaty system to Yugoslavia and Rumania, and in making the Little Entente a French instrument against Germany.

The customs union threatened this arrangement. Yugoslavia and Rumania being politically bound to France were, on purely economic grounds, more attracted by Germany. Both countries met with great difficulties in finding markets for their surplus agricultural products. Germany as a highly industrial country offered a solution to their problems. They looked at participation in the Austro-German customs union from a different standpoint to that of Czechoslovakia, because their political relations with France were less intimate.

Opinion within the Yugoslav government was for this reason split over which policy to follow. A part regarded support for Germany, or at least neutrality, as advantageous. The Yugoslav Prime Minister Marinkovitch, on the other hand, thought it essential to support the French policy, reasoning that Yugoslavia depended financially and in armament deliveries on France, and he offered his resignation should the cabinet not agree with this course.[1] He realized, however, that the Austro-German project gave him a good bargaining position in his negotiations for a French loan.

The Rumanian government especially welcomed the economic aspects of the customs union. It was already negotiating with the German government for a treaty by which Germany would undertake to buy annually a fixed quota of Rumanian cereals, in return for a Rumanian undertaking to buy an equivalent quota of German manufactures. A participation in the customs union would have been only a logical extension of this policy, and according to one rumour Briand had to exercise pressure on the Rumanian government to restrain them from accepting the Austro-German invitation.[2]

---

[1] Hassel's report, 14 April, GD, 3086H/D615380; Rieth's report, 22 April 1931, ibid., D615444.
[2] *Survey of International Affairs, 1931,* p. 305, note 4.

On 27 April the French minister of finance, Flandin, declared that France had either to organize the economic life of the successor states within the political framework of the treaties, or she would expose herself to all the dangers resulting from the agitation for revision and from the discontent of the central European population. The essence of the French counterplan, of which the British government received on the same day a first account, was therefore to find measures against the economic attractions of the Austro-German customs union.

Accordingly the *plan constructif* proposed: (*a*) measures dealing with the Danube cereal surplus and a plan envisaging a system of preferences for the food exporting central European states; (*b*) the development of industrial cartels to organize markets and to restrict competition; (*c*) an organization for short-term land credits for the countries in Eastern and central Europe under the auspices of the League; (*d*) a preferential tariff for certain Austrian goods offered by the principal clients of Austria in order to remedy her special situation.[1] The French plan was by its very nature concentrated on the economic situation in central Europe.

The British government being interested in finding an acceptable alternative for the Austro-German scheme immediately criticized the inherent weakness of the *plan constructif*.

While making every effort to secure considerable advantages for Austria, the French proposals do little or nothing to secure the more important end of satisfying Germany.[2]

Unless Germany received some real advantage from the French proposals, she would certainly try to conclude the customs union. Advocating the interests of the overseas countries the British government pointed out that the grain exporting countries would raise difficulties over the proposed preference system. As far as the industrial cartels were concerned, it could not see how they could bring immediate relief to the economic situation. The British critical reply ended with the conclusion that a general reduction of tariffs would still be the best contribution to economic co-operation.

[1] See the *plan constructif* in BrD, 2nd Ser., Vol. II, enclosure in No. 31; US, 1931, Vol. I, p. 583.
[2] British *aide-memoire*, 4 May 1931, ibid., enclosure in No. 37; Vansittart to de Fleuriau, 27 April, No. 31.

c

The German reaction was similarly negative. It emphasized that France being a highly protectionist country could not offer preferential treatment. French industry disposed at that time of 90 per cent of its production in the home market. France was nearly self-sufficient in her food supply. The only country, therefore, which could make concessions, was Germany. The German government rejected for this reason Francois-Poncet's offer that Austria and Germany should give up their project and only pursue it if the realization of the *plan constructif* proved to be impossible.

The Austrian government viewed the French plan more favourably. Peter, on behalf of the Austrian government, proposed to the German Ambassador that they should wait with the conclusion of their treaty and see what would come out of the French initiative.[1] As the Germans insisted, however, on complete freedom in the negotiations the French counterplan failed to replace the Austro-German customs union.

The French proposals succeeded on the other hand in the more urgent aim of keeping in line Yugoslavia and Rumania, which threatened to break out of the carefully built up French defence system. The annual conference of the Little Entente was approaching and it was important to secure a unanimous policy. At this moment France played her financial trump. On 23 April she granted a loan of about $50,000,000 to Czechoslovakia and on 8 May a loan of over 1,000,000,000 French francs to Yugoslavia. In between, on 5 May, the conference of the Little Entente was held in Bucharest, at which, as a result of the French influence, Yugoslavia, Rumania, and Czechoslovakia decided that the Austro-German customs union should be opposed at the forthcoming meeting of the League.

France had the ground well prepared when the Austro-German project came up for consideration before the commission of inquiry for European union on 15 May at Geneva. She could expect that England, Italy, and the Little Entente would support her line of action. The meeting began in an unpropitious way. Briand arrived fresh from his defeat at the Presidential elections two days before, on 13 May, when he took the chair at the meeting. He had been defeated by the politically far less distinguished but more conservative candidate M. Doumer by a margin of forty-one votes

[1] Rieth's report, 5 May 1931, GD, 3086H/D615564

and he left no doubt that he saw in Curtius the scapegoat for his defeat.

The discussion on how to remedy the existing economic crisis once again resulted in a repetition of the two controversial schemes: the formation of small groups of countries which would grow progressively larger, or the general adoption of a plan which excluded regional agreements. On 18 May the Council began to consider the legal aspects of the Austro-German customs union. Curtius presided over the meeting, which prevented him from taking a leading part in the discussion. There was a general tendency to treat Briand with consideration because of his recent defeat. The main issue had, however, already been settled beforehand in negotiations between Henderson, Briand, Grandi, and Curtius. The Germans and Austrians agreed to Henderson's proposal that the matter be referred to the Permanent Court of International Justice for an advisory opinion, if the Austro-German project was compatible with article 88 of the Treaty of St. Germain and with the Geneva protocol of 1922. The discussion on the legal point re-emphasized the opposite positions. Briand asserted that the customs union infringed Austria's independence. This was denied by Schober who replied with some justification:

If, however, by a far-reaching interpretation of the Geneva protocol, the anxiety for our independence were pushed so far that we lost all freedom of action in our relations with foreign countries, then that attitude would indeed deprive us of our independence.[1]

The real bone of contention was whether the Council should have the right to examine the political aspect of the dispute after the Court had reached a decision. Following their policy of limiting the discussion to the legal aspect, and optimistic with regard to the Court's decision, Curtius and Schober disputed the Council's right to discuss the political side. But Briand left no doubt that the Council would have to consider the political implications later, and he was supported in this by the representatives of the Italian, Czechoslovak and Yugoslav governments.

With the meeting of the League Council the second round

[1] League of Nations, *Official Journal*, *12th year*, minutes of the 63rd session of the Council, 1931, p. 1070.

came to an end. Paris had paralysed the Austro-German action. Curtius believed he had achieved a success by limiting the discussion to the legal aspect. But he had in fact given way to the French, who had gained time and were not going to miss their chance during the months to come. The decision had only been postponed.

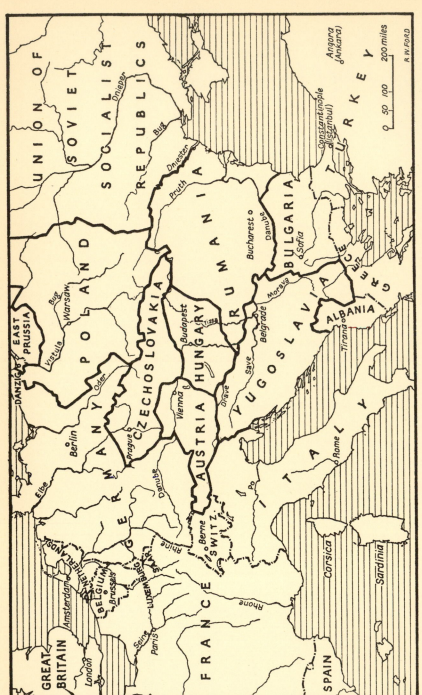

II. Austria and Hungary after 1919, and the new states of Poland, Czechoslovakia, and Yugoslavia

CHAPTER II

FRENCH PRESSURE ON AUSTRIA AND GERMANY

Ce que nous percevons maintenant, dans les coulisses autrichiennes, montre que, dans les semaines qui suivront le 19 mars, l'initiative austro-allemande ne peut pas resisté à l'emploi le plus modéré de l'arme financière française.

Echo de Paris, 21 May 1931

COLLAPSE OF THE AUSTRIAN *CREDITANSTALT*

The session of the League Council on 18 May coincided with the first signs in Europe of the world financial crisis. The outstanding event was the collapse of the Austrian *Creditanstalt*. In April 1931 the German government had become aware of the weakness of the Austrian bank and the inherent dangers for the Austro-German project. Curtius asked Luther, the president of the *Reichsbank*, to open an account of 20,000,000 Schillings with the *Creditanstalt* in order to strengthen its position.[1] But though Schober expected a strengthening influence the credit proved to be a drop in the bucket.

On 11 May the Austrian government had to announce that the *Creditanstalt* faced failure. The balance-sheet for 1930 showed a loss of 140,000,000 Schillings.[2] One cause for the crash was that the *Creditanstalt* in 1921 under government compulsion had taken over the rival *Boden Creditanstalt*, which was at that time insolvent. Its situation in 1931 still arose from that decision. But a fuller explanation is to be found in the same reasons which led to the crisis in 1921: the dismemberment of the Austro-Hungarian Empire, which by impoverishing Austria deprived the *Creditanstalt* of the source of its capital, exposed Austria to the high tariff barriers of the successor states, and forced it to rely entirely on foreign loans. The loans given to Austria had remedied the effects rather than the causes of her economic instability.

[1] Curtius to Luther, 14 April, GD, 6075H/E449661.
[2] League of Nations, *Official Journal*, *No. 12*, Annex 1325b. 2nd Supplementary report submitted to the Council on 25 Sept. 1931, pp. 2407ff.

The failure of the *Creditanstalt* would have meant a breakdown of the Austrian financial structure, because it dominated Austrian economic life and possessed a large amount of shares in Austrian industry. The repercussions of a complete failure would not have been limited to Austria, as the bank's foreign debts alone amounted to 76,000,000 Schillings in 1931.[1] The Austrian government tried to prevent the collapse of the *Creditanstalt* and, together with the Austrian National Bank, came to the rescue, the government subscribing 100,000,000 Schillings for shares of the bank. During the meeting of the League at Geneva from 18–20 May Schober was still confident and he assured Curtius that the crisis could be overcome.[2]

But the Austrian government had difficulties in persuading the financial market to take up the shares. The critical position of the *Creditanstalt* and the subsequent risk which a purchase involved, made a normal sale of the shares impossible. It was clear that anyone who bought the shares would do so for political reasons. Germany's own financial situation prevented Berlin from taking advantage of the situation. The offers which Paris made, however, were rejected by Vienna because it feared the influence which France would consequently have on the management of the bank and on Austrian financial policy. Being unable to sell the shares on a wider scale the Austrian government hoped to obtain new credits through the issue of treasury bills to the amount of 150,000,000 Schillings.

Thus the financial crisis, starting with the failure of the *Creditanstalt*, gave France the opportunity of taking full advantage of her financial superiority. Since Poincaré had assumed office in August 1926 the financial situation in France had gradually improved. In June 1928 the Bank of France had gold reserves of 5,543,000,000 francs, besides several milliards of foreign currency which were mostly deposited in London and New York. In 1928 Pandele prophesied in his book *La Repartition de l'or dans le monde*:

In the new world-redistribution of gold, France plays and will play a considerable role. The total of her assets abroad exceeds one milliard

---

[1] *The Times* reported on 24 July 1931 that Great Britain had assets of £27,000,000, the United States £24,000,000, France, Holland, and Switzerland £6,000,000 and Germany £5,000,000.
[2] Curtius, *Bemühung um Österreich*, p. 54.

dollars; the realization of which could be performed overnight and would place English and American money markets in a most embarrassing position indeed. One cannot sufficiently stress the powerful position in which such a situation places France and the influence which her monetary policy will consequently have.[1]

In 1931 Paris proved that it had learned this lesson. France was yet but little affected by the economic crisis. As she was the only country capable of lending money, she could attach any political strings she liked to her loans. The history of the defeat of the customs union is mainly an account of the French financial pressure put on Austria and Germany.

As long as the French files remain closed there is no conclusive evidence of how far the rumours were justified according to which the crash of the *Creditanstalt* was due largely to the deliberate withdrawals of credits by French bankers. Hoover estimates that in order to bring pressure to bear, the short-term bills presented for payment to Austria and Germany by Paris amounted to $300,000,000.[2] On the other hand, according to the report of the German embassy in Vienna on 12 May, French finance had no influence on the collapse of the *Creditanstalt* and no French capital had been withdrawn to any degree worth mentioning as the French assets were rather small.[3] This again does not give us the final answer, as France might have indirectly exercised pressure by withdrawing money from England and the United States which in their turn had lent the same money to Austria at a higher rate. But there is sufficient evidence that Paris did nothing to remedy and everything to precipitate the economic crisis, from which it drew its political strength.[4]

The Austrian government had to be authorized by the committee of the guarantor states of the Geneva loan in 1922 for the planned issue of treasury bonds to the amount of 150,000,000 Schillings. During the meeting of the committee on 15 and 16 May the representatives of France and Czechoslovakia tried to bring pressure to bear on Austria by refusing their consent unless Austria made concessions in the customs union question. They

---

[1] P. 241 (my translation).
[2] Hoover, *The Great Depression*, p. 62.
[3] Note on telephone conversation, GD, 6075H/E449678.
[4] Bennett, op. cit., p. 100, does not think that the collapse of the bank was caused by French intrigue.

hoped to delay a decision in the meeting until the discussions of
the Austro-German project before the European commission and
the League Council had come to an end. But the British representative resented this blackmail. He insisted on an immediate
consultation and on 18 May the committee sanctioned the issue of
the treasury bonds.

The authorization was only the first obstacle to overcome; far
more difficult was the task of disposing of the bonds. Neither the
German nor the British and American money markets were
capable of raising the necessary money without French co-operation. Claudel, the French ambassador in Vienna, made it perfectly clear that a renunciation of the customs union was a *sine
qua non* for any French loan.[1] Suggestions in the French press
confronted Austria repeatedly with the alternative either to give
herself up to France or to continue her co-operation with Germany facing final disaster as a consequence.

Italy feared the dominant part which France was going to play
in Austria's internal affairs. Rome contemplated financial steps to
counter the French influence. But nothing came of this. In England especially financial circles were opposed to the French
attitude. During his visit to Chequers on 7 June Curtius had met
Montagu Norman, governor of the Bank of England, who regarded the situation in Vienna as exceedingly critical, and who
feared a catastrophe which would spread to the neighbouring
countries and particularly to Germany. Montagu Norman resented the political considerations which dominated the French
credit policy. And he declared to Curtius that the Bank of England
would not tolerate any exploitation of French financial power for
political aims in Central Europe.[2]

In the meantime Paris continued to sabotage the Austrian
attempt to raise the necessary credit. At French insistence the
Bank for International Payments made it a condition for granting
the second instalment of the Austrian loan that Vienna should
find a market for its treasury bonds. As this in turn depended upon
French co-operation a complete deadlock in the Austrian financial
situation had been reached. The degree of the crisis is disclosed

---

[1] Report, 30 May 1931, GD, 6075/E449775; von Neurath's report, 3 June 1931,
ibid., E449797.
[2] Curtius's memorandum on the conversation, 10 June 1931, GD, 6075/
E449852.

by the fact that the Austrian government did not succeed in persuading anyone to take over the direction of the bank. Several candidates who were approached refused the ungrateful task.

The Austrian government now became convinced that the Austro-German project could not be carried through. The only solution remained the English proposal for an alternative plan. On 2 June Schober asked Henderson to invite an informal meeting of experts to consider what action could be taken for some satisfactory substitute to the customs union.[1] As hitherto the French banks had evaded the Austrian demands for a credit by pointing out that they could not take up the Austrian treasury bonds unless the French government expressed a wish to this effect, Vienna decided to force the issue into the open. On 11 June the Austrian government asked the French government formally to give the consent without which the French banks were unable to act.[2]

On 16 June Paris answered with an ultimatum. The French were willing to agree, if Vienna accepted the following conditions:[3]

1. The Austrian government would consent to submit Austria's economic and financial condition to an examination by the League of Nations. It would agree to accept in advance whatever measures were proposed to her by the League Council.

2. This undertaking would imply a formal renunciation of the intention to enter any economic or political arrangement which would modify the international status of Austria. The Austrian government would authorize the French government to publish this condition at any time if it thinks necessary.

Provided that Vienna gave a satisfactory reply by 8 p.m. on the same day the French government promised immediate steps by the French banks.

The decision to dispatch the ultimatum was made at the ministerial council on 16 June. Briand had opposed the procedure and criticized the second condition, which amounted to an

---

[1] BrD, 2nd Ser., Vol. II, No. 59.

[2] von Hoesch's report, 11 June 1931, GD, 6075H/E449862.

[3] Rieth's report, 17 June 1931, ibid., E449893; Atherton's report, US, 1931, Vol. I, p. 23.

immediate renunciation of the customs union.[1] But he was finally forced to agree. It is interesting in this context that on the same day an attack was delivered on Briand because of his inclusion in the newly formed cabinet, which had formally resigned after the Presidential elections. The French government thought its goal had been reached and was sure of the success of the ultimatum. Flandin, the Minister of Finance, and Briand asked the German ambassador repeatedly if he was not authorized to renounce the project.[2]

But Paris had overstepped its limits. No Austrian government could agree to terms, which implied complete surrender. The failure of the *Creditanstalt* had already caused a cabinet crisis. The Austrian Minister of the Interior refused to assume responsibility for a state guarantee of the old debts of the *Creditanstalt*. Consequently, on 16 June, the cabinet handed in its resignation. Schober used the resignation to evade the French ultimatum, declaring that the Austrian government was dissolved and could give no answer.

Schober decided to counteract. He instantly informed the British, Italian, and German ambassadors of the French ultimatum and handed them copies. The news caused indignation in the different capitals. Montagu Norman made good his declaration given to Curtius at Chequers. On the same day the Bank of England telephoned to Vienna and Berlin denouncing the French procedure as intolerable and informing them that the Bank of England would advance the necessary 150,000,000 Schillings (£4,300,000) to the Austrian National Bank in order to provide the latter with the funds for meeting the foreign liabilities of the *Creditanstalt*. The advance should be repaid out of the proceeds of the Austrian loan when floated.

The action of the Bank of England did not, however, reflect the official policy. The advance was a move in the 'independent foreign policy' of the Bank of England, anti-French and pro-German.[3] The British Foreign Office was reserved in its reaction to the French ultimatum, though privately MacDonald and Henderson were outspoken in their criticism of the French 'black-

[1] According to Berthelot Briand declared '*Je suis battu*'. Berthelot to Grünberger, GD, 6075H/E450126.

[2] von Hoesch's report, 17 June, GD, 6075H/E449898.

[3] Hugh Dalton, *Call Back Yesterday*, 1953, p. 254.

mail'. It emphasized that the Bank of England had itself taken the initiative for the intervention and that when consulted the Foreign Office had only given its approval.[1] Asked in the House of Commons if he would do everything in his power to help Austria, Henderson replied somewhat evasively 'that he approved of the action of the Bank of England, and that he hoped it would have that effect'.[2]

Vienna received the money as relief at the last minute. As an immediate effect it ended the government crisis in Vienna. After a short interlude with Seipel as Chancellor from 18 to 20 June, Buresch formed a new government. The Germans were successful in helping Schober to enter the government as Foreign Minister against the expressed French desires.

But Schober had given up any hope for the Austro-German project. He realized that Austria was too weak to carry it through against the French resistance. On the other hand he was aware of the fact that the project strengthened his position with Paris. He decided therefore to pursue the scheme as a bargaining counter in Paris. He left Berlin in the dark and declared on 16 June that 'neither he nor any other Austrian minister could accept the French conditions'. They should insist on the project.[3] But on the other hand he admitted on the same day to the English ambassador Sir Eric Phipps, 'though he could not say so officially, that there could no longer be any question of putting the customs union plan into execution, even should the decision of the Hague court be favourable', and Schober informed the Austrian Chancellor accordingly.[4]

The intervention of the Bank of England saved Austria from complete breakdown. It robbed Paris of the success of its pressure. But Montagu Norman's aim of forcing the French hand and making the French government accept an international loan without the previous strings attached to it failed. Paris knew that the Austrian treasury bonds had still to be taken up, as London had only made a temporary advance. Paris could afford to wait and did not comprehend the action of the Bank of England.

---

[1] von Hoesch's report, 18 June, GD, 6075H/E449922; Atherton's report, 18 June, US, 1931, Vol. I, p. 24.
[2] *Parliamentary Debates*, 22 June, Vol. 254, col. 30.
[3] Rieth's report, 17 June, GD, ibid., E449894.
[4] Sir Eric Phipps's report, 17 June, BrD, 2nd Ser., Vol. II, No. 59.

On 22 June the French ambassador de Fleuriau told Vansittart
that

Austria would in any case have to address herself to the League.
The question of a new loan would arise and that would be the occasion
for his government to renew the condition they had laid down as to
renunciation of the customs union; but the condition might be put in
a milder and a more tactful form.[1]

Montagu Norman's attempt to dispose of the Austrian bonds
through his commissioner Louis Fleischmann in Paris met with
equal incomprehension, because 'the attitude of the French banks
had not changed'.[2]

The ill success of Montagu Norman's action, which had been
partly motivated by the strong financial commitment of the
English banks to Austria, was caused by the growing weakness of
the British money market itself. The intervention was the last
independent measure before the financial crisis hit London to its
full extent. The loan contributed to the subsequent difficulties of
the British money market. Throughout July there was a heavy
drain of gold from the Bank of England to France, whose demands according to *The Times* 'appeared insatiable'.[3] On 15 July
£3,000,000 of gold were withdrawn, followed by £5,000,000 the
next day. During the subsequent fortnight the Bank's losses
averaged nearly £2,500,000 a day and amounted to £17,000,000
on 22 July.[4]

No conclusive evidence is available as to whether these withdrawals were made in order to put pressure on the Bank of England not to advance any more credits and to recall the Austrian
loan, or whether they were caused by a general lack of confidence in the financial strength of London.[5] If we take into
account how much French banking policy had been influenced by
political motives hitherto, the first assumption seems probable.
The pressure on London had, however, the effect of making the

---

[1] Vansittart's note, BrD, 2nd Ser., Vol. II, enclosure in No. 76.
[2] Flandin to Gruenberger, v. Hoesch's report, 2 July, GD, 6075H/E499999.
[3] 23 July 1931.
[4] Snowden at the London conference, 22 July, BrD, 2nd Ser., Vol. II, p. 460.
Toynbee, *Survey of Intern. Affairs, 1931*, p. 216.
[5] This was assumed by Sacket, the American ambassador in Berlin, Stimson's
memorandum, 15 July, US, 1931, Vol. I, p. 261. Lord Tyrrel's inquiries in
Paris, whether the French action had political motives, had no result; his report,
16 July, BrD, 2nd Ser., Vol. II, No. 207.

financial circles reluctant to grant any further credits unless some basis for French co-operation could be found. *The Times* pointed out that

. . . the risks in making loans had been increased by the danger of sudden financial attacks from Paris carried out with the object of exerting political pressure and taking the form of withdrawals of short-term credits.

Austria drew the only possible conclusion from this situation. One month after the ultimatum, on 16 July, the French government intimated that the French demands had been '*trop directe et trop brutale*'. The French government did not insist on the acceptance of the conditions provided Austria herself 'made a satisfactory declaration'. It proposed that the Austrian government should apply directly to the League. Meanwhile the Bank of England urged the refund of the loan of 150,000,000 Schillings and Vienna promised to pay the first instalment on 1 September.[1] For Schober there was no alternative. The same day on which the French government had made the suggestion, Schober informed the General Secretary of the League that Austria was going to apply for a loan.

Nearly ten years after the Geneva protocols of 1922 Austria found herself in exactly the same position. Vienna could only expect financial help from the League if it gave up the idea of an economic Anschluss with Germany. After Schober's appeal to the League the final renunciation of the proposed customs union was only a matter of time. The Austrian Minister in Berlin left Curtius in no doubt on 28 July that if necessary the Austrian government would make this concession.[2]

THE HOOVER MORATORIUM

The complete loss of confidence which the collapse of the Austrian *Creditanstalt* involved forced the banks to cash other foreign balances in order to cover their position. This attempt to liquidate foreign assets seized upon Germany as its next victim, as her financial houses were closely connected with those of Austria and Hungary. The German Reichmark became very weak and by 23 June the *Reichsbank* had lost 979,000,000 Reichsmark from its

[1] Curtius memorandum, 31 August 1931, GD, 3086H/D616011.
[2] Ibid., GD, K49/K5617.

gold reserve and 93,000,000 Reichsmark from its reserve of foreign currencies.

The United States realized that her economic recovery was bound up with the recovery of Europe. A collapse of the German financial structure would have struck the United States hard, because 41 per cent of the total German foreign debts, or $2,370,000,000, were owed to United States citizens at the end of July 1931.[1] President Hoover became convinced that nothing short of a general moratorium on foreign debts could save the German financial system. On 20 June Hoover proposed a one-year moratorium on all inter-governmental payments, both debts and reparations.

While the other countries welcomed Hoover's initiative, it was attacked in Paris. The following period was mainly dedicated to attempts at winning French approval. The French government endeavoured to use its key position to impose the following political conditions on Germany:[2]

1. The abandonment of the so-called German pocket battle-ship.

2. The abandonment of the Austro-German customs union project.

3. The cessation of German activity in the French spheres of influence in central Europe and in the Balkans.

The other European countries soon fell in with the French line. Beneš made it clear that, though he approved of Hoover's plan and though his country had everything to gain by a postponement of payments, the proposal would only be accepted on the terms agreeable to Czechoslovakia's ally France.[3] The same attitude was taken by Italy, who since the meeting of the League Council in May was disposed to follow the same policy as France towards Austria. Grandi, fearing the combined pressure of Germany and Austria at Trieste at the head of the Adriatic, emphasized that Italy would oppose anything that might help Germany to extend her hegemony over Austria.[4]

The British government hoped to facilitate the acceptance of

---

[1] Ferrell, *American Diplomacy in the Great Depression*, 1957, p. 117, note 17.
[2] Edge's report, 28 June 1931, US, 1931, Vol. I, p. 96.
[3] Ratshesky's report, ibid., p. 201.
[4] Garrett's (Rome) report, ibid., p. 219.

the Hoover proposal by persuading Germany to get the customs union question out of the way. The Germans should avoid the impression that 'they were taking everything and giving nothing'.[1] Henderson tried to win American assistance for his representations with the German government in this direction.

This attempt to tie up the Hoover moratorium with the customs union failed because of the American and German resistance, though each had different motives. Dealing with European political problems was something that the American diplomatists had carefully avoided doing. American post-war diplomacy was based on non-interference in European affairs. It had little understanding of Germany's policy of revision, and less of the impact it had on Germany's internal affairs. 'The United States,' Hoover believed, 'could not afford to be dragged into European entanglements.'[2]

Washington was therefore very reluctant to express any opinion in the Franco-German dispute. It did not want any explanations from the French or the Germans. America's main interest was whether the most-favoured nation clause of her commercial treaty with Germany was affected, though unofficially Stimson mentioned that '. . . he could not altogether blame Germany; everybody knew that the tariff situation in Central Europe had been intolerable since the end of the war and yet nobody had done anything.'[3]

It followed from the American policy that the United States refused to consent to the use of the moratorium as a lever to obtain political concessions from Germany. It protested against the attempt to connect political bargaining with a relief measure as 'contrary to the spirit of the President's suggestion'.[4] The only concession Washington made was agreeing to intimate, if the Germans made an approach, that the views of the British

---

[1] Henderson to Lindsay and Newton, 26/29 June, 1 July, BrD, 2nd Ser., Vol. I, No. 87, 93, 105, 113.

[2] Hoover to Stimson, 11 April 1919, quoted in Myers, *The Foreign Policies of Herbert Hoover*, pp. 16–17.

[3] Stimson to Grandi, 9 July, ibid., p. 540.

[4] Stimson to Garrett, 23 June, US, 1931, Vol. I, p. 220. The American policy was not consistent insofar as it demanded the abandonment of the construction of the battleship, which it did not, however, regard 'as a political question'. Memorandum, 29 June, ibid., p. 97.

government with regard to the customs union were shared by itself. This, however, the Germans carefully avoided doing.

The Germans opposed the linking up of Hoover's proposal and the customs union mainly for internal reasons. In face of the growing strength of the extremist parties especially on the right, and without a workable majority in the Reichstag Brüning's government had to rely more and more on the support of the army and the President. The memory was still vivid of the trial in Leipzig, the year before, of the army officers Ludin, Scheringer, and Wendt, who had been charged with spreading Nazi propaganda in the army; this had shown that the army was responsive to Hitler's agitation. Brüning and Curtius made it clear that they could not renounce the customs union because 'any sign of yielding in regard to the matter must be resented by the Reichswehr, on whose loyalty they depended in the last resort'.[1] They feared a humiliation would endanger this ultimate stronghold.

On 30 June the negotiations were near breaking-point. The United States threatened to propose to their individual debtors a postponement of all payments for one year, provided they took a similar measure. The German government indicated that it would declare a moratorium should the negotiations break down. It was in the face of this combined pressure that the French government, fearing isolation from the other countries, accepted Hoover's proposal.

When finally on 6 July an agreement was signed, it was already too late to restore confidence. The delay in settling the plan lessened its value. The protracted negotiations only made the financial world more suspicious of Germany's condition. The run on the banks continued. On 13 July the Darmstädter Bank, the second largest private bank in Germany, closed its doors. The German government had to intervene and only a banking moratorium saved the banking system from complete ruin. As a result huge volumes of foreign short-term credits were practically frozen, which was precisely the sort of thing the Hoover moratorium had hoped to prevent.

Paris hoped that Germany's deteriorating economic position would present an occasion for enforcing upon Germany the political concessions which President Hoover had excluded from

---

[1] Curtius to Newton, 3 July, BrD, 2nd Ser., Vol. II, No. 120. Brüning to Sacket, 2 July, US, 1931, Vol. I, p. 130.

his moratorium. Accordingly the French government suggested that, in order to ensure the stability of the Reichsmark, a short-term credit of $500,000,000 should be granted to Germany, which would be repaid through the floating of an international loan for ten years, guaranteed by France, Great Britain, and the United States. The German government should, in return, secure the loan by a mortgage on the German customs. It should agree to a political moratorium over the same period of ten years. These political guarantees should include: an undertaking not to change the situation established by the Peace Treaties, the cessation of the construction of the pocket battleship, and the renunciation of the customs union.

There was no hope of success for this plan. Stimson emphasized once again that the American government would not go into a guarantee which related to a political question in Europe, 'as it would involve us in the kind of European questions we had always kept out of'.[1] Nor were the United States and England financially strong enough to participate in the loan.

Brüning continued to steer between the Scylla of French financial assistance and the Charybdis of German Nationalism. His position was the same as during the negotiations about the Hoover moratorium. He was convinced that an acceptance of the French conditions would result in the fall of his government. During his negotiations with Laval in Paris on 18–19 July he refused the French proposal. Laval himself acknowledged Brüning's difficulties, but was bound by the opposition of Tardieu and Maginot within the cabinet. He emphasized that France could not help the Germans without political safeguards and his frankness even disarmed the Germans.[2] In fact the French did not 'care to lend money to Brüning and then have it spent by Hitler'.[3]

The London conference on the German financial situation proposed by Henderson was foredoomed to failure when it met on 20 July. Its outcome was meagre in spite of the participation of the world's leading statesmen. Laval's tactics were simple and efficient. He had made it a condition for his presence at the conference that agreement was reached in principle between the

[1] Stimson's memorandum, 15 July, US, 1931, Vol. I, p. 258.
[2] Schmidt, *Statist auf diplomatischer Bühne*, p. 222.
[3] Stimson's memorandum, ibid., p. 258.

French and German governments and that their relations did not admit of mediation by a third party. In the preceding conversations with Brüning in Paris, Laval insisted on tying up the financial and political problems. For the conference in London he demanded the separation of the two issues.[1] For once Laval's condition corresponded with the American principle of not mixing finance and politics. The London conference remained confined to the financial aspect of the German situation.

Thus Laval succeeded in establishing a superior position at both conferences. He avoided any political pressure from countries which might have come down on the German side. The French had only to maintain the political conditions (a gulf which could not be bridged between the Germans and the French, and a topic which could not be touched at the London conference), in order to reduce the London conference to nullity.

Paris is relieved [commented *The Times* on 23 July] that the French representatives were able to hold to their refusal to lend more money to Germany without any of the political guarantees which is their object to obtain, and this feeling is linked with the hope that an opportunity will occur later to insist on them with better hope of success.

THE TARDIEU PLAN

Since the Austrians pursued the project only for bargaining purposes, the German government fought a losing battle. Throughout August Vienna continued its double game, still leaving Berlin some hope of success. According to Schober the negotiations for a loan through the League did not necessarily affect the Austro-German project. While Curtius still insisted on the scheme, Brüning's attitude was more realistic. On 16 July he indicated that a replacement of the customs union would be possible.[2]

The final negotiations for the renunciation took place in the course of the September session of the commission for European union at Geneva early in September. Brüning urged Curtius that he should separate himself from the Austrians, leaving it to them to renounce the project in order to avoid humiliating Germany.

---

[1] Henderson's memorandum, 19 July, BrD, 2nd Ser., Vol. II, No. 193, minute 27.
[2] Brüning to Rumbold, BrD, 2nd Ser., Vol. II, No. 210, 215. GD, K49/K5625.

But Curtius, with a strong feeling of solidarity, refused: *'Österreich konnte den schweren Gang des Verzichts nicht allein gehen.'*[1] He thought it necessary, in the future interests of Austro-German relations, to renounce the project together with the Austrians.

On 3 September Schober declared the renunciation by saying that '. . . the customs union might raise obstacles to confident co-operation between European states and that the Austrian government did therefore not intend to pursue the project.' Curtius emphasized that, expecting a successful outcome of the more general schemes for European co-operation, the German government would not persist with the plan originally contemplated.

How much the political aspect dominated the judicial is shown by the fact that two days later, on 5 September, the opinion of the World Court was made public, at a moment when the fate of the customs union had already been decided. By an eight to seven majority, they came to the conclusion that the projected customs union was incompatible with Austria's undertakings, because it menaced the economic independence of Austria. The court's opinion was criticized as having been influenced by political considerations as the nationalities of the judges forming the majority and minority showed. As the decision had no political impact, it is beyond the scope of this book to discuss the legal arguments which were used in support of the controversial opinions.

In Germany the reaction was despairing. Since the customs union had become the vehicle of German revisionist policy, its defeat destroyed whatever illusion may have remained that a reversal of the Treaty of Versailles was possible under the system of Versailles. Both ways had been explored, co-operation with France and action against France, and both had ended in failure. With the defeat of the Austro-German customs union, the foreign policy of the Weimar Republic faced its final disaster. It was easy for Hitler to exploit the defeat. He had only to recall his words of April 1931, when he had predicted that the German government could not face up to France. According to him Germany needed a man of his determination. He wrote in the *Völkischer Beobachter* on 6 September:

[1] Curtius, *Sechs Jahre Minister*, pp. 202–203.

After this terrible defeat only one act can express the protest of the oppressed German people: the immediate resignation from an office which the members of the government are no longer equal to.[1]

The defeat of the Austro-German customs union seemed to prepare the way for the French and Czechoslovakian Danubian plans. In October 1931 Beneš approached the Austrian Minister at Prague and suggested the establishment of some kind of customs union. He proposed that Schober should take the initiative in this respect. But this approach was rather maladroit, and Schober was certainly the wrong person to address. He replied bitterly that 'he had been sufficiently punished for one year for exercising his initiative in such matters and that similar proposals should in the future come from other quarters'.[2]

The French schemes had a more ambitious character. Tardieu advocated a variation of the unsuccessful *plan constructif* and proposed a complete reorganization of the Danube area. He was determined that France should take advantage of her momentary financial superiority and realize the scheme.[3] His plan envisaged the *rapprochement* between the countries of the Little Entente on one side, and Austria and Hungary on the other. These countries should organize a special economic system, which should consist of a preferential tariff reduction of 10 per cent, the abolition of all import and export prohibitions between them, the cancellation of exchange restrictions, and possibly the establishment of a common currency. In addition France proposed a reconstruction loan to which it was willing to contribute £10,000,000.

The predominance in this plan of the Little Entente and, in the last resort, of France, over Austria and Hungary meant that it ran up against opposition from different sources. In Vienna, Schober adhered to his policy that Austria should not enter into any combination of states from which Germany was excluded. Since Schober had become by now a continuous obstacle to the extension of French influence in Austria Paris insisted on his removal. At French insistence and because of the objections of the financial committee of the League, Chancellor Buresch dismissed Schober from his government. Buresch thereby weakened his

---

[1] Quoted in Wedel, *Die deutsch-österreichische Zollunion im Spiegel der reichsdeutschen Presse*, Diss. Heidelberg, 1937, p. 50 (my translation).

[2] Stockton's report, 21 October 1931, US, Vol. I, pp. 846–847.

[3] See the minutes of his conversation with Heeren and Dosse, 17 March 1932, GD, 3086/D616227–235.

position, because the Pan-Germans had been only willing to co-operate upon the condition that Schober remained in the government. Consequently they withdrew their support and Buresch had to base his government on a minority of Christian Socials and the *Landbund* (Agrarian League).[1] In March 1932 Tardieu threatened that Austria could not expect a loan from the League unless the 'Tardieu plan' was accepted in its basic structure.

But it was not only Austria's reluctance that had to be overcome. Rumania raised the same doubts as the year before when the *plan constructif* had been under discussion. Argetorianu, the Rumanian Minister of Finance, stressed the fact that a union of the grain-producing countries, namely Rumania, Hungary, and Yugoslavia, could not increase the grain-consuming powers of the two remaining countries, Austria and Czechoslovakia. Rumania held therefore that the participation of Germany was essential.

Italy feared that a realization of the 'Tardieu plan' would bring Austria and Hungary under French tutelage. This would, as Grandi emphasized, destroy her expectation of an Italo-Austro-Hungarian customs union, which, as she hoped, would replace the defeated Austro-German project.[2] On behalf of the British government, the Foreign Secretary, Sir John Simon, expressed the main criticism that the French were making a political approach towards an economic issue. Tardieu paid a visit to London in order to win him over, but failed in his mission.[3] It was to be expected that Germany would receive the French initiative with especially strong suspicion. As far as the German government could, it raised obstacles. Thus, Berlin proposed the inclusion of Bulgaria in the scheme in order to counterbalance the weight of the Little Entente.[4]

Although the resistance of these countries was of importance, they lay outside the Balkan area and could not have prevented the French Danubian plans if the Danubian countries themselves had been willing to co-operate. In this respect the Hungarian demand for revision formed the stumbling block to each project for a *rapprochement* with the Little Entente. Moreover, the financial strength of France was vanishing. The world depression

---

[1] Curtius, *Bemühung um Österreich*, p. 208.
[2] Grandi to Schuberth, Schuberth's report, 16 May 1932, GD 6001/E442869.
[3] Bernstorff's reports 15 and 30 March 1930, GD, 3086/D616209/D616289.
[4] Bülow's telegram, 7 March 1932, GD, 3086/D616183.

from which France had thought herself secure struck her with full force by 1932 and with her economic difficulties the central European Countries doubted whether France could initiate a reorganization of the Danubian area. The Danube conference, from 4–8 April 1932, of Great Britain, France, Germany, and Italy was therefore doomed to failure, and ended over mere questions of procedure.

With the resignation of Tardieu's government on 4 June the sponsor of the French Danubian plan had gone. Herriot, the new French Premier, was most critical of Tardieu's policy and doubted the reasonableness of loans at the present moment.[1] Nevertheless, although he was sceptical about the ultimate advantage of support to Austria, he nevertheless thought a loan necessary in order to prevent the Anschluss. He continued with the policy of loans within the framework of the League. In return the Austrian government promised, on 9 June, to abstain from any attempts at an Anschluss.[2]

The League Council had meanwhile referred the Austrian financial problem to the Mixed Committee of Treasury Representatives and members of the Financial Committee. This Committee held a special session at Lausanne in June 1932 and considered the raising of a guaranteed loan of 300,000,000 Schillings over twenty years to Austria. The British government, however, was reluctant to consider a new financial commitment in Austria, especially since the 100,000,000 Schillings lent during the crisis of June 1931 by the Bank of England had still not been repaid. It was ready to participate in the guarantee with a portion of the 100,000,000 Schillings, only under the condition that the previous loan should be repaid out of the proceeds of the new one. Consequently the British share represented no new money, but merely resulted in the transformation of a short-term into a long-term loan guaranteed by the British government. The rest of the 200,000,000 Schillings was to be raised under the guarantees of France up to 100,000,000, Italy 30,000,000, Belgium 5,000,000, Holland, 3,000,000, and of other countries who it was hoped would participate in the floating.

Germany refused to take part in the loan because she objected

---

[1] Herriot to Papen, Bülow's memorandum, 17 June 1932, GD, 3086/D616365.
[2] Herriot, *Jadis*, Vol. II, p. 313.

to the linking of the loan with the Anschluss question. The German government's main motive, however, was to save face and to placate the German nationalists. Papen's government, pressing for the German equality of rights in armaments, did not want to get involved in this problem. Papen sympathized with Dollfuss and his government:

> If he needed this loan to put Austria on a sound economic footing, then he should take it on any terms, even if he would have to accept certain limitations on Austria's right to self-determination in the event of Anschluss with Germany. For a great historical event like the Anschluss would not be prevented by the terms of a loan agreement.[1]

Papen went still further. On 9 July he asked the German ambassador in Vienna to persuade the Pan-German leaders that they should raise no difficulties for Dollfuss,[2] but this intervention had no effect. The terms of the loan, under which Austria should again undertake not to alienate her independence, nearly caused its failure. Resentment in Austria was strong, since the Austro-German customs union project had been defeated. The Pan-Germans opposed the Lausanne protocols violently and they were supported in their opposition by the Socialists. Dollfuss, who had succeeded Buresch as Chancellor on 10 May 1932 and who, like his predecessors, based his government on the Christian Socials, secured only a vote of 82 to 80 in favour of the Lausanne protocols, and that only after bringing the Landbund into his government.

In the French chamber the Lausanne protocols were equally criticized. Flandin said that France would be reproached for buying the liberty of the Austrian people for 300,000,000 francs. Marin, still further to the right, doubted whether French financial pressure could prevent the Anschluss in the last resort. Prime Minister Herriot on the other hand emphasized that they had only the alternative of either accepting the Anschluss or the policy of the League. Moreover, Italy began taking an increased interest in Austrian affairs, and it was Italy to which Paul-Boncour referred when he spoke of 'certain other influences'. These arguments finally secured the ratification in the French chamber.

---

[1] Starhemberg, *Between Hitler and Mussolini*, pp. 98–99; Papen, *Memoirs*, p. 178.
[2] Bülow to Rieth, 9 July 1932, GD, 3086/D616374.

Similarly the terms of the loan were ratified in Great Britain and Italy before the end of 1932.

Ten years after the Geneva Protocols a similar remedy had been devised for the Austrian problem. Lausanne reiterated the old policy, but this time with less perceptible effect. As we have pointed out, the premise of Austria's independence was that France, England, and Italy should co-operate and abstain from interfering in her affairs. An essential condition of this premise was that England and Italy should follow the lead of France in Austrian matters. In 1932 this condition no longer existed.

The British government had only taken a nominal part in the Lausanne loan and had shown reluctance to assume new financial commitments towards Austria. Since the formation of the National Government under MacDonald England had made herself financially independent through the repayment of credits to Paris and New York. The habit of co-operation with France was continued on the whole. But London was no longer prepared to subordinate its policy to Paris in order to satisfy the French claim for security, as had been the case when Henderson guided foreign policy. In disarmament the German demand for equality had begun to occupy the foreground of the problem. The main question was no longer how to achieve French disarmament, but how to prevent German rearmament. This necessarily diverted the attention of the British diplomats from Paris to Berlin. On 6 February 1933, von Hoesch, now German ambassador in London, commented:[1]

One of the most significant characteristics of world developments in the past year seems to me to be the fact that the role of political leader in Europe has passed over more and more from France to England. A comparison between the French hegemony under Laval in the autumn of 1931, with England in a state of almost total financial impotence and greatly impaired political activity, and the present situation, which shows England to be active and France to be in an increasingly defensive position, provides clear proof of the changeover that has taken place.

[1] von Hoesch's report, 6 February 1933, GD, Ser. C, Vol. I, No. 13.

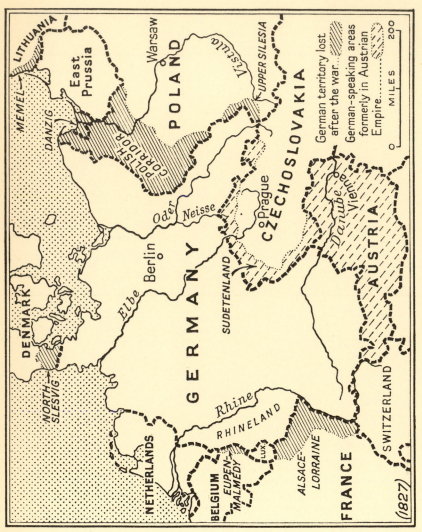

III. Germany after 1919

CHAPTER III

THE GERMAN–ITALIAN CONFLICT
FOR INFLUENCE OVER AUSTRIA

I have become convinced that in Austria is occurring a true re-
awakening of patriotic feeling, which is polarized around the ideas
of the independence of the state and the historic mission of German
Austria.

Mussolini to Dollfuss, 1 July 1933

THE CHANGE IN MUSSOLINI'S AUSTRIAN POLICY

The decline of French leadership coincided with greater
activity in Italian foreign policy. Mussolini became opposed to international co-operation. His Foreign Minister,
Grandi, had been hitherto the main advocate of solidarity with
France and England, but acknowledged that he was opposed 'by
a strong party both inside and outside the government which
wished to throw Italy into the arms of Germany'.[1] After the
breakdown of the Franco-Italian naval negotiations Grandi had
offered his resignation 'in case Mussolini thought somebody more
suitable could be found'.[2] That time Mussolini had refused to
accept the resignation, but a year later he thought a change in the
Foreign Ministry necessary. He arrived at the conclusion that
Grandi 'had permitted himself to become the prisoner of the
League, had conducted a pacific and internationalist policy, and
had acted the ultra-democrat and League of Nations man'.[3] On
21 July 1932 Mussolini therefore dismissed Grandi, gave him the
London embassy, and took over the Foreign Ministry himself.

Until Grandi's dismissal Mussolini had contented himself with
French and English co-operation within the framework of the
League in order to safeguard Austria's independence. His initial

[1] Grandi to Beaumarchais, Graham's report, 25 June 1930, BrD, 2nd Ser.,
Vol. I, No. 220.
[2] Grandi to Graham, Graham's report, 28 March 1931, ibid., Vol. II, No. 334.
[3] Mussolini, *Storia di uno anno*, p. 161; quoted by Gilbert, 'Ciano and his
Ambassadors', in *The Diplomats*, p. 513.

support for the Austro-German customs union, when he had overridden Grandi's advice, is an exception to this rule. Grandi's removal from the Foreign Office now became the starting point for a more active policy in south-east Europe. The new course was very much the result of the influence of Suvich, the Under-Secretary of State in the Foreign Ministry. Since Mussolini could not take complete charge of foreign affairs, Suvich's advice became highly influential in shaping his opinions. As a former citizen of the old Austria, from Trieste, Suvich objected to the Anschluss; being of Jewish origin he detested National Socialism. The question of Austria, he once said to the British ambassador in Rome, Sir Eric Drummond, was causing him as much preoccupation as if it were his own country which was at stake.[1] It was Suvich who proposed a closer political and economic cooperation between Austria, Hungary, and Italy. The Italo-Hungarian side of this triangle was already formed, since his championship of revision had given Mussolini a strong hold over Hungary. Hungary relied on Italy as a counterbalance against the Little Entente, which had French backing.

It now remained to draw Austria into the triangle. After the defeat of the Austro-German customs union in September 1931 and the failure of Tardieu's plan in 1932 the obstacles to a solution of the Austrian problem in the Italian sense seemed to have been removed. For his purpose Mussolini had to establish a firmer grip on Austria's policy. The *Heimwehr* organization with its fascist leanings provided the necessary instrument for achieving this aim. The influence of the *Heimwehr* on Austro-Italian relations makes the development of the organization, since it had first stated its anti-democratic intentions at Korneuburg on 18 May 1930, worth examining in more detail.

The fascist beliefs of the *Heimwehr* posed the question of whether the organization should lean towards the National Socialists in Germany or towards Italy. Both tendencies were present. The earlier relations with fascist Italy go back to April 1930 when Steidle, the leader, travelled to Italy and secured financial support. Opposed to this course was Prince Starhemberg, a wealthy young Austrian aristocrat. Having taken part in the Kapp *putsch* and in the fights of the *Freikorps* in Upper

---

[1] Suvich to Drummond, Drummond's report, 28 January 1934, BrD, 2nd Ser., Vol. VI, No. 222.

Silesia, Starhemberg was the type who 'wanted to go on fighting almost anyhow'.[1] He said about himself: 'As long as politics meant fighting, and the arena was a political platform, I found them very interesting.'[2] On 6 October 1930 he declared:

We are all conscious that we are a part of the German people; we want to make the old *Ostmark* German and Christian again; this will be only the first stage, until a greater German Empire comes into being, which will last for many thousand years.[3]

Starhemberg therefore criticized the financial support coming from Italy and in September 1930 he forced Steidle to resign. He became leader himself and took the obligation – 'to lead the *Heimwehr* under the Pan-German idea against the parliamentary parties'.

The elections in November 1930 confronted the organization with the problem of whether it should make common cause with the National Socialists or the Christian Socials. The *Heimwehr* was split over the issue. The leaders in Styria and Salzburg advocated an alliance with the National Socialists, while others were in favour of a common front with the Christian Socials. His negotiations with the National Socialists having failed, Starhemberg decided that the *Heimwehr* should form its own electoral front. But the result of the election proved that the party had no popular support. The *Heimwehr* gained only eight seats. However, Starhemberg found some consolation in the hundreds of thousands who had voted against the existing régime and added:

I count also the votes of the Hitler movement. The Hitler movement is a strong ally of ours with which, sooner or later, we shall quite certainly unite ourselves.[4]

During the provincial elections in April 1931 the *Heimwehr* did not win a single seat and began to disintegrate. Starhemberg had financed the greater part of the movement and the election campaign himself and his estates no longer covered the expenses. Owing to his financial difficulties and to the pressure of the more

[1] Vansittart, *The Mist Procession*, London 1958, p. 490.
[2] Starhemberg, *Between Hitler and Mussolini*, 1942, p. 136.
[3] Quoted in Winkler, *Die Diktatur in Österreich*, 1935, p. 136 (my translation).
[4] *Neue Freie Presse*, 17 November 1930, quoted by Gulick, *Austria: From Habsburg to Hitler*, 1948, p. 912.

national-minded group within the party, Starhemberg had to
resign. He was succeeded by Pfriemer, the exponent of the
national-radical section. Pfriemer was opposed to the financial
policy of the government. On 4 September 1931, a day after the
renunciation of the Austro-German customs union, Pfriemer declared that because of the increasing enslavement to foreign
countries the political situation had to be solved by force.[1] But
his *putsch*, in September 1931, failed and Starhemberg reassumed
the leadership.

Starhemberg had learned two lessons from his own and
Pfriemer's failures: he needed financial subsidies from outside
and collaboration with a political party in order to obtain political
power. He could find both by supporting the Christian Socials
and Mussolini's policy in Austria. In June 1932, according to him
with Dollfuss's consent, Starhemberg went to Mussolini and
asked for money, arms, and diplomatic support in exchange for a
pro-Italian policy. Mussolini strengthened Starhemberg in his
new course:

> Our highest ideal in Fascist Italy is 'Italianata', that is the incarnation
> of the Italian consciousness. You must create something of the sort in
> Austria . . . Austria must play a new historic role in Europe.[2]

But more important for Starhemberg Mussolini promised the
necessary financial support. It was arranged that Austrian rifles
and machine-guns, seized as war booty in 1918, were to be sent
to the Austrian arms factory at Hirtenberg. A part of these
arms should be transported to Hungary, whereas Starhemberg
should keep 50,000 rifles and 200 machine-guns in Austria.

Knowing that the arms were destined for the *Heimwehr* and
fearing a strengthening of their worst opponents, the Austrian
Socialists disclosed the arms importations in order to provoke an
intervention of the Little Entente and France. In January 1933
the Little Entent urged in Paris and London that the matter
should be investigated by the League Council to decide whether
or not the disarmament clauses of the Treaty of St. Germain had
been violated.

Nothing could be more unwelcome to the French and British

---

[1] Quoted by Winkler, op. cit., p. 35.
[2] Starhemberg, op. cit., p. 105.

governments. They had no interest in rendering relations with Italy more difficult. Paris and London promised the Little Entente to take steps in Rome and Budapest, and particularly to take strong action in Vienna. This intervention was, however, completely unsuccessful; the Italian and Hungarian governments denied outright having anything to do with the arms delivery. In order to prevent the Little Entente from raising the issue at the League, Paris and London had to undertake immediate action. Both capitals sent a sharp ultimatum to Vienna, on 11 February 1933, demanding either the destruction of the weapons or their return to Italy within two weeks and proof under oath that this had been affected. Vienna informed Rome of the ultimatum and asked for stronger protection, with the reminder that the Italians were partly responsible for the affair.

This offered Rome the chance of turning diplomatic defeat into diplomatic success. Without previous consultation with Vienna it had the note containing the news of the ultimatum published by the *Giornale d'Italia* on 18 February. The indignation of public opinion made it impossible for the Austrian government to consider the note and it flatly rejected the demands.[1] An Italian statement that Italy was prepared to take the arms back and a hint from London that the Little Entente should not pursue the matter further in the League of Nations closed the event.

The incident, though of minor importance, revealed the British and French reluctance to invoke the League against Italian interference in Austrian affairs. France had taken up an ambiguous position between the Little Entente and Italy, which caused disillusion with French leadership. Finally Austria was further estranged from France. Vienna especially resented the fact that Paris had withheld the money of the Lausanne loan in order to exercise pressure in the affair. Though England, France, and Italy had ratified the Lausanne protocol by 31 December 1932 there was no money forthcoming.

Meanwhile Dollfuss was in a precarious position, with only a bare majority in the assembly. When on 4 March 1933 a motion of the Socialists against a government proposal to penalize workers who had taken part in a recent railway strike was carried by one vote, Dollfuss seized the opportunity to dissolve the parliament. His supporters contested the validity of this action, whereupon

[1] See Rieth's report, 18 February 1933, GD, 6057/E446816–26.

the Pan-German president of the assembly resigned his office. Dollfuss now offered his resignation to President Miklas, who consented to a government by emergency decrees. From the middle of March 1933 onwards Austria found herself under semi-dictatorial rule.

This was another reason for the French Socialists to obstruct the Lausanne loan. In 1932 they had only voted for its ratification on condition that Dollfuss would maintain democratic institutions.[1] Their votes were still needed to make the loan fluid and they refused to strengthen a government which was turning fascist. On 9 April Dollfuss protested against these delays in making the loan available. But the *Populaire* replied that the French Socialists were in complete solidarity with their Austrian comrades: 'Not one groschen to the Austria of Dollfuss and Starhemberg.'[2]

The failure in Dollfuss's calculation was that he had begun an authoritarian revolution without having the instrument to carry it through. The conditions of his government were in this respect similar to those of the Papen government in Germany before Hitler's rise to power.[3] Two rival forces had the necessary machinery for Dollfuss's dictatorial policy: the *Heimwehr* supported by Italy, and the National Socialists backed by Germany. In April 1933 Dollfuss turned to Italy and started negotiations with Mussolini.

During Dollfuss's visit to Rome from 11 to 17 April Mussolini put forward the main conditions for Italy's support and, as he carefully pointed out, there was a connexion between his ideas about the future development of the campaign which he devised for Austria and the help which Italy was providing.[4] In return for this help Mussolini expected Dollfuss to pursue a policy corresponding with his own aims. With regard to internal measures Mussolini asked Dollfuss 'to carry through a programme of

---

[1] Renner, *Österreich von der ersten zur zweiten Republik*, Vienna, 1953, pp. 117, 132.

[2] Quoted by Gulick, op. cit., p. 1051.

[3] In October 1932 Dollfuss declared to Papen that the situation had become so difficult that he had to form a government similarly to that one in Germany, Bülow's memorandum, 12 October 1932, GD, 3086/D616417.

[4] Mussolini to Dollfuss, I July 1933, *Geheimer Briefwechsel Mussolini—Dollfuss*, p. 17 (hereafter quoted as *Briefwechsel*), translation in Braunthal, *The Tragedy of Austria*, London, 1948, p. 184.

effective and basic internal reforms in the decisive Fascist sense'.[1] Immediately after his visit to Rome Dollfuss proceeded to fulfil this condition. He strengthened the position of the *Heimwehr* within the cabinet; on 10 May the party leader Fey was appointed Minister of Public Security and thus gained full control over the police. Neustädter-Stürmer, a *Heimwehr* member of the parliament, became state secretary for 'work creation'. In the middle of May Dollfuss, with the help of Starhemberg, created the Fatherland Front (*Vaterländische Front*), a fascist organization which should stand above parties and make them superfluous. On 19 May Dollfuss announced: 'In the new constitution there will be no room for a parliament as it has hitherto existed.'[2] And to Mussolini he wrote:

I am honoured to be instructed by Your Excellency. The fatherland front will be built on the Führer principle; I myself am the Führer of the front.[3]

On foreign policy Mussolini put forward his demand for a closer accord between Austria and Hungary. Mussolini wrote:

This co-operation in both political and economic matters, must, as Italy views it, start off with a formal agreement by both governments to follow a common policy.[4]

Here again Dollfuss hastened to fulfil Mussolini's wishes. He invited the Hungarian President Gömbös to Vienna and the visit took place on 9 July. Dollfuss and Gömbös agreed that Vienna would keep the Hungarian government informed about all Central European questions. In this way Gömbös hoped to prevent Austria from slipping away to the group under French influence.[5] With respect to the economic questions Dollfuss reported to Mussolini that

. . . they are fully agreed that they must continue to develop and broaden their commercial relations. The indispensable corollary for such a development will, I am convinced, be provided by Italy.[6]

---

[1] Mussolini to Dollfuss, 1 July 1933, Braunthal, op. cit., p. 185.
[2] Quoted by Winkler, op. cit., p. 57 (my translation).
[3] Dollfuss to Mussolini, 22 July 1933, Braunthal, op. cit., p. 190.
[4] Mussolini to Dollfuss, I July 1933, Braunthal, op. cit., p. 186.
[5] Köpke's memorandum, 14 July 1933, GD, Ser. C, Vol. I, No. 363.
[6] Dollfuss to Mussolini, 22 July 1933, Braunthal, op. cit., p. 192.

Full agreement between Dollfuss and Gömbös was, however, prevented by their different relations with Germany. Having a common interest in revision and being opposed to the Little Entente, Germany and Hungary were on friendly terms, whereas Austria was necessarily opposed to the idea of revision. But Dollfuss emphasized that this '. . . cannot impair common action by both countries on the question of the economic systematization of the Danubian area'.[1]

GLEICHSCHALTUNG INSTEAD OF ANSCHLUSS

The second new aspect of the Anschluss problem, in addition to Mussolini's active Austrian policy, was Hitler's rise to power in January 1933. Basically the event did not involve any radical change in Germany's foreign policy. Hitler was in no position to realize the ambitions expressed in *Mein Kampf.* He considered the consolidation of his power as his overriding objective.[2] 'At first he had to make Germany entirely National Socialist, and this would take about four years. Only then could he trouble about foreign policy.'[3] Already, in his speech before the German industrialists on 27 January 1932, he had criticized the primacy of foreign politics under Brüning's government:

> In contrast to our own official government I cannot see any hope for the resurrection of Germany if we regard the foreign politics of Germany as the primary factor: the primary necessity is the restoration of a sound national German body-politic armed to strike.[4]

Hitler had no interest in precipitating the resistance of the other countries and still less in giving cause for armed conflict. In view of Germany's military inferiority he stressed at a conference of his ministers on 8 February 1933 that for the next four or five years the main principle must be: everything for the armed forces.[5] And a few days earlier, on 3 February, he declared to leading officers of the *Reichswehr*:

---

[1] Braunthal, op. cit., p. 192.

[2] See Bullock, op. cit., p. 292; Bracher, 'Das Anfangsstadium der Hitlerschen Aussenpolitik', *Vierteljahreshefte für Zeitgeschichte*, V (1957), p. 65. Taylor, *The Origins of the Second World War*, London, 1961, p. 72.

[3] Quoted in Nadolny, *Mein Beitrag*, 1955, p. 130 (my translation).

[4] Baynes, *Hitler's Speeches*, Vol. I, p. 828.

[5] Minutes of the Conference of Ministers, 8 February 1933, GD, Ser. C, Vol. I, No. 16.

The most dangerous period is that of the rebuilding of the armed forces. Then we shall see whether France has statesmen; if so, she will not leave us time but will fall upon us [presumably with eastern satellites].[1]

Hitler was therefore never tired of reassuring the other countries about Germany's good intentions. His tactics were the complete opposite of Brüning's: everything aggressive said by Brüning had been for home consumption, while everything peaceful said by Hitler had been for foreign consumption. Already in April 1933 Hitler envisaged an understanding with Poland.[2] As the revision of the eastern frontiers had been a major objective during the Weimar Republic it shows to what extent Hitler was willing to make sacrifices in order to gain international confidence.

His attitude to Austria contrasted with his general approach. The Anschluss was one of his principal aims and Hitler was already writing in *Mein Kampf* that he – himself an Austrian – felt called upon to reunite the two German states. Hitler did not impose upon himself the same restrictions as he did with regard to the other revisionist aims. Immediately after his rise to power he speculated on the possible collapse of the Viennese government and its replacement by the National Socialists: the *Gleichschaltung*[3] preceded the Anschluss. He could not support the Dollfuss cabinet in any circumstances, Hitler declared to the Italian ambassador Cerruti in March 1933, '. . . elections would have to take place in Austria which would create clear-cut conditions and, in particular, give the National Socialist movement in Austria the place to which it was entitled'.[4] Austria's internal *Gleichschaltung* would obviate the need for an actual Anschluss.[5]

[1] Statement made according to notes by Lieutenant-General Liebmann quoted by Thilo Vogelsang, 'Neue Dokumente zur Geschichte der Reichswehr', *Viertelj. für Zeitgeschichte*, II (1954), p. 435 (translation GD, Ser. C, Vol. I, No. 16, note 7).

[2] Dirksen, *Moskau, Tokio, London*, 1949, p. 123.

[3] As a political term *Gleichschaltung* was used mainly by the National Socialists. It signified a policy which, while respecting the independence of another state, aimed at its internal co-ordination. In the case of Austria this meant that the Austrian institutions should be similar to the German, and the Austrian government formed by National Socialists.

[4] Köpke's memorandum, 23 March 1933, GD, Ser. C, Vol. I, No. 112; Neurath to Hassel, 27 March 1933, ibid., No. 128.

[5] Hitler at the cabinet meeting, 26 May 1933, Minutes of the meeting, ibid., No. 262.

E

No doubt this radical interference in Austrian policies was liable to arouse foreign resistance, since a *Gleichschaltung* amounted, as much as the Anschluss, to a German domination over Austria. The reasons for this inconsistency between Hitler's general caution and his policy in Austria were twofold.

The first is to be found in the history of the National Socialist movement in Austria, which at the beginning led a separate existence from its German counterpart. But by 1924 the Austrian faction was receiving financial support from Germany, and in 1926 had split over the question of continuing its separate existence or of becoming incorporated into the German party. In August 1926, at a meeting in Munich under the presidency of Hitler, the executive of the Austrian National Socialists placed itself unconditionally under Hitler's leadership.[1] From then onwards the Austrian organization constituted a branch of the German Nazi party. The union of the two parties thus anticipated the union of the two countries. After the nomination as Gauleiter for Vienna, on 27 January 1930, of Alfred Frauenfeld, who had been a clerk in the Vienna Bodenkreditanstalt and who had lost his job when the bank failed, the party was reorganized. In three years the Vienna branch increased its membership from three hundred to forty thousand. In July 1931, Theo Habicht, up to then Gauleiter for Wiesbaden, was nominated Provincial Inspector for Austria. The propaganda immediately increased and led to a strengthening of the party.

As the Austrian National Socialists formed an integral section of the German Nazi party it seemed a necessary implication that the National Socialists would take over power as their comrades had done in Germany. Frank, the *Reichskommissar* for Justice, declared in a broadcast from Munich on 18 March 1933:

Austria is the last part of Germany where German aspirations can still be suppressed with impunity. I wish to warn the Austrian government in all friendship and fraternal sympathy not to force the National Socialists of the Reich to take upon themselves the task of securing the liberty of their fellow-countrymen in Austria.[2]

---

[1] *The Death of Dollfuss, An official history of the revolt of July 1934, in Austria,* p. 18 (hereafter quoted as *Official History*); the major part of it is a translation of the Austrian publication *Beiträge zur Vorgeschichte und Geschichte der Juli revolte,* Vienna, 1934 (quoted as *Beiträge*).

[2] Quoted in *Official History,* p. 46.

The Austrian Chargé d'Affaires in Berlin protested in vain against this speech. No sufficient explanation being given, the Austrian Minister Tauschitz made another protest on 12 April. But he received the reply that Frank had obviously not spoken in an official capacity. The matter was not to be considered as interference in Austria's internal affairs. 'It was simply an attitude taken by the National Socialist Dr. Frank with respect to the struggle of his fellow-party members in Austria.'[1]

The second reason for Hitler's lack of caution on the Austrian question was that he personally estimated that the Dollfuss government would give in easily and come to a compromise favourable to the Nazis. At the cabinet meeting on 26 May 1933 he declared that the goal of the Austrian régime was the expulsion of the nationalist-minded opposition in Austria. There was a great danger that 'Germany thereby might definitely lose six million people who were becoming something like the Swiss'. 'The contest with the Austrian government would be decided before the end of the summer of 1933.'[2]

The position of Dollfuss's government and his relations with his own party, the Christian Socials, seemed indeed to justify this expectation. A part of the Christian Socials resented the growing dependence upon the *Heimwehr*. At the party conference of the Christian Socials from 6–7 May 1933 the party elected Vaugoin instead of Dollfuss as its party chairman, though it had been the tradition, if the Chancellor was Christian Social, to nominate him for the post. This created hostility between Vaugoin and Dollfuss, while it confirmed the latter in his decision to abandon the party as a basis. Moreover, the Christian Socials watched with apprehension the creation of the Fatherland Front. It meant a decrease of their influence and destroyed their illusion that they would take over the function of the state party with a totalitarian character.

A strong wing of the Christian Socials therefore favoured negotiations with the National Socialists and hoped by coming to terms with them to elude the *Heimwehr* influence. For the discussions the Christian Socials formed a committee consisting of Vaugoin, Buresch, and Rintelen, while Schuschnigg took part

[1] Köpke's memorandum, GD, 8643/E605165.
[2] Minutes, 26 May 1933, GD, Ser. C, Vol. I, No. 262.

as Dollfuss's personal confidant. On the side of the National Socialists the negotiations were conducted by Habicht. During these negotiations in May 1933 the Christian Socials offered the Nazis two ministerial posts in the government. Habicht demanded the elimination of the *Heimwehr* from the cabinet and its replacement by three or at the most four men of his group. This reorganization was to be followed by elections, but Habicht conceded that however the elections resulted Dollfuss would remain as Chancellor.[1]

Though Dollfuss personally intervened and had two conferences with Habicht, they could reach no agreement. The crucial point was the demand for new elections. Dollfuss could make no concessions on this score. He had no illusions about the prospect that the Nazis would materially increase their vote. In fact, the municipal elections in Innsbruck at the end of April 1933, which resulted in the Nazis winning nine out of twenty seats, had just provided a strong warning. And the Austrian government announced thereupon that no more municipal elections would take place until further notice.

Not only the Christian Socials, but the *Heimwehr* itself also tried to strike a bargain with the National Socialists. Starhemberg had contacts with Göring through the former *Heimwehr* minister Huber, who went to Berlin on 5 April 1933, though without any results.

Whatever the outcome of these contacts Hitler determined not to relax the pressure on the Austrian government, considering that a continuation of the struggle could only strengthen his bargaining position. He therefore gave his consent to the increase of activities against the Austrian government. His tactics were an application of the method he had used on his way to power in Germany. By demanding new elections and exerting pressure upon the Austrian government he hoped to force the participation of the National Socialists in the cabinet.

On 13 May 1933, Frank, the Bavarian Minister of Justice, arrived in Vienna by aeroplane, accompanied by Kerrl, the *Reichsminister* of Justice. Since the question of Frank's broadcast on 18 March was still left unsettled the Austrian government regarded his arrival as a provocation. On landing Frank was informed that

---

[1] Schuschnigg, *Dreimal Österreich*, pp. 240–242; Langoth, *Kampf um Österreich*, p. 106; Winkler, *op. cit.*, p. 54.

his visit 'was not especially desired'.[1] In spite of this Frank proceeded to Graz on 14 May. He attended a National Socialist meeting, at which he greeted the party members on behalf of Hitler. In his speech he declared that reprisals would be taken for the reception he had been given by the Austrian government and the insult to the German government. He urged the audience to resist the Austrian police, threatened that no German would come to Austria this summer during the tourist season, and repeatedly described Dollfuss as a 'Pocket Metternich'.

The tourist boycott, forecast by Frank, was decided in the cabinet meeting on 27 May. A special tax of 1,000 Marks was imposed on all citizens making journeys to Austria. Hitler ordered that as a matter of tactics a statement should be issued that the German government felt constrained to inaugurate a visa requirement for German tourists going abroad, in order 'to preclude visits by German guests, not wanted by Austria, which might possibly lead to diplomatic complications'. By stopping the tourist traffic the Austrian economy was struck at its weakest point. Furthermore, Hitler ordered that the Austro-German negotiations on preferential tariffs which, due to Austrian concessions, were near final agreement, should not be concluded. The delay should, if possible, be explained by non-political reasons.[2]

The assignment of Habicht, the provincial inspector for the Austrian National Socialists, to the German legation in Vienna as Press Attaché on 27 May was to be a further move against the Austrian government. As an official of the Austrian Nazis pointed out, the assignment was only temporary and for the sake of appearances. Habicht would not be able to devote himself to press matters or any other business at the legation, as he was completely occupied with his activities in the Austrian party office.[3] But the Austrian government considered it impossible to grant diplomatic privileges and thereby special protection to one of its most aggressive opponents. It refused to take cognizance of the appointment.[4] On 29 May the German Minister Rieth protested

---

[1] GD, Ser. C, Vol. I, No. 234, note 1.
[2] Ritter's memorandum, 25 April 1933, ibid., No. 187, see marginal note by Neurath, No. 187, note 3.
[3] Völcker's memorandum, 19 May 1933, GD, 3086/D616495–97.
[4] Verbal note of the Austrian government, 27 May 1933, GD, Ser. C, Vol. I, No. 267.

against this decision. Two days later, upon being informed by Habicht that the police had made a search of his apartment in Linz, Rieth made another protest. In its reply on 31 May the Austrian government refused again to grant Habicht 'such privileges in Austria as would result from investiture with a diplomatic function'.[1]

After Dr. Steidle, the leader of the *Heimatschutz* in Tyrol, had been shot at by von Alvensleben, a German member of the National Socialists, on 11 June, and after several Nazi riots had taken place on 12 June, the Austrian government arrested about eighty German National Socialists and expelled Habicht from the country. Hitler ordered that the Press Attaché to the Austrian legation in Berlin, Wasserbäck, should leave Germany by way of reprisal.[2] During the night of 13–14 June the Prussian police arrested Wasserbäck and took him into custody. As a consequence of these events the German Nazi party was prohibited in Austria on 19 June. Thereupon the propaganda campaign from Germany was increased and conducted through the Munich broadcasting station. On 5 July a regular series of talks was introduced 'designed to keep listeners in Austria informed in regard to the position in Austria'. The first talk was given on the same day by Habicht:

The whole of Austria, the whole world, shall see and understand that the National-socialism is a living force in Austria and that no power on earth can remove it . . . The organisation in its new form is complete. Let us take up the struggle which the Dollfuss government has thrust upon us and carry it through ruthlessly and relentlessly to victory. With us are a thousand years of German history, behind us stands the whole German people, but before us lies, as our goal, the liberation of Austria and the establishment of the German nation.[3]

During the period from 5 July 1933 until February 1934, eighty-four similar propaganda speeches were broadcast.[4]

In addition to the radio propaganda German aeroplanes started dropping leaflets and propaganda pamphlets on Austrian towns on 17, 25, and 27 July. The Austrian minister made several protests against these violations and the German Foreign Ministry

[1] Rieth's report, 31 May 1933, GD, 3086/D616512–14.
[2] Memoranda, 9 and 13 June, GD, Ser. C, Vol. I, Nos. 298, 306.
[3] Broadcast on 5 July 1933, *Documents on Intern. Affairs*, pp. 387–388.
[4] *Official History*, p. 59.

could no longer deny these incidents. But the Foreign Ministry had no power to stop them. On 1 August a German official admitted that a violation had occurred. He indicated however that the whole matter was a party affair and declared that the party

. . . did not regard Austria as a foreign country, and their propaganda would not stop at frontiers which had been forced upon them. The point of view of the party was, therefore, that this was no interference with the affairs of a foreign country, but the fight of the opposition party against the government in power.[1]

But Austro-German affairs were not purely a domestic issue, as Hitler pretended, and the German Foreign Ministry was well aware of this. The party activities ran strictly against the policy advocated by the German professional diplomats. As this was the first clash between the Foreign Office and the party, the outcome of the clash was decisive for the question of how strong the influence of the Foreign Office would be in determining the objectives of German policy.

On 22 March Köpke, director of the south-eastern department, wrote that Germany 'must absolutely abstain from broaching the Anschluss question' and 'scrupulously avoid any appearance of influencing Austrian domestic policy'.[2] In a memorandum of 19 May he stated that he considered the Austrian complaint about the conduct of Frank during his speech at Graz as justified, and that he was concerned about the assignment of Habicht to the German legation in Vienna.[3] Heeren, senior council in the same department, objected likewise to the appointment of Habicht and the tourist ban.[4] And State Secretary Bülow pointed out to Neurath that

. . . the struggle with Austria, which has lasted so much longer than we had expected, is extremely costly to us. We are losing the sympathies of all the smaller powers, which must be telling themselves that we might proceed against them with similar methods.[5]

But Foreign Minister Neurath failed to combat the party policy. In February 1933 he had declared to the British ambassador, Sir

[1] *Official History*, pp. 63–64.
[2] Köpke to Rieth, 22 March 1933, GD, Ser. C, Vol. I, No. 107.
[3] Köpke's memorandum, 19 May 1933, ibid., No. 249.
[4] Heeren's memorandum, 20 May 1933, ibid., No. 256.
[5] Bülow to Neurath, 1 August 1933, ibid., No. 385.

Horace Rumbold, that 'Hitler was proving reasonable' and that he had only accepted his post 'on condition that he was given a free hand and that no experiments in foreign policy were to be tried'.[1] The developments up to August 1933 proved that Neurath had deluded himself, and had failed to stand up for his own policy. He claimed at the Nuremberg trial that he opposed Hitler's Austrian policy,[2] but his resistance was lame. Neurath expressed his agreement in principle with the travel ban, though he had some misgivings about the economic aspects. He gave the necessary instructions for the appointment of Habicht as Press Attaché. He indeed suggested that Frank should be stopped from speaking in Austria, but abandoned the subject when Hitler ordered that nothing should be done.[3]

The party went ahead with its Austrian policy, and during the London economic conference in the middle of June Neurath was extremely perturbed by the hostility which he met. On 19 June Neurath warned Hitler that Paris was following the Austro-German conflict closely and was trying to create an atmosphere of intervention, even of a military kind. He underlined that 'this tendency must be kept in mind in our conduct toward Austria'.[4]

THE ATTEMPT AT JOINT ANGLO-FRENCH–ITALIAN INTERVENTION

The continuance of the Nazi attacks on the Austrian government in defiance of Austrian protests alarmed the Western capitals. During the economic conference in London in June 1933 Dollfuss's speech was received with demonstrative applause which expressed the widespread friendly feeling for Austria among the members of many delegations.[5] Eden, then Parliamentary Under-Secretary of State for Foreign Affairs, declared in the House of Commons, on 21 June, that Dollfuss had the sympathies of the British government and of public opinion 'in his efforts to establish the finances of Austria on a sound basis and to maintain the authority and independence of the state'.[6] In

---

[1] Rumbold to Simon, 4 February 1933, BrD, 2nd Ser., Vol. IV, No. 235.
[2] *The Trial of German Major War Criminals*, London, 1947, Part 17, p. 121.
[3] Lammer's memorandum, 15 May 1933, GD, 8674/E606944.
[4] *Trial of the German Major War Criminals*, Vol. XL, doc. Neurath, Part 12, pp. 469–470.
[5] Neurath to Bülow, 15 June 1933, GD, Ser. C, Vol. I, No. 313.
[6] *Survey of International Affairs, 1934*, p. 444.

order to achieve this aim the British government advised Dollfuss to strengthen his political position by coming to some working arrangement with the Socialist party.[1]

But since the Austrian Socialists had eliminated the demand for an Anschluss from their party programme as a consequence of Hitler's rise to power and turned to the Little Entente and France for support, a reconciliation between Dollfuss and the Socialists was conditional upon a rejection of Italian Fascism. Such a course ran straight against Dollfuss's *rapprochement* with Italy, and he was unwilling to sacrifice his new friendship with Mussolini in order to come to terms with the Socialists.

The moral support which Dollfuss found was however of no avail as long as it did not express itself in stronger political action. In this respect Sir John Simon, the British Foreign Secretary, was reluctant to take the risks involved in a strong central European policy. When the question of joint action by England, France, and Italy against Berlin arose, he dismissed the idea. He thought the 'attitude of the press and public opinion would be sufficient to dissuade the German National Socialists from their present course'.[2] The German government seemed more likely to yield to this pressure 'than to diplomatic representations which would in fact make it harder for them to save their faces'.

Nor was the French attitude more promising. Foreign Minister Paul-Boncour reiterated the position of the French Socialists, which excluded any support for Dollfuss as long as he pursued his pro-Italian policy. Paul-Boncour declared himself for a postponement of the Lausanne loan until 'the Austrian government's internal position was strong enough to guarantee the maintenance of independence'.[3] Moreover, at the end of June the possibility of getting the loan issued in France in the near future was viewed pessimistically on account of the growing deterioration of the French government credit, which in turn was due to the weakness of the French government.[4]

An additional cause for alarm in Vienna was the number of

---

[1] Sargent's note, 29 June 1933, BrD, 2nd Ser., Vol. V, enclosure in No. 233.
[2] Simon to Phipps, 17 June 1933, BrD, 2nd Ser., Vol. V, No. 214.
[3] Quoted in *Survey of International Affairs, 1934*, p. 443.
[4] Rost, appointed by the Financial Committee of the League to the Austrian government, to Sargent, Sargent's note, 29 June 1933, BrD, 2nd Ser., Vol. V enclosure in No. 233.

Austrian National Socialists who fled into Bavaria in order to escape persecution by the Austrian government. These refugees, numbering between 5,000 and 6,000, were assembled in Bavarian camps, trained in the SA service and formed the so-called Austrian Legion. Dollfuss feared that a violent incursion of Nazi bands into Austrian territory might take place. Since the Italians made no secret of their intention that, in the event of a German invasion, they would react with military measures and send troops to the Austrian frontier,[1] Dollfuss rightly apprehended that a German incursion could easily lead to an Italian instead of a German occupation.

Dollfuss sought protection from too much patronage. By bringing the Austrian question before the League, he hoped to escape from his growing dependence upon Italy and to internationalize the problem. On 29 June 1933 Dollfuss sent Rost, the League financial adviser to the Austrian government, to London, with the suggestion that England, France, and Italy, in order not to be caught by surprise, should agree in advance on the action they would take in defence of Austria's independence, if it were suddenly attacked. Dollfuss suggested as a possible countermeasure a concerted appeal to the League.[2] Simon welcomed the proposal and sounded Paris and Rome on their reactions on 4 July. The French equally approved of the idea. But the Italian government, resenting the Austrian attempt to detach herself from Italy's exclusive tutelage, refused co-operation.[3] Simon thereupon pointed out to the Italians that the Italian remedy of armed intervention, 'amounting to a general race by troops to the Austrian frontier, is particularly dangerous, is just what we want to avoid, and is precisely what the League exists to prevent'.[4]

In the late summer of 1933 the British Foreign Office made stronger attempts to promote effective protection of Austria, but this policy was more the result of the initiative of Vansittart, Permanent Under-Secretary of State for Foreign Affairs, in charge of the Foreign Office during Simon's holidays from 15 July to 29 August, than a reflection of the general course. Even before Hitler's advent to power Vansittart had advocated a strong anti-

---

[1] Suvich to Graham, 11 July 1933, BrD, 2nd Ser., Vol. V, No. 246.
[2] Sargent's note, 29 June 1933, ibid., enclosure in No. 233, minute 4.
[3] Graham to Simon, 11 July 1933, ibid., No. 246.
[4] Simon to Graham, 12 July 1933, ibid., No. 249.

German policy. Hitler's aggressive Austrian policy confirmed him in this attitude. Vansittart warned the British government that Austria confronted it 'with a European crisis of the first magnitude', 'with Hitler's first trial of strength'.

Austria has only been chosen for the first break-through of the renewed will to power because it is the easiest and weakest point . . . The future of Europe turns largely on the fashion of our facing the German challenge over Austria, in which we are at present likely to lose. The seriousness of the challenge can only be realised if it is not seen as an isolated case, in which the country has no direct interest, but as the first of a series of challenges, each one of which will carry with it a nearer threat to this country.[1]

Subsequent events have borne out Vansittart's warnings. At the time, however, the effectiveness of his advice was diminished by the fact that he was already in his own words 'tarred as an alarmist'. It was difficult to distinguish how much the warnings were based on foresight and how much on his anti-German feelings, of which he made no secret. Moreover, Vansittart's pessimistic outlook weakened his argument, as he himself conceded that 'we are all backing a losing horse in Austria'.[2]

Vansittart regarded the prevention of an Anschluss as the primary objective and his policy towards Italy and France followed from this. Only Dollfuss and the *Heimwehr* promised to be a challenge for the National Socialists and both therefore deserved backing. France and Italy, having a common interest in maintaining Austria's independence, had to find a basis for co-operation. Vansittart overlooked, however, that this common interest was of a purely negative character. Italy suspected that, by saving Austria from Germany, France wanted to force Austria into an alignment with the Little Entente. France, on the other hand, distrusted Italian intentions and feared the formation of an Austro-Hungarian–Italian bloc. There was ample evidence for both these suspicions. But Vansittart dismissed these considerations. He held Italian support against Germany 'so essential that France ought to be prepared to pay for it in this and other matters where she is in a position to make concessions'.[3]

---

[1] Vansittart's memorandum on the 'Present and Future Position in Europe', BrD, 2nd Ser., Vol. V, No. 254.

[2] Ibid., p. 549.

[3] Vansittart to Tyrrel (Paris), 11 August 1933, BrD, 2nd Ser., Vol. V, No. 322.

On 24 July, against Mussolini's urgent advice,[1] Dollfuss requested the British to support his government openly and to make representations in Berlin in order to stop the interference in Austrian internal affairs. On 25 July, he sent similar requests to Paris and Rome.[2] This gave Vansittart the opportunity for action. He emphasized that the British government took so serious a view of the situation that the case could be brought before the League as 'a circumstance affecting international relations which threatens to disturb international peace'. Since Italy had only recently expressed her reluctance to invoke the League, Vansittart refrained from such a measure. No friend of the League himself, he proposed instead that France, Italy, and England should make common representations in Berlin urging the German government to put an end to all subversive activities.[3] The French government again followed suit. On 29 June it approved the British note and promised its support.

This pressure on Italy for common action placed Mussolini in a difficult position. Though he was opposed to German domination over Austria, he wanted to maintain good relations with Germany; he wanted to run with the hare and hunt with the hounds. His German policy became a decisive element in the explanation of his Austrian policy, which in turn accounts for his reluctance in supporting the British initiative.

Already in 1932 Mussolini had, as a consequence of his revisionist attitude, advocated the German demand for equality of rights in armaments and advised the German government on the right course to take. In order to placate public opinion and French opposition the Germans should declare that they would only claim equality of rights *after* the prospect of disarmament by other countries had disappeared. But naturally such a declaration was only meant *pour la vitrine*.[4] With Hitler's rise to power ideological solidarity strengthened Mussolini in his pro-German policy. The Fascist Grand Council recognized in National Socialism

[1] Mussolini to Hassel, Hassel's report, 8 August 1933, GD, 6113/E53783–84.
[2] Vansittart to Harvey and Graham, 25 July 1933, BrD, 2nd Ser., Vol. V, No. 270; see Bülow's memorandum, 31 July 1933, GD, Ser. C, Vol. I, No. 383.
[3] BrD, 2nd Ser., Vol. V, No. 271.
[4] Mussolini to Schuberth, 29 July 1932, GD, 6001/E442882.

... the affirmation of a new spirit which, directly or indirectly, derived from the whole of doctrines and institutions thanks to which Italy had created the modern state, the state of the people.[1]

By supporting Germany in the face of France Italy could exercise a stronger influence. French attention would be diverted from central Europe.

Mussolini was aware of the fact that Germany needed time to regain her strength. On 28 March he declared to the German ambassador, Hassel, that it was absolutely necessary to get through the next few months without a conflict. Towards the end of 1933 Italian armaments would be considerably stronger, so that one could then calmly face anything, and he referred in this context to a possible co-operation of the two air forces.[2] Support for Germany was likewise Mussolini's motive when he proposed the Four Power Pact between Italy, England, France, and Germany in March 1933:

> Except for Italy's friendship, Germany was at the moment completely isolated. The all-important thing was to break through this ring quickly and effectively. A prompt conclusion of the pact, which would strike the weapons from the enemy's propaganda, was the best means toward that end.[3]

Since the British government recommended the Four Power Pact for exactly the opposite reasons, namely as the basis for a closer understanding between France and Italy,[4] the paradoxical situation arose that the four contracting countries undertook, under the terms of the pact, 'to make every effort to pursue a policy of active co-operation between all Powers' while on second thoughts they were directing the pact against each other. Ultimately the only effect of the pact was to estrange the Little Entente, especially Poland, from France, an effect which was one of Mussolini's and Hitler's explicit aims.

In strengthening Germany, which aimed at Austria's *Gleichschaltung*, Mussolini actually pursued a policy which was

---

[1] Quoted by Anchieri, 'Les rapports italo-allemands pendant l'ère nazi-fasciste'; *Revue d'Histoire de la Deuxième Guerre Mondiale*, 25 (1957), p. 6.

[2] Hassel's report, 28 March 1933, GD, Ser. C, Vol. C, No. 122.

[3] Aloisi to Papen and Hassel on the basis of Mussolini's memorandum, 19 and 20 April 1933, ibid., Nos. 164, 171.

[4] Simon to Tyrrel, 26 May 1933, BrD, 2nd Ser., Vol. V, No. 171; Vansittart to Graham, 15 July 1933, ibid., No. 254.

irreconcilable with his own objective of an Austria dependent upon Italy. Mussolini discovered a solution to this inconsistency without sacrificing one policy to the other. His idea was to defeat National Socialism in Austria without fighting it. This is where the Austrian Socialists had to play their part. Mussolini proposed to Dollfuss that he should outstrip the National Socialists and win over their followers. Since the fight against Marxism was one of the major principles of the Nazis, Dollfuss had to forestall them and to crush the Socialists.[1] Not that Mussolini believed that the Socialists presented any danger to the Austrian régime. They themselves were threatened by the National Socialists and in view of this danger they would, as Mussolini pointed out to Dollfuss in his letter of 1 July 1933, 'be obliged, as always, to march along the line chalked out by Your Excellency'. But that was not the essential point:

If the Social Democratic Party is treated with consideration, it appears to me that the much greater and more concrete danger exists that thereby the anti-Marxist weapon will be delivered into the hands of the Nazis and they will be enabled at a given moment to play the role of the saviours.

Dollfuss had to make full use of this tactic:

I am convinced that, as soon as you appeal to all sound national forces in Austria, and strike a blow at the Social-Democrats in their stronghold, Vienna, and extend the purge to all centres, and press hard against all the disruptive tendencies which are in opposition to the authoritarian principle of the state, then many of those who today are active in the ranks of the Nazis will come over to the circle of the national front.[2]

As a secondary measure, Mussolini tried to dissuade the Germans from their course. They should not play the game of the French, who were speculating on the German–Italian antagonism in the Austrian question. The problem of the relations between Austria and Germany was not acute and they could agree on a common policy in the south-east without discussing Austria.[3]

---

[1] Mussolini to Dollfuss, 1 July 1933, Braunthal, op. cit., p. 185; already on 20 April 1933 Mussolini had mentioned to Hassel that he had told Dollfuss that he had to crush the Socialists, if he wanted to remain at the helm, Hassel's report, 20 April 1933, GD, Ser. C, Vol. I, No. 171.

[2] Quoted in Braunthal, op. cit., pp. 184–187.

[3] Mussolini to Hassel, Hassel's reports, 20 April 1933, GD, Ser. C, Vol. I, No. 171; 30 June 1933, ibid., No. 343.

Hassel strongly supported Mussolini in this line. The idea of an economic co-operation in the Danube Basin was his current theme. According to him the economic activity in the south-east should be divided between the two countries. ·

These advances found no response in Berlin. The German Foreign Office held the Austrian question to be the decisive one and saw no possibility of by-passing it. It had no interest in being drawn into collaboration or even an alliance with Italy and Hungary, because such a combination would be inferior in power politics and inevitably be detrimental to Germany. Co-operation could even erect a barrier which would prevent Germany from increasing her influence and deprive her of her own initiative.[1]

Mussolini's tactics of competition in anti-Marxism in Austria as a challenge to the Nazis, and his intention of using Germany against France, explain why Mussolini did not respond to the British request of 29 July for concerted action in Berlin. In fact he did exactly the opposite. Before making a reply to London he informed the German government of the British intentions and the contents of the British note. He consulted the German government on how the British initiative could best be obviated and for this purpose suggested a German assurance to Rome that the activities objected to in the British note would cease. Mussolini offered as a counter-concession that the two large parties, the National Socialists and the Christian Socials, would form a new cabinet in accordance with the probable ratio of strength in the population, but without new elections.[2]

Mussolini's proposal was considered at a meeting of Bülow and other officials of the Foreign Office with Habicht on 31 July. Negotiations with the Austrians under Mussolini's tutelage were regarded as premature, because Habicht emphasized that 'from three different quarters in the Austrian cabinet feelers had been put out in order to explore the possibility for such a compromise'. On 4 August Neurath drew Hitler's attention to the intended intervention. Hitler now ordered a greater moderation in Habicht's radio propaganda and a stop to all aeroplane propaganda. The economic pressure, however, was to be continued in

[1] Neurath to Hassel, 7 February 1933, GD, Ser. C, Vol. I, No. 14; Köpke to Hassel, 20 February 1933, ibid., No. 27.
[2] Bülow's memorandum, 31 July 1933, ibid., No. 383.

all its severity.[1] The Italian ambassador was informed accordingly on 5 August.[2]

Vansittart's reaction was that 'the Italians had stolen a march on us in order to avoid a step with us'.[3] But Mussolini's hope that the German reply would obviate the French and English representations was disappointed. The English and French ambassadors made their *démarche* on 7 August. It was, however, easy for Berlin to play off the Italians against the French and the English. Bülow could point out that the necessary assurances had been given and that he could not understand this belated action.[4] Thus Mussolini's beliefs in his 'special position' in Berlin caused the failure of the intervention. No further measures were taken. Vansittart was opposed to an appeal to the League since this 'would be foredoomed to futility, because Italy was not yet in line'.[5]

Mussolini found no reward for his restraint. The aeroplane propaganda did indeed cease as a consequence of Hitler's interference, but on 9 August Habicht delivered another broadcast on the Munich radio. He sharply attacked Dollfuss 'for having arranged this foreign intervention in a purely German quarrel. Her action,' he said, 'disclosed that the Austrian government was facing collapse.'[6] Not only Mussolini's policy, but his prestige was now at stake. He became 'quite unusually excited and attached extreme importance to the matter'.[7] But Hitler declared that he 'would not stand for that sort of tutelage'.[8] He had only promised that the propaganda would be kept in check and this had been done. He was not going to be coerced by Mussolini.

---

[1] Neurath to Bülow, GD, Ser. C, Vol. I, No. 390.
[2] Bülow's memorandum, ibid., No. 391.
[3] Memorandum, 28 August 1933, BrD, 2nd Ser., Vol. V, No. 371.
[4] Bülow's memoranda, 7 August 1933, GD, Ser. C, Vol. I, Nos. 392, 393; Newton's report, 7 August 1933, BrD, 2nd Ser., Vol. V, No. 312.
[5] Vansittart's memorandum, BrD, ibid., No. 371, minute 26.
[6] On instruction from Habicht a text of this speech was sent by his office to Neurath personally and Neurath read the text to Hitler, GD, 3086/D618826–35.
[7] Cerruti to Heeren, 12 August 1933, GD, Ser. C, Vol. I, No. 401.
[8] Hitler to Neurath, 14 August 1933, ibid., No. 402.

CHAPTER IV

FAILURE OF HITLER'S AUSTRIAN POLICY, 1934

The contest will be decided before the end of the summer. The sacrifices which Germany must make now are nothing compared to the sacrifices which would have to be borne if the development in Austria continued in its present course.

Hitler at the Conference of Ministers on 26 May 1933

THE NEGOTIATIONS BETWEEN DOLLFUSS AND HABICHT

Committed to his course of challenging National Socialism in Austria alone, Mussolini attributed the failure of the intervention in Berlin not to his own policy, but to the insufficient application of his principles. In seeking British and French assistance Dollfuss had shown himself to be less than pliant. The actual pace of Dollfuss's internal measures did not satisfy Mussolini's expectations, and he decided to establish a firmer grip on Dollfuss's policy. For this purpose another meeting was arranged between Dollfuss and Mussolini at Riccione on 19 and 20 August 1933. Suvich participated on the Italian side, while Starhemberg went to Venice and was in constant touch with Dollfuss.

Mussolini left no doubt about his intentions:

The third trip to Italy – more unexpected and more sensational than the previous ones – must not result in things being left in their present static condition, but must signalize the beginning of a new course in Austrian domestic and foreign policy.[1]

Mussolini declared to Dollfuss that, though he did not expect a German invasion, Italy would react with military measures in such an event.[2] He also set forth a detailed programme for

[1] Note to Dollfuss for his consideration, undated, Braunthal, op. cit., p. 192.
[2] Dollfuss's *Amtserinnerung*, notes made for the Austrian Foreign Office file of his discussions with Mussolini at Riccione, 19 and 20 August 1933, Braunthal, op. cit., p. 194.

F

Austria's internal policy. Upon his return from Riccione Dollfuss should announce an important speech for early September, followed by a *putsch*. In order to make the speech efficient, it ought to be preceded by the following series of actions:

(*a*) Immediate strengthening of the government by bringing in new elements (Steidle, Starhemberg) who will remove the present government's character of being composed simply of a residue from the old régime.

(*b*) Fusion of all forces and of all fronts into a single national front with the motto: the independence of Austria and the renovation of Austria.

(*c*) Pronounced dictatorial character of the government.

(*d*) Government commissioner for the city of Vienna.

(*e*) Propaganda on a large scale.[1]

Over the participation of the *Heimwehr* in the government disagreement developed between Dollfuss and Mussolini. Dollfuss noted that 'Mussolini exerted pressure on him to get a fuller participation', but he succeeded in evading this. Starhemberg was not at all pleased with this outcome and returned to Italy, where he stayed at Rome from 1 to 8 September and had several conferences with Mussolini. Mussolini fully supported Starhemberg's point of view. Shortly after Starhemberg returned to Vienna another letter from Mussolini arrived, in which he expressed his misgivings that Winkler and Schumy, both members of the *Landbund*, 'who are not thought to have the will or the intention to bring the country out of the morass of liberalism and democracy, remain in the government and participate in all official Austrian demonstrations of a political character'.[2]

Dollfuss could no longer evade Mussolini's demands. On 11 September he made, as scheduled in Riccione, his famous speech outlining his constitution reform programme in the direction of 'a Social Christian German state with a corporative basis'. The Vatican had by now decided that Dollfuss's new course was worth supporting, a fact which found its echo in Dollfuss's advocacy of the encyclical letter *Quadragesimo Anno* as the model for building a corporate state. Dollfuss, however, still avoided making the

---

[1] Note to Dollfuss, Braunthal, op. cit., p. 192.

[2] Mussolini to Dollfuss, 9 September 1933, Braunthal, op. cit., pp. 195–196; *Briefwechsel*, pp. 70–72.

final move against the Socialists. Starhemberg gave him a sharp reminder in his speech on the following day, 12 September, demanding that 'Dollfuss should chase the Socialists out of the Vienna city hall'.[1]

By keeping Winkler and Schumy in the cabinet Dollfuss had until then counterbalanced the influence of the *Heimwehr* ministers and played off the *Landbund* against them. Under Starhemberg's and Mussolini's pressure he had to reorganize his government. Vice-Chancellor Winkler, Schumy, and Army Minister Vaugoin had to resign on 20 September. In addition to the chancellorship Dollfuss assumed the Ministries of Foreign Affairs, Public Security, Defence, and Agriculture; while Fey, leader of the Vienna *Heimwehr*, became Vice-Chancellor.

Dollfuss felt that Mussolini's influence was becoming intolerable.[2] By occupying the major ministries he had considerably strengthened his position within the government, but he lacked more than ever any support outside. Having abandoned the democratic parties one after the other and finally parliament itself, he was forced into increasing dependency upon the *Heimwehr*. By trying to strengthen his position through authoritarianism he had actually weakened it and found himself the prisoner of his own policy. Dollfuss realized that his course could ultimately result in his own fall.

He therefore tried to loosen the bonds which tied him to Rome. He let Mussolini know that 'he marches quickly, but does not like to have his friends push him from behind – that disturbs the march'.[3] Nor did he receive Mussolini's praise for his speech on 11 September with his usual gratitude. He replied on 22 September that he would 'translate his programme into action with especial regard for Austrian conditions'.[4]

The question for Dollfuss was in which direction should he turn. His anti-socialist outlook excluded a compromise with the Socialists, his authoritarian policy ruled out a revival of the

---

[1] Winkler, op. cit., p. 69; Renner, op. cit., p. 132; this declaration is in contradiction to Starhemberg's account in his memoirs, op. cit., p. 120: 'First let it be understood that neither Dollfuss nor I had the slightest wish to bring about a collision with the armed elements of the Social Democratic party.'

[2] Peter, Secretary General for Foreign Affairs, to Rieth, Rieth's report, 13 December 1933, GD, Ser. C, Vol. II, No. 124.

[3] Braunthal, op. cit., pp. 196–198.

[4] Braunthal, op. cit., pp. 198–199.

parliamentary system. The only alternative left was a compromise with the National Socialists. Dollfuss found himself under constant pressure from their side to conclude an agreement with them. State Secretary Gleissner, convinced of the hopelessness of the struggle against the Nazis, induced Dollfuss to try this course.

Two advances, one on a governmental and the other on a party level, were made. On 26 September, in Geneva, Dollfuss asked for a meeting with Neurath. The German Foreign Minister was willing to meet him. He arranged with Kanya, the Hungarian Foreign Minister, that he would have a conversation with Dollfuss at his hotel. The plan failed, however, because they could not agree who should pay the first visit. Dollfuss was only prepared to come 'if Neurath left his calling card at his hotel'.[1]

The negotiations with the Nazi party started more successfully. On 27 September Habicht met Foppa, the chairman of the Pan-German party, and Langoth, one of its members, in Czechoslovakia and authorized them to enter into negotiations with Dollfuss should they materialize.[2] On 13 October Foppa and Langoth discussed with Dollfuss the possibilities of an arrangement. Though at the beginning Dollfuss was still reluctant to negotiate with Habicht personally and preferred direct contact with Hess and Hitler, he finally drew up an outline of his position and made arrangements to facilitate a further journey by Foppa and Langoth, this time to Germany. They met Habicht again on 20 October in Munich.

Habicht emphasized that Dollfuss could only negotiate through him and that he had the full authorization of the Führer to act on behalf of the National Socialists. Believing himself on the point of achieving success, Habicht called all his *Gauleiters* together at Munich and told them that he was holding them personally responsible that not the slightest incident should occur in Austria during the next few weeks. On the other hand he asked the Foreign Ministry to avoid anything which the Austrian government might interpret as a strengthening of its position.[3]

---

[1] Völcker's memoranda, 26 and 28 September 1933, GD, Ser. C, Vol. I, No. 450; GD, 3086/D616956.

[2] No documents can be found in the German archives with regard to these earlier negotiations. There is, however, the published account of Langoth, one of the two emissaries, Franz Langoth, *Kampf um Österreich; Erinnerungen eines Politikers*, 1951, pp. 120–132.

[3] Hüffer's memorandum, 21 October 1933, GD, Ser. C, Vol. II, No. 20.

After their return from Germany Foppa and Langoth had a meeting with Dollfuss in Vienna on 25 October.[1] The preliminary talks had by now so far developed that both sides made their positions clear for a final meeting between Dollfuss and Habicht. Habicht accepted Dollfuss's conditions that the participation of the National Socialists in the Austrian government must automatically settle the relationship between Austria and Germany, and that Vice-Chancellor Fey would have to remain in the new cabinet. Habicht on the other hand demanded that the new cabinet should be formed by Dollfuss's and his own group, 50 per cent each, with Dollfuss as Chancellor and himself as Vice-Chancellor – after he had become naturalized in Austria. The ban on the Nazi party and its organizations would have to be lifted. In internal policy he demanded the opening of the most vigorous struggle against Marxism, in foreign policy the establishment of friendly relations with Germany. Furthermore, Habicht announced a truce, limited to a fortnight, during which all agitation would cease, as soon as the negotiations between him and Dollfuss had begun. But Habicht left no doubt that should his proposals be rejected he would resume the fight in an intensified form.[2]

Habicht, however, had overreached himself. Dollfuss regarded his demands as far too excessive, and he thought he had found a way of circumventing Habicht by dealing with Hanfstaengl, the Chief of the Nazi party press office, and others, such as von Alvensleben and Count Trautmannsdorff, who had contacted him. Hanfstaengl presented a nine-point plan of pacification to the Austrian legation in Berlin and Dollfuss calculated that by playing off the Nazi intermediaries against each other he could obtain better conditions. Consequently Dollfuss had Foppa and Langoth informed that there could be no question of any contact with Habicht. He was only willing to negotiate either with autonomous national groups in Austria or directly with the German government.

When Hitler was informed of Hanfstaengl's interference he expressed strong disapproval and ordered that Habicht alone was competent to negotiate in his behalf. Habicht was therefore confident of his final success and told Foppa and Langoth that '. . . he had to leave it entirely to Herr Dollfuss to try out possibilities

[1] See Langoth, op. cit., pp. 136–140.
[2] Hüffer's memorandum, 30 October 1933, GD, Ser. C, Vol. II, No. 35.

of a new way, but he was convinced that this way would be worthless for Herr Dollfuss. He would soon have to come back to him. Moreover, he could await this new interlude at his leisure.'[1]

Dollfuss's attempt at reconciliation was not the only feeler put out from Vienna. At the request of Vice-Chancellor Fey, Prince Max Hohenlohe-Langenburg on 29 September made soundings at the Reich Chancellery and the Foreign Ministry about settling the Austro-German conflict. The relations between Dollfuss's and Fey's negotiations can only be reconstructed with difficulty. It remains obscure whether they were directed against each other. The German documents fail to cover all the facts and the reports involve contradictions. The fact that Fey opened the negotiations at the time when he lost the Ministry of Public Security in the cabinet reorganization of 20 September and had been given the politically less important Vice-Chancellorship seems to suggest that Fey resented the decrease of his influence. On the other hand both Dollfuss and Fey envisaged their respective participation in a future coalition with the National Socialists. It is therefore more probable that Fey's initiative was caused by his personal antagonism to Starhemberg and the tensions within the *Heimwehr*.[2]

Fey, by descent a German of Brandenburg origin, had an ambitious character. As leader of the Vienna *Heimwehr* he held an influential position. He resented the strength which Starhemberg gained through his connexion with Mussolini and tried to counterbalance his influence by establishing contact with Berlin. Another emissary of Fey's was Count Alberti, leader of the party in Lower Austria. With Hitler's consent Habicht sent a plenipotentiary to Hungary, where he had discussions with Alberti about a possible reorganization of the Austrian government on the basis of *Heimwehr* and National Socialists.[3] But the negotiations ended without any agreement, because Fey demanded a truce before he entered into personal negotiations with Habicht.

In the light of Dollfuss's tactics we have to reassess the pictures which have been drawn of him by his apologists as by his critics. Dollfuss was neither the courageous defender of Austria's independence, the imaginative creator of the authoritarian state, nor

---

[1] Hüffer's memorandum, 16 November 1933, GD, Ser. C, Vol. II, No. 71.
[2] Hüffer's memorandum, 5 October 1933, GD, 6114/E454081–83.
[3] Hüffer's memorandum, 13 October 1933, GD, Ser. C, Vol. I, No. 497.

the ruthless suppressor of the Socialists and parliamentary democracy. He played the part of a skilful tactician, who embodied
the unsteady equilibrium of Austrian politics. As soon as he had
made a fundamental decision, however, he tried to escape from
its consequences. He remained at the helm because neither of the
main forces, pulling in different directions, could gain the upper
hand.

Searching for another counterweight against the *Heimwehr*
after the ill success of his negotiations with Habicht, he tried to
reverse his decision of September and bring the *Landbund* back
into the government. After this attempt had failed he reopened his
contact with Berlin. Since Hitler had again ordered, on 11 December 1933, that 'in the relationship with Austria the party question
had to be straightened out first, before any negotiations about the
restoration of normal negotiations could be conducted from
government to government',[1] Dollfuss had no alternative but to
deal with Habicht directly. In fact the German minister in Vienna,
Rieth, had been strictly instructed to avoid any discussion of the
Austro-German problem.

On 1 January 1934 the Austrian Minister Tauschitz informed
the German government of Dollfuss's conditions. Dollfuss insisted that the 'interview should be requested by Habicht and
take place with the knowledge, consent, and authorization of
Chancellor Hitler. Habicht would be given safe conduct and travel
strictly incognito.' To this Hitler immediately consented. The
date of the meeting was left open. Neurath proposed that the
date for the discussions with Habicht should be fixed after
Suvich's forthcoming visit to Vienna because 'more good is
likely to come of it if the rush of Suvich's visit be allowed to
pass'.[2]

But it was just because of Suvich's visit that Dollfuss wanted
the meeting with Habicht so urgently. He anticipated that he
would find himself under strong pressure because he had fulfilled none of the obligations undertaken by him at Riccione in
August 1933. The Socialists had not been liquidated, nor had an
agreement with Hungary been concluded. Dollfuss realized that
his last chance for an escape from Suvich's demands was to con-
front him with an agreement with the National Socialists. Dollfuss

---

[1] Neurath's memorandum, 11 December 1933, GD, Ser. C, Vol. I, No. 115.
[2] *Official History*, pp. 94–95.

therefore insisted that he should see Habicht before Suvich's arrival and 8 January was fixed for the conference.

So far Dollfuss's forthcoming meeting with Habicht had been successfully kept secret from the *Heimwehr* and precautions had been taken that the discussions would take place without its knowledge. A leakage in Vienna destroyed this plan. On 7 January the party leaders got information about Habicht's visit. They immediately called a meeting with Dollfuss on the same night.[1] Starhemberg told Dollfuss 'that their ways would lie apart if he really held a discussion with Habicht', while Fey threatened that 'he would have the whole group arrested' if the meeting took place.[2] The Italians likewise intervened. The Italian Minister in Vienna at this time was Preziosi, but more important was Morreale, nominally Press Attaché at the Italian legation but whose real function was to serve as contact man between Suvich and Starhemberg.[3] Morreale protested vigorously to Dollfuss, since Italy had everything to fear should Dollfuss come to terms with the Nazis. Being exposed to this pressure Dollfuss was no longer master of the situation. He was forced to call off the meeting with Habicht and a diplomatic pretext was easily found in recent terrorist acts by the National Socialists.[4]

Habicht faced his second failure with much less complacency. On the morning of 8 January the German Foreign Office informed him of the cancellation of his visit to Vienna. Habicht insisted on taking the plane on his own responsibility.[5] The Foreign Office thereupon informed Hitler that Habicht had left for Vienna against its urgent advice. Hitler refused to have his hand forced and ordered Habicht's return. This was transmitted by radio and reached Habicht just in time to prevent his landing in Vienna.

Nevertheless, Habicht managed to persuade Hitler that further conversations with Dollfuss were desirable and on 11 January,

---

[1] There are various accounts of the *Heimwehr* intervention, see Starhemberg, op. cit., pp. 117–118; Schuschnigg, *My Austria*, pp. 224–227; Winkler, op. cit., pp. 86–88; Pertinax (Otto Leichter), *Österreich 1934*, p. 245; though they differ in details they all agree that Dollfuss had to cancel the meeting because of the *Heimwehr* pressure.

[2] Pertinax, op. cit., p. 245.

[3] About Morreale's personality, see Wiskemann, op. cit., p. 39; his function marginal note in memorandum by Maur, GD, Ser. C, Vol. II, No. 263, note 11.

[4] Starhemberg, op. cit., p. 119.

[5] Renthe-Fink's memorandum, 8 January 1933, GD, Ser. C, Vol. II, No. 166.

with Hitler's consent, sent Prince Waldeck as his emissary to Vienna, where he had a conference with the National Socialist leaders Schattenfroh and Frauenfeld, and the *Heimwehr* leader Alberti. On the same day the portfolios of public security and defence were transferred to Fey. He now carried out his previous threat and arrested the whole group, among them Alberti, through whom he himself had formerly contacted the National Socialists. Waldeck had to return to Germany, whereas Frauenfeld and Schattenfroh, together with Alberti, were sent to a concentration camp.

Dollfuss now relied more than ever on the forces which co-operated with Italy. He might still have had a chance of a reconciliation with the Social Democratic party, which still represented a strong force and was backed by France and the Little Entente. According to the available evidence, however, Dollfuss made no attempt to co-operate with the Socialists. This may have been his biggest mistake, though it is an open question how far he was still free in his actions. Probably such an attempt would have met with the same fate as his negotiations with the National Socialists.[1]

When Suvich arrived on 18 January 1934 Dollfuss could do nothing but accept his verdict. After an investigation of the extent to which Dollfuss could still be trusted, Suvich confronted him with the alternative of either following the Italian lead or being abandoned for another candidate. Suvich gained the impression that 'the government was in a position to dominate the situation, even though it had reached a critical point, particularly in the provinces'.[2] In his letter to Dollfuss of 26 January 1934 Suvich summed up the circumstances in which he 'considered the cause of Austrian independence and the régime embodied by Your Excellency capable of being saved'. He reminded Dollfuss that 'his great

[1] The question of whether Dollfuss still had the possibility of a compromise with the Social Democratic party has been the subject of much controversy. Braunthal, op. cit., p. 8, denies the question and writes: 'The deeper reason for the crisis was an ideological antagonism which could have been resolved only if the Social Democrats had ceased to remain true to their principles.' Gulick, on the other hand, puts the blame on Dollfuss (op. cit., Vol. II, p. 1237): 'At any rate Dollfuss could at least have tried a program of uniting Reither, Renner, and other anti-Fascists in a coalition cabinet.' The controversy appears somewhat academic. In view of the pressure on Dollfuss during his contacts with the Nazis it seems that Dollfuss was no longer master of the situation.

[2] Suvich to Dollfuss, strictly confidential and personal, 26 January 1934, Braunthal, op. cit., p. 199.

popularity was due above all to the conviction that he was the man who would clean away all the rubbish of the former democratic Austria'. In Suvich's catalogue of renovations the fight against Marxism was listed first, and Suvich stressed that 'the moment for carrying out this more decisive work could no longer be postponed'. Finally Dollfuss was reminded of the still pending negotiations with Hungary 'which were expected of him in accordance with the Riccione agreements'.[1]

THE RESULTS OF ITALIAN DIPLOMACY: SUPPRESSION OF THE SOCIALISTS AND THE ROME PROTOCOLS

Since Dollfuss was internally the complete prisoner of the *Heimwehr* he again tried to involve the League of Nations, to which he always turned in the last resort. On 17 January 1934, the day before Suvich's arrival in Vienna, he notified the German government that 'unless the illegal activities ceased, Austria would have to bring the question of Austro-German relations before the League'.[2] By informing the Western powers of this step Dollfuss hoped to regain his freedom of action. On 1 February Berlin rejected the demand. Unless Dollfuss wanted to lose face he had to appeal to the League. But since his former attempts to secure the support of London and Paris had been unsuccessful the failure of a similar action was a foregone conclusion. The same story repeated itself, though with the roles exchanged.

This time the French government welcomed the Austrian initiative and encouraged Vienna to go ahead with the appeal.[3] Paris realized that a move before the League was as much directed against Italian as against German interference:

In the French view the two most urgent considerations are

(1) to evade an immediate direct clash between the Powers and Germany,

(2) to obviate the risk of isolated Italian action.

The appeal to the League will in some measure do both inasmuch as it will decentralize the dispute and bring its further development under the League control.[4]

[1] Braunthal, op. cit., p. 201.
[2] Austrian note, 17 January 1934, GD, Ser. C, Vol. II, No. 188 enclosure; BrD, 2nd Ser., Vol. VI, appendix to No. 201.
[3] Herriot's account of the cabinet meeting, Herriot, *Jadis*, Vol. II, p. 384.
[4] Campbell (Paris) to Simon, 28 January 1934, BrD, 2nd Ser., Vol. V, No. 221.

Barthou, who became Foreign Minister after 6 February 1934, developed a strong foreign policy and hoped to reconstruct France's alliances in face of Germany. He regarded the situation in foreign affairs 'as nearly as serious as in July 1914',[1] and was therefore in favour of energetic action.

The British government was much more reluctant. It hoped to re-establish a basis for co-operation with Germany, since Germany had withdrawn from the League of Nations and the Disarmament Conference in October 1933. Prime Minister MacDonald even suggested a visit by Hitler to London in November and thought such a visit would be a way to restore international contact.[2] In February 1934 Eden, then Parliamentary Under-Secretary of State for Foreign Affairs, emphasized that 'His Majesty's Government were anxious for Germany's early return to the League' and he asked Mussolini 'if he could assist them by bringing pressure to bear in Berlin on this issue'.[3] In these circumstances London could have no interest in rendering relations with Germany more difficult by using the League against Germany in the Austrian question.

Sir John Simon remained opposed to a strong Austrian policy. He declared to Mussolini on 4 January 1934:

> We regard the integrity of Austria as an object of our policy, and will use all our influence to this end. We can not, of course, intervene more actively.

He now recalled that 'last summer the Italian government, by their attitude, rendered unavailing the policy of joint representations at Berlin and he did not wish to repeat that experience'.[4] The decision to appeal would 'rest on the responsibility of the Austrian government alone'.[5]

Moreover, the British attitude was hesitant because the reinforcement of Austria's independence and the strengthening of Italy's anti-democratic course within Austria now went hand in

---

[1] Herriot, op. cit., p. 384.
[2] von Hoesch's report, 10 November 1933, GD, Ser. C, Vol. II, No. 283.
[3] Drummond to Simon, 27 February 1934, BrD, 2nd Ser., Vol. V, No. 320; see also Hassel's conversation with Eden, 27 February 1934, GD, Ser. C, Vol. II, No. 283.
[4] Simon to Drummond and Campbell, 27 January 1934, BrD, 2nd Ser., Vol. V, No. 213.
[5] Simon to Drummond, 12 February 1934, ibid., No. 269.

hand. Suvich made no secret of his intentions in this respect. He told the British ambassador that the suppression of the socialist municipality of Vienna was necessary and claimed 'that even the Socialists were more or less resigned to this. It was now a question of life or death'.[1] Suvich looked forward to an intervention in Austria:

The most satisfactory thing might be an invasion by German Nazis of Austrian territory. If this happened Italy, Czechoslovakia, and Yugoslavia could react energetically and would either threaten or in fact send troops unless the invaders retired.[2]

The threat of an Italian domination over Austria had just the opposite effect in London to that which it had in Paris. It decreased the readiness to help Austria. Simon warned the Italian government that if Dollfuss established a Fascist régime in Austria 'there was bound to be a very marked cooling in the unanimity of the support hitherto given to Austria by the press and public opinion', and further attempts to assist Dollfuss 'might be rendered increasingly difficult'.[3] Vansittart, never really a friend of the League, pointed out that 'our criticism is not so much that Italy objects to Austria going to the League', but that Italy's attitude was ambiguous. He could quite understand Suvich's feeling that the suppression of the Socialist party 'would be the proper and most effective solution of the Austrian problem, but it is equally clear that it is not one to which this country and France can lend themselves'.[4]

Meanwhile Suvich made contradictory remarks with regard to the Italian intentions. He declared that he was against placing the matter before the League,[5] but emphasized on the other hand that 'if such an appeal were made, he trusted we should fully support Austria'.[6] The reason was that he was playing for time in which to dissuade Dollfuss from his course. On 2 February he pointed out to Vienna that Germany had left the League, which therefore would have to make a decision without the participation of one of the states directly interested. Furthermore, the League proceed-

---

[1] Drummond to Simon, 25 January 1934, BrD, 2nd Ser., Vol. V, No. 205.
[2] Drummond to Simon, 28 January and 2 March 1934, ibid., Nos. 222 and 326.
[3] Simon to Drummond, 12 February 1934, ibid., No. 270.
[4] Vansittart to Drummond, 13 February 1934, ibid., No. 276.
[5] Hassel's report, 15 February 1934, GD, Ser. C, Vol. II, No. 255.
[6] Drummond's report, 28 January 1934, BrD, 2nd Ser., Vol. V, No. 222.

ings would take too long. Suvich requested Vienna 'to do nothing until the Italian government had time to study the matter'.[1]

Dollfuss's endeavours to place the Austrian problem in the lap of the League Council, and his continued contact with the National Socialists convinced Rome that the liquidation of the Socialists was overdue. This action would finally tie Dollfuss to the fascist course and prevent his turning back. It would compromise his attempt for an appeal to the League. The final execution lay in the hands of the *Heimwehr*. On 11 February Fey gave the signal for action and declared in a speech before the *Heimwehr* of Vienna and Lower Austria:

> The discussions of yesterday and the day before have given us the certainty that Chancellor Dr. Dollfuss is ours. I can tell you even more, even if only briefly: tomorrow we shall go to work, and we shall make a thorough job of it.[2]

The fighting between the government forces and the Socialists, which lasted from 12 to 16 February, and the defeat of the Socialists had important consequences for the Austrian government both in its relations with the National Socialists and in its international position.

The fight confronted the Nazis with the question of which tactic would be the best for turning the struggle to their advantage. They had several possibilities: they could co-operate with the government, operate independently of both parties, or simply remain neutral. On 12 February a conference took place in the Viennese apartment of Gilbert In der Maur, an Austrian journalist and SA liaison officer between Munich and Vienna, at which the question was discussed. Besides In der Maur were present Türk, representative of the Munich SA, Count Kirchbach, Chief of Staff of the Austrian SA in Munich, and Prince Schönberg, a National Socialist and son of the Austrian State Secretary for National Defence.

The SA leaders agreed that from a military point of view the Austrian government forces would be able to suppress the Socialists. This excluded right from the beginning a co-operation with them, even if ideological considerations could have been overcome. From a political point of view there was a consensus of

[1] Rintelen's report, 2 February 1934, Braunthal, op. cit., pp. 203–204.
[2] Quoted by Gulick, op. cit., p. 1265.

opinion that the position of the Austrian government should be exploited and that the old conditions for co-operation should be put forward again. For this purpose Schönberg approached his father, while In der Maur had a conversation with von Horstenau, who informed Schuschnigg.[1] Schönberg's father refused every attempt at mediation, whereas Schuschnigg passed on the proposal to Dollfuss. Dollfuss rejected this attempt at reconciliation. The Austrian government felt victorious, and even if Dollfuss wanted to come to terms he could no longer act independently, since Fey had taken the action into his hands.

The possibility of an independent action was likewise discussed at the meeting on 12 February, but was dismissed in favour of a neutral attitude which promised, in the estimation of the SA leaders, the best returns. They calculated that a neutral attitude could involve certain momentary, purely tactical disadvantages. After the elimination of the Socialists the Austrian government would be able to concentrate its forces and direct them solely against the Nazis. But they reckoned that the advantages far outweighed the disadvantages:

For, owing to this wait-and-see attitude, the hands of the NSDAP would remain free of the blood of the citizens, and the NSDAP therefore formed the natural reservoir into which the insurgent masses of German workers would be channelled.[2]

Habicht in Munich equally thought that a participation by the Nazis in the uprising in any way whatsoever had to be absolutely avoided. Being completely cut off from the party members in Austria during the fighting he saw the only possibility for restraining the Austrian Nazis from action as being the proclamation of an eight-day truce in the feud with the Austrian government. This he made in a broadcast from Munich on 19 January. He thus gave the Viennese government a breathing-space for the consolidation of its position.

Mussolini's tactics resulted in the very opposite of the desired effect. After the defeat the workers turned away from their own state in a mood of resignation. They came to the conclusion that if Fascism were unavoidable, the anti-clerical variety of the

[1] Memorandum by Gilbert In der Maur, 16 February 1934, GD, Ser. C, Vol. II, No. 263.
[2] Ibid.

Germans was preferable to that oriented towards Italy and the Church.[1]

The Austrian government's position was now heavily compromised. Public opinion in England and France unanimously condemned the suppression of the Socialists. There could no longer be any question of an appeal to the League. On 15 February the Czechoslovak government declared that to deal with the Austrian complaint about Nazi activities appeared senseless and ridiculous in view of the civil war. The possibility of a *Gleichschaltung* could no longer, according to Prague, be excluded.[2] The Yugoslav government reacted similarly.[3] Only France still supported the idea of bringing the Austro-German conflict before the League, but being isolated Paris could achieve nothing on this issue.

As an alternative procedure to an appeal to the League the Italian government proposed that separate but concordant statements should be issued recognizing Austria's independence. The British government did not feel that such a measure was likely to dissuade the German government from its course.[4] But at the insistence of the French, agreement was finally reached on the terms of a joint declaration, made public on 17 February 1934, which said that the three governments

... took a common view of the necessity of maintaining Austria's independence and integrity in accordance with the relevant treaties.[5]

But this declaration had only a face value. France, weakened by internal crisis, could give no force to these words. On the part of the British government Simon hastened to reveal that they had barely any meaning. Questioned in the House of Commons on 21 February, 'whether he had made it clear, both to the Italian and French governments, that we shall raise not a finger to protect the independence of the Austrian government', Sir John Simon replied that

... the statement was one of general principles and that it was specifically limited by saying, 'In accordance with the relevant treaties.'[6]

---

[1] Renner, *Denkschrift über die Geschichte der Unabhängigkeitserklärung Österreich's*, Vienna, 1945, p. 15; quoted by Sweet, *Mussolini and Dollfuss*, p. 183.

[2] Koch's report, 15 February 1934, GD, 6113/E453975.

[3] Henderson to Simon, 5 March 1934, BrD, 2nd Ser., Vol. VI, No. 331.

[4] Simon to Drummond, 15 February 1934, ibid., No. 269.

[5] Drummond to Simon, 17 February 1934, ibid., No. 290.

[6] Answer to a question by Colonel Wedgewood (Labour), *Parl. Debates*, House of Commons, 21 February 1934, Vol. 286, col. 318.

Parallel with its pressure for internal reforms in Austria the Italian government pushed on the plans for the political and economic *rapprochement* of Austria, Hungary, and Italy. Ever since the failure of the Tardieu plan Rome had aimed at a customs union of the three states, while as a long-range goal it envisaged some sort of union between Austria and Hungary. However, Mussolini considered the time highly inopportune for a restoration and advised the Monarchists to play a waiting game.[1]

Meanwhile Rome tried to dispel the apprehensions of the French and British governments. It flatly denied that any closer economic ties between Austria, Hungary, and Italy were planned and emphasized that in her efforts to maintain the independence of Austria 'Italy had no ulterior motives either political or economic such as a desire to establish a special position for herself'. If the Italian government had supported Dollfuss in his policy of suppressing the Socialist party without consulting France, this was 'because it realized that the French government would for internal reasons find it difficult to commit themselves on this point'.[2]

Paris did not delude itself about Italy's real intentions, but had resigned itself to Italian domination over Austria and Hungary as the only way of keeping Austria detached from Germany. It decided to support Italy actively in her efforts to solve the central European problem and exerted strong pressure on the Little Entente with a view to securing its collaboration.

As it was, resistance against the Italian scheme came from the Hungarian side. The government in Budapest had too strong a sense of proportion not to realize that an exclusive Italo-Hungarian alignment could never be a substitute for Germany's assistance in her revisionist aims. It therefore stressed its absolute neutrality in the Austro-German conflict.[3] Moreover, when it became apparent that France and Italy, whose respective influences over the Little Entente and Hungary were based upon the mutual antagonism between these countries, were moving towards a

[1] Mussolini to a leading Austrian Monarchist, Phipps's report, 2 June 1933, BrD, 2nd Ser., Vol. V, No. 197.

[2] Simon to Drummond, 12 March 1934, ibid., Vol. VI, No. 344.

[3] Kanya to Suvich, Mackensen's report, 26 February 1934, GD, Ser. C, Vol. I, No. 279.

rapprochement, Hungary was prompted to reinforce her relations with Germany.

In February 1934 Admiral Horthy, Regent of Hungary, expressed as his conviction both to Dollfuss and Suvich that the Austrian *Gleichschaltung* was a natural necessity which would in the end overcome all resistance.[1] Kanya, Hungarian Minister in Berlin from 1925 till February 1933, and now Foreign Minister, proposed on 11 January 1934 an oral agreement or a secret exchange of notes containing German–Hungarian economic relations and a consultative pact with respect to the mutual policy towards the Little Entente.[2]

The German Foreign Office considered a consultative pact as 'a one-sided pleasure – and that merely on the Hungarian side'. It had no interest in binding itself politically. Berlin realized, however, the danger of a customs union between Austria, Hungary, and Italy. Hassel had repeatedly sent him warnings from Rome to this effect.[3] Knowing that from an economic point of view its position was much stronger than the Italian one the German Foreign Office decided to play this trump. In a conference of the heads of the competent departments on 17 January 1934 it was agreed to change over to a new system of commercial policy, in which the economic terms should be decisively influenced by reasons of foreign policy.[4]

Since all the concessions which Germany might make to Hungary would, on the basis of the most-favoured-nation treatment, be claimed by the other treaty states, a unilateral tariff reduction in a veiled form was considered for Hungary. In a confidential agreement with the Hungarian government of 21 February 1934 means were provided for refunding to a certain extent the customs proceeds accruing in the export trade of Hungary with Germany. This enabled Hungary not only to evade the German duties, but also to equalize the differential between the lower world market prices and the higher Hungarian domestic prices. The agreement, which included other economic advantages, could be terminated upon three months' notice 'if conditions should come about that

[1] Mackensen's report, 28 February 1934, GD, Ser., C, Vol. I, No. 290.
[2] Bülow's memorandum, 11 January 1934, ibid., No. 175.
[3] Hassel's reports, 29 June 1933, GD, 8076/E579472–74; 7 August 1933, 3086/D616471.
[4] Minute by an official of the Reich Chancellery, 17 January 1934, GD, Ser. C, Vol. II, No. 189.

G

are likely to produce basic changes in the premises of the agreement'.[1] The German government left no doubt that it would regard as such a condition the conclusion of an Austro-Hungarian or Italo-Hungarian customs union.

After the preliminary visits of Suvich to Vienna on 18–20 January and to Budapest on 21–23 February, and of Dollfuss to Budapest on 7–8 February the final negotiations between Austria, Hungary, and Italy took place in Rome from 13–16 March. By exerting strong economic pressure on Austria and granting privileges to Hungary the German government had right from the beginning driven a wedge between the partners. In the economic field Hungary refused to commit herself too strongly and her opposition caused the failure of the Italian scheme of a customs union.

Austria on the other hand hoped to avoid far-reaching political undertakings. Vienna had received warnings from Paris and London that no further support could be expected, if it tied itself entirely to Rome. But since this support had proved itself inefficient, and with economic help only forthcoming from Rome, Dollfuss could not maintain his position as the Hungarian government did. On the third day of the negotiations he gave up his resistance and agreed to a formal consultative pact.

The result was that whereas the Rome Protocols of 17 March 1934 were more concrete in the political sphere, they were unexpectedly sparse in the economic sphere. The three countries undertook to develop:

> . . . a concordant policy which shall be directed towards effective collaboration between the European states and particularly between Italy, Austria, and Hungary. To this end the three governments will proceed to common consultations each time that at least one of them may consider this consultation opportune.[2]

The news that a consultative pact had been signed came as a complete surprise to the Little Entente and France. Mussolini's speech on 18 March, in which he sympathized with Hungary's territorial aims, increased the resentment. Mussolini dismissed this criticism of his policy:

---

[1] The Foreign Ministry to the State Secretary of the Reich Chancellery, strictly confidential, 13 March 1934, GD, Ser. C, Vol. II, No. 322 and enclosure.
[2] *Survey of International Affairs, 1934*, pp. 499–500.

Why cannot the French and the Little Entente understand that I am compelled to talk of revisionism if I am to hold the Hungarians and prevent them passing into the German camp? It is essential to keep both Austria and Hungary under my influence and the French and the Little Entente ought to understand this. They cannot themselves provide any other method of obtaining the above end.[1]

THE NAZI *PUTSCH* OF 25 JULY 1934

Mussolini had miscalculated when he believed that his grip upon Austria's policy was now firmly established. The chief obstacle which he encountered was the rivalry within the Austrian triumvirate consisting of Fey, Starhemberg, and Dollfuss. As soon as Rome was leaning predominantly upon one of them, it drove the other two into opposition and into a *rapprochement* with the Nazis. Suvich's visit to Vienna from 18–21 January strengthened Fey's position considerably, which was resented by Starhemberg. On 21 January Starhemberg therefore took up negotiations with the *Landesleitung Österreich* through the representative of the arrested member of the Federal Council, Schattenfroh. Starhemberg indicated in this connexion that he himself claimed the Federal Presidency, whereas Habicht could take over the office of the Federal Chancellor. Dollfuss should receive a cabinet post.[2]

The fight against the Socialists in February interrupted this contact, but the discussions were resumed soon afterwards. As a result of the suppression of Socialism and the part which Fey had played, his influence had been further increased. By enrolling a considerable number of the unemployed youth and middle class, who were led by ex-officers and non-commissioned officers without jobs, Fey had won control over the armed *Heimwehr* detachments. This in turn reaffirmed Starhemberg in his opinion that he had to come to terms with the National Socialists.

He decided that it was time to take concrete measures. On 26 March 1934 Major Kaltenboeck, Starhemberg's former press secretary, made a detailed proposal on Starhemberg's behalf. He set forth the following conditions, which should form the basis for negotiations between Starhemberg and the Nazis:[3]

---

[1] Mussolini quoted in Drummond's report, 20 March 1934, BrD, 2nd Ser., Vol. VI, No. 358.

[2] Hüffer's memorandum, 24 January 1934, GD, Ser. C, Vol. II, No. 213.

[3] Memorandum 26 March 1934, GD, 4938/270021–26 (my translation); Starhemberg made the same offer twice. On 27 March 1934 von Marnegg visited

1. Hitler expresses confidentially his consent to the *Heimwehr* or Starhemberg, that Starhemberg would become Reich Regent (*Reichsverweser*). His position as Regent is to be interpreted in the sense that Starhemberg would remain Regent for the Reich until the Anschluss had been achieved.

2. Austria undertakes to conduct her foreign policy in strict agreement with the Foreign Office in Berlin.

3. The Austrian SA and SS become incorporated in the *Heimatschutz*, formalities being left to later discussions. Uniforms of the SA and SS could not be kept; the swastika, however, would be introduced everywhere.

4. Until the *Machtergreifung* the Reich pays subsidies to the *Heimatschutz* in intervals of 8–14 days. The *Heimatschutz* would undertake to accept no further payments in future from Italy or the Dollfuss government. Envisaged is a monthly payment of 40,000 Reichsmarks. (At the moment the *Heimatschutz* receives 100,000 Schillings from the government.)

Starhemberg maintained these contacts for over a month and on 27 April he was, again through Kaltenboeck, in direct contact with the Austrian SA leadership in Munich, whereas Habicht was excluded from the negotiations. The premises for a discussion having been settled, it was agreed that a conference should take place in Vienna. On 3 May Count Kirchbach arrived with several SA emissaries at Vienna. The discussions were postponed from one hour to another. Finally, according to Winkler's account, Starhemberg had to cancel his appointment, because Dollfuss had been informed of the forthcoming meeting and intervened.[1]

Parallel with Starhemberg's efforts, Fey himself entertained relations with the Nazis through Wächter, Habicht's personal representative in Vienna.[2] Similar to the feud between Fey and Starhemberg there existed a rivalry in the Nazi camp between

---

Erbach at the German legation in Vienna and repeated the proposal. In contrast to Kaltenboek he pretended, however, that Starhemberg did not know about the approach. This was most probably only a precautionary measure, Erbach's memorandum, 27 March 1934, GD, 4938/E270026.

[1] Winkler, op. cit., p. 141; Starhemberg, on the other hand, writes, op. cit., p. 135, 'Dollfuss bade him to pursue the connexion with due discretion'. This does, however, not explain, why his planned conference with Count Kirchbach failed. Starhemberg of course denies that he ever had the intention to come to a real agreement with the Nazis. His detailed proposal shows that he in fact did consider a settlement with them.

[2] Starhemberg, op. cit., p. 135; see also Hüffer's memorandum, 15 March 1934, GD, Ser. C, Vol. II, No. 328.

Habicht, who was a Reich German, and Reschny, the leader of the Austrian Nazis, who had fled to Germany. Hence the two different feelers from the side of the National Socialists. Whereas Habicht hoped to reach an agreement with Fey, Reschny tried to come to terms with Starhemberg.[1]

From the Austrian side a meeting between Hitler and Fey was suggested. Hitler could now either exploit the personal antagonism between Fey and Starhemberg and tip the scales by coming to an agreement with one of them; or he could simply wait and hope that events would make up his mind for him. Less as the result of a conscious or deliberate decision as of his instinctive feeling that the situation in Austria had to clarify itself, and that first a trustworthy and authoritative party had to emerge, Hitler chose to wait.

He decided that no immediate solution could be envisaged and that the party had to prepare itself for a long-range struggle. The fight in Austria should be conducted on a new basis. Hitler ordered on 15 March the use of force as well as direct attacks on the Austrian government in press and radio were to be strictly avoided. The main emphasis should be put on increased propaganda within Austria and on the building up of the party organization. Habicht was instructed not to make any more aggressive speeches of any kind against Austria.[2]

The actions directed from Germany had been Habicht's most important weapon. He felt himself decisively curbed in his influence and warned that the 'Austrian government for its part was working more actively and now, not being hampered by any counteraction, with increasing success'. But when Neurath saw Hitler after the new directives had been issued, and mentioned Habicht's anxieties, Hitler emphasized that he was well aware that in Austria a certain spirit of resignation was taking hold in some National Socialist circles and that they felt abandoned by the Reich. 'But this had to be accepted in the bargain. This attack of weakness would and must be overcome.'[3]

During March and April the Austrian Nazis followed Hitler's order that all extreme activities were to be stopped. When these

---

[1] Starhemberg, op. cit., p. 135.
[2] Köpke to Rieth, 15 March 1934, GD, Ser. C, Vol. II, No. 328; Köpke's memorandum, 16 March 1934, ibid., No. 329.
[3] Köpke's memorandum, 16 March 1934, ibid., No. 329.

tactics yielded no immediate results the Austrian radical elements resumed their terrorist activities. They argued that Hitler had issued his order only for tactical reasons and inwardly welcomed every firm act of opposition.[1] By the end of May a new campaign had begun. Attacks were made on railways and public buildings. On 29 May Wächter, Habicht's Deputy in Austria, declared that it was difficult to keep the Austrian Nazis in hand and to prevent wild attempts at insurrection. There was a complete lack of united leadership. For this reason he took the position that 'if acts of insurrection should be inevitable, an organized revolt was to be preferred'.[2]

This was the first open hint that the patience of the Nazi leaders was becoming exhausted. They had negotiated hard with Dollfuss, only to be robbed of success at the last minute. The Nazi party in Austria was beginning to lose its younger, more radical members to the militant Communist organization, elements which had to be won back by strong action.[3] The terrorist activities of the Austrian Nazis, now conducted independently from the leadership at Munich, deprived Habicht of his remaining influence.[4]

The German Foreign Office was aware of the danger of a *putsch* and hoped to avoid it. In his memorandum of 9 April for Hitler, State Secretary Bülow stressed:

It is presumably clear that Germany is not in a position now to put through internationally a solution to the Austrian question in a German sense. By solution in the German sense is meant not only the direct achievement of the Anschluss but even *Gleichschaltung* on the Danzig pattern. All German attempts in this direction will founder on the solid opposition of all the European Great Powers and the Little Entente. In these circumstances we shall have to take the position that in the Austrian question we want nothing except that natural political developments should continue to be given free play. We can, for our part, calmly renounce all militant methods. . . .[5]

[1] Wächter to Köpke, Köpke's memorandum, 31 May 1934, GD, 6112/E453423–26.
[2] Wächter to Renthe-Fink, 29 May 1934, GD, Ser. C, Vol. II, No. 469.
[3] Secret, unsigned memorandum from Austria, end of August 1934, by an apologist of the *putsch*, GD, 6114/E454320–41.
[4] Rintelen, the Austrian Minister in Rome, who was always in close contact with Habicht, mentioned that he had been told positively that Hitler had dropped Habicht. Weydenhammer's memorandum, 7 March 1934, GD, Ser. C, Vol. II, No. 308.
[5] Bülow's memorandum, 9 April 1934, ibid., No. 389 enclosure.

The Foreign Minister Neurath also warned Hitler about the trend of terrorist activities. He took steps to decrease tension on the Austro-German frontier – the result of heavy concentrations of *Heimwehr* formations on the Austrian side, and the so-called Austrian Legion consisting of Austrian Nazi refugees on the Bavarian side. At Neurath's demand the Minister of the Interior, Frick, ordered the removal of the Austrian Legion from the frontier on 14 June. From Vienna the German Minister Rieth repeatedly called attention to the dangerous developments and on 5 June his Military Attaché, Muff, warned 'that the international consequences of a violent attack were immeasurable'.[1]

But these efforts to avoid an increase of violence, with its inevitable consequences, were to no purpose. The party warfare in Austria was conducted independently of the Foreign Ministry, which had no power over the party officials. Neurath had to declare to Suvich in June that 'there were violent quarrels proceeding between the Austrian SA and SS and that the situation was completely out of the control of the government'.[2] This leads us back to Hitler himself, the only person who could have intervened successfully.

Hitler's meeting with Mussolini in Venice on 15 and 16 June 1934 raised hopes for a negotiated solution. For already in *Mein Kampf* Hitler had proclaimed an alliance with Italy as one of his chief objectives in foreign policy.[3] Hitler realized that Austria formed the main obstacle towards this goal, but was not willing to sacrifice the Anschluss for a friendship with Mussolini. As early as 1926 he considered that a renunciation of South Tyrol would suffice in order to win Italy over, and he violently attacked the Germans who were not ready to make this concession.[4] Advances had been made by Göring who had assured Mussolini in April 1933 that 'Hitler regarded the question of the South Tyrol frontier as finally liquidated by the peace treaties'.[5] Mussolini was not caught this way. He had made it clear that he would consent

[1] Muff's report, 5 June 1934, GD, 6111/E452851–53.
[2] Drummond's report, 20 June 1934, BrD, 2nd Ser., Vol. VI, No. 462.
[3] See in greater detail Walter Pese, 'Hitler und Italien 1920–1926', *Vierteljahreshefte für Zeitgeschichte*, 1955, pp. 118–124.
[4] In 1926 Hitler published the pamphlet 'Die Südtiroler Frage und das deutsche Bündisproblem'.
[5] Simon to Graham, 25 April 1933, BrD, 2nd Ser., Vol. V, No. 90.

neither to the Anschluss nor to the *Gleichschaltung* in return for a simple reaffirmation of the Tyrol frontier.

The meeting in Venice of 15 and 16 June revealed both Hitler's and Mussolini's desire to find a basis for a common policy and their division over Austria. When Hitler arrived in Venice his position was rapidly defined. As he explained to Mussolini, the Austrian question could only be settled on the following basis:[1]

1. The question of the Anschluss was of no interest since it was in no way acute and, as he was well aware, internationally not feasible.

2. He must insist that a personage of independent outlook, that is to say not bound to any political party, should be at the head of the Austrian government.

3. This personage would have to proclaim an election as soon as possible so that the attitude of the Austrian people would be made clear.

4. After this National Socialists would have to be taken into the government.

5. All economic questions in Austria should be handled by Germany and Italy in closest consultation.

Hitler's proposal to Mussolini, amounting to a recognition of Austria's *Gleichschaltung*, found no response. Mussolini obviously thought these points not worth a detailed discussion. Both Hitler and Mussolini emphasized 'that the Austrian question must not and would not be an obstacle in the shaping of their relations'. But, with each of them actively supporting one of two rival movements, which were daily engaged in a fierce fight, the solution of the Austrian problem was a premise for successful negotiations, which could not be circumvented. Back in Rome Mussolini let the German ambassador know that 'in view of the acts of violence against the Austrian government he could not advise Dollfuss to start negotiations with the National Socialists'.[2]

The negative result of the Venice conversations confirmed those Nazi elements which believed only in a solution by force. On 25 June Habicht held a conference at Zürich with his Chief of Staff Weydenhammer, his deputy Wächter and Glass, the leader of the newly formed Austrian SS Standarte 89, a unit consisting of ex-soldiers of the Austrian army who had joined the National

---

[1] Neurath's memorandum, 15 June 1934, GD, Ser. C, Vol. III, No. 5; unsigned memorandum approved by Hitler, which gives a shorter version, ibid., No. 7.
[2] von Hassel's report, 5 July 1934, ibid., No. 62.

Socialists. It was Glass who now submitted his *putsch* plan to the German Nazi leaders.[1] He suggested that the SS Standarte 89 should take the Federal President and the entire Austrian cabinet prisoner. At the same time it should seize the Austrian radio transmitter and the Vienna telephone headquarters. In the resulting vacuum a National Socialist government should be formed under the Austrian Minister at Rome, Rintelen, who was in close contact with the Nazis and who had already stated earlier that he was 'unconditionally prepared to follow the directives of Habicht'.[2]

But no decisions were taken at this meeting. Glass made it a precondition that the Austrian regular army units would actively support the plot and in this connexion he promised the services of a 'higher General Staff officer'. Habicht approved of the plan in principle and Glass was told to concentrate on winning over more Nazi sympathizers in the Austrian army and police force in Vienna. Glass left Zürich with the promise of further arms deliveries from Habicht's headquarters in Munich.

Meanwhile the struggle within the Austrian government continued. Dollfuss and Starhemberg, seeing themselves menaced, combined against Fey's rising influence.[3] They decided to sidetrack him. But Fey flatly refused to accept the cabinet's offer of an appointment as Austrian minister to Budapest and, relying on the support of the leaders of the *Heimwehr*, succeeded in remaining in the cabinet. As a compromise Starhemberg replaced Fey as Vice-Chancellor during the cabinet reorganization on 1 May, while Fey retained the strategically important post of Head of the Ministry of Public Security.

Fey was not the man to retreat without putting up a determined resistance. From two different sources came information that he planned violent action against Dollfuss. When Starhemberg visited Budapest on 1 and 2 June, Gömbös, the Hungarian Minister President, warned Starhemberg against an impending Nazi *putsch* and against Fey, whom he connected with these plans.[4] And one of Habicht's informants reported that when

[1] Details of the plan are contained in the unpublished Weydenhammer report to Hitler on the *putsch* which is extensively quoted in Gordon Brook-Shepherd, *Dollfuss*. London, 1961, pp. 234 *seq.*, and on which the following account is based.
[2] Weydenhammer's memorandum, 7–8 March 1934, GD, Ser. C, Vol. II, No. 308.
[3] Starhemberg, op. cit., pp. 135–136.
[4] Starhemberg, op. cit., p. 144.

Fey came to Budapest himself on 12 and 13 June, he had inquired what action Hungary would take in case of a *coup d'état* against Dollfuss.[1]

Realizing this danger, Starhemberg demanded the arrest of Fey and his final removal from the government. Yet Dollfuss still hesitated. According to Starhemberg's account Dollfuss planned a great political purge, when all these questions would be settled. But before taking action he wished to discuss the matter with Mussolini during his forthcoming visit to Riccione at the end of July.

However, there appears to have been more than one reason for Dollfuss's reluctance to resort to more drastic measures. In June 1934 the internal crisis in Germany, resulting from the conflict between the SA and the *Reichswehr*, and the rivalry between Roehm and men of Hitler's entourage like Himmler and Göring, was coming to a head. Dollfuss, apparently, hoped to turn this conflict to his own advantage.[2] He tried to revive his earlier connexions with Roehm, dating from November 1933.[3] In Vienna it was Neubacher, the president of the Austrian–German Volksbund, who was especially convinced that 'the Austrian question could ultimately be solved only by the SA with Roehm, but excluding Habicht'. Dollfuss supported Neubacher in this opinion and in a conversation with him he promised that, if Neubacher were to become *Landesleiter* of the party in Austria, he 'would at once give the party four ministerial seats and would remove the Legitimist Ministers from the cabinet'.[4]

How strong the connexion between Dollfuss and Roehm was remains a matter for speculation. According to available evidence only preliminary advances were made. During a visit to Berlin Neubacher tried to have a conversation with Roehm and in fact received an invitation from him, but was warned by Habicht against entering into such a discussion.[5] Whatever hopes Dollfuss may have had that he could come to terms with Roehm were destroyed by Roehm's death during the purge of 30 June.

[1] Enclosure in Habicht's letter to Hüffer, 18 June 1934, GD, Ser. C, Vol. III, No. 17.
[2] Winkler, op. cit., p. 151; Langoth, op. cit., p. 174.
[3] Langoth, op. cit., pp. 144–147; Winkler, op. cit., p. 86; Hüffer's memorandum, 16 November 1933, GD, Ser. C, Vol. II, No. 71.
[4] Habicht's letter to Hüffer, loc. sit.
[5] Ibid.

Dollfuss now decided to deal the second blow to Fey. On 10 July he made another attempt at ousting him from the cabinet. Though it was impossible to expel him, because leading *Heimwehr* members such as Lahr and Neustädter-Stürmer (the third *Heimwehr* Minister in the cabinet) expressed their solidarity with him, Dollfuss succeeded in curbing his position decisively. Fey was reduced to Minister without Portfolio and appointed to General State Commissioner for Security, with Dollfuss himself taking over the ministries of Security and National Defence.

Seeing his influence on the decline Fey used the tactics which had just failed Starhemberg.[1] He tried to oppose Dollfuss and Starhemberg by coming to terms with the Nazis. As a first step he voted against the new decree of 12 July 1934, which made death the only penalty for using or even possessing explosives and which was mainly directed against National Socialist activities. On 18 July Lahr declared on Fey's behalf to a representative of the Vienna section of the party that Fey resented the part forced upon him by Dollfuss as hangman of the Socialists and Nazis. Fey was ready to open negotiations with the aim of forming a transitory national government stressing 'that he would be a much more convenient partner for the Nazis than Dollfuss'.[2]

It is still an open question whether or not Fey resorted to the extreme measure of participating in the preparations for a Nazi *putsch*, which went on parallel to the intrigues within the Austrian government. The information coming from Budapest, which warned against Fey in connexion with a possible *putsch*, his contacts with the Nazis before the fact, his own position – endangered by Dollfuss, and his later attitude during the *putsch* all seem to indicate that he was involved in the plot.[3] But there is no conclusive evidence that Fey was implicated. Most probably he planned his own action and was sitting on the fence ready to step down on the side of the Nazis should they succeed.

[1] Hitler ordered that he be handed over all the material concerning the negotiations of the SA in Munich with Starhemberg and Fey. He reserved to himself the decision to publish the material at a suitable moment. Hüffer's memorandum, 29 August 1934, GD, 6115/E454893–94.

[2] Unsigned memorandum, 19 July 1934, GD, 4938/E270049–51. The party official, who wrote the memorandum, advised that its contents be kept secret from the German Foreign Office.

[3] See *Survey of International Affairs, 1934,* p. 473, note 1; Gordon Brook-Shepherd, op. cit., pp. 247–251, 263–271; Gulick, op. cit., pp. 1666–1667; Winkler, op. cit., pp. 162 *seq.*

In the Nazi camp the Austrian minister in Rome, Rintelen, who was losing patience, urged a solution before the end of July. When Weydenhammer visited him in Rome on 11 July Rintelen warned that Dollfuss's forthcoming visit to Mussolini, planned for August in Riccione, and the meeting between Dollfuss and the French Foreign Minister Barthou, could endanger German policy. He himself could not possibly postpone his leave in Vienna beyond the end of July and said it was unlikely that he would be returning to his post in Rome afterwards.

An additional argument for early action was the support promised by Lt.-Colonel Sinzinger, Chief of Staff at the garrison headquarters in the Austrian capital. On 16 July, according to Weydenhammer's report, the last and decisive conference took place in Habicht's flat in Munich. Besides Habicht and Weydenhammer were present the Gauleiter-designate for Vienna, Frauenfeld; the head of the Austrian SA organization, Reschny; the leader of the SS Standarte 89, Glass; and as a personal representative of Sinzinger, a Major Egert of the De-coding Department of the Austrian War Ministry. Glass had encouraging news: in the meantime he had had 'positive negotiations' with Dr. Steinhausl, a senior pro-Nazi of the Vienna police, with the commander of the police emergency squad, and with two unnamed army staff officers. The final line of action was decided upon and the afternoon of 24 July fixed as the time for the *putsch*.[1]

There was still Hitler's opposition to overcome. The available evidence suggests that these preparations had been made without his knowledge, and that he had not changed his policy ordering the party to conduct a long-range struggle.[2] Habicht cheated in order to obtain Hitler's consent. He falsely led him to believe that the Austrian armed forces were prepared to undertake action on their own in order either to force the government into accepting the Anschluss or else to overthrow it. This interpretation corresponded exactly with Hitler's temperament. He thought he could score a success by letting others do the work for him. He therefore agreed that if the armed forces would take action and the party in Austria would support the armed forces along these lines, such

---

[1] Gordon Brook-Shepherd, op. cit., pp. 235–236.

[2] Köpke to Rieth, 15 March 1934, GD, Ser. C, Vol. II, No. 328; Köpke's memorandum, ibid., No. 329. Gordon Brook-Shepherd, op. cit., thinks that Hitler planned the *putsch* long beforehand. But he produces no convincing evidence to support his thesis.

action would have the *political* support of the party in Germany.[1] But what actually happened was that not the Austrian army, but the SS Standarte 89 consisting of dismissed Austrian soldiers prepared the revolt, hoping to carry the army along.

The conspirators now executed their plans. Weydenhammer, disguised as a British businessman 'Mr. Williams', joined Wächter in Vienna on 23 July. Rintelen, being 'on holiday', was already staying at the Imperial Hotel in Vienna. The former *Landbund* leader, Winkler, was in contact with the conspirators, and his role was to travel immediately to Prague in order to reassure the Czech government that the removal of Dollfuss had been inevitable and that Rintelen commanded a trustworthy government.

Everything was set for action on 24 July, when the group received information from Buresch, the former Austrian Chancellor, that the cabinet meeting had been suddenly postponed until noon on 25 July. Plans were readjusted and the *putsch* fixed for the following day.

At one o'clock on 25 July 1934, lorries with 154 members of the SS Standarte 89 disguised in Austrian army and police uniforms drove up to the Chancellery. They followed the regular military police guard and were admitted without difficulty. Then they overwhelmed the guard and within a few minutes had gained control of the whole building. At the same time a group of fifteen Austrian Nazis occupied the radio station and announced that the Dollfuss cabinet had resigned and that Rintelen had been appointed Chancellor.

The insurgents had hoped to force the resignation of the government without bloodshed and calculated that the army could be won over for the prospective new government. If this was the plan, the *putsch* had already failed. Information had leaked out and reached Fey, who did not, however, pass on all he knew to Dollfuss and his ministers gathered at the cabinet meeting. But, acting on his own, Fey did order one of his *Heimwehr* regiments to march immediately back to town, and finally gave Dollfuss a general warning that a *coup d'état* was planned.[2]

Dollfuss thereupon interrupted the cabinet session. When the

---

[1] Evidence by Göring, *The Trial of German War Criminals*, London, 1947, part 9, p. 102; von Neurath, ibid., part 17, p. 121; von Papen, *Memoirs*, p. 339.
[2] Gordon Brook-Shepherd, op. cit., pp. 247–249.

insurgents occupied the building they found only Dollfuss, Fey, and the State Secretary for Security, Karwinsky. The majority of the cabinet had escaped capture and was able to carry on the functions of the government in the Ministry of Defence. Major-General Zehner had the army firmly under control and before two o'clock the Chancellery was already surrounded by detachments of police and the army. Schuschnigg, the senior among the ministers, telephoned President Miklas who immediately declared that he would not accept any conditions from the rebels. Miklas ordered that Schuschnigg, as provisional Austrian Chancellor, bring the situation under control.

Meanwhile, at the Chancellery, Dollfuss had tried to escape from the building through a side entrance. But he found the door closed when he reached it, and he was shot after a short struggle by one of the insurgents who broke into the room.

Fey on the other hand played for high stakes, for only thus could he hope to win. On learning of the *putsch* he knew that only a deadlock between the Nazis and the government would give him the chance to dictate his conditions to one of the two parties. Hence it seems probable that he had warned Dollfuss of the *putsch* in order to prevent a complete Nazi success. Now it was high time to try co-operation with them. When the rebel leader offered him the post of Minister of Security in a Rintelen government, with the police, the *Heimwehr*, as well as the Austrian SA and SS under his command, he no longer hesitated and accepted.[1] He gave orders that a Major Reidl should deputize for him as head of the Vienna *Heimwehr*, that there should be no firing on the rebel forces, and that immediate contact should be made between the party and the Nazis 'to discuss common action'.

But time elapsed, and seeing that the *putsch* had failed, the Nazis in the Chancellery started negotiating for free conduct. Agreement was reached with the delegated Minister Neustädter-Stürmer that the conspirators be granted free passage to the German frontier under military escort, provided that they evacuated the building without causing loss of life. The invaders insisted that the German Minister Rieth should come and witness the agreement. Rieth consented, and though he emphasized that he 'would not do so in his official but in his private capacity

---

[1] Gordon Brook-Shepherd, op. cit., p. 266, on the basis of the testimony of ex-insurgents.

only',[1] he gave the impression that the German legation was involved in the plot.

Hitler, who was attending the Wagner festival in Bayreuth, was furious about Rieth's action and the way he had compromised himself and indirectly the German government. No doubt he would have accepted a success; but seeing that the *putsch* had failed he could not forgive the way he had been cheated. Twice in the day, at 10 and 11 p.m., he telephoned to the Foreign Ministry to say that Rieth should have nothing to do with the transport of the rebels and that he would have them arrested if they arrived at the frontier, and transferred to a concentration camp.[2] Late in the night Hitler ordered Rieth's immediate recall from Vienna, and this was finally followed by Habicht's dismissal.

Among the Western governments Mussolini was the only one who took active counter-measures. He had been expecting Dollfuss to visit him in two days' time in Italy, where Dollfuss's family was already staying with him. He regarded the *putsch* and Dollfuss's murder as a personal blow. 'Hitler is the murderer of Dollfuss, Hitler is the guilty man, he is responsible for this,' he exclaimed to Starhemberg.[3] During the afternoon of 25 July Mussolini ordered that four divisions, consisting mainly of artillery and numbering about 100,000 in all, and which were already training not far from the Austrian border, should be moved right up to the Brenner and the Carinthian border. In Vienna Morreale took charge of the situation. He committed the Austrian ministers by arranging for the publication of an anti-Nazi minister's statement from which it was impossible to retreat.[4]

While the insurgents in Vienna had surrendered, having obtained the assurance of free conduct, the fighting continued for about three days in some provinces, and especially in Carinthia and Styria. But the leaders had been so sure of success in Vienna that no concerted action had been planned. The timing came as a complete surprise to the Austrian Nazis in the provinces, who found themselves with insufficient arms and no ammunition. The

[1] Rieth's report, 26 July 1934, GD, Ser. C, Vol. III, No. 119; see also memoranda of Rieth's telephone conversations on 25 July 1934, GD, 3086/617246–49.
[2] Bülow's note, 26 July 1934, GD, Ser. C, Vol. III, No. 115.
[3] Starhemberg, op. cit., p. 170.
[4] Wiskemann, op. cit., p. 39, on the basis of articles by U. Grazzi, Italian Chargé d'Affaires in Vienna in 1934.

signal for action had come too early. At best they saw a chance for a successful uprising in about two months' time.[1]

The Italians regarded the fighting between the Nazis and the government forces as a welcome pretext for military intervention. On 27 July the Italian Consul in Klagenfurth twice asked the Carinthian provincial government 'whether he should let the soldiers march. . . . Modern equipment had been prepared, so that the affair would be done within a couple of hours'.[2] But the Austrian government saw no reason to avoid a Nazi success by accepting Italian domination, fearing a chain reaction and a race of armies into Austria.

In fact the Yugoslav government would not tolerate Italian troops on her Austrian frontier and declared that if the Italian army entered Austrian territory the Yugoslav army would invade Carinthia at once;[3] they considered that the League of Nations alone could decide whether the Nazi uprising called for international action. Since the League had repeatedly proved its inefficiency in Austrian matters, this suggestion amounted to a proposal of inaction. Convinced that if it came to a choice between German and Italian rule over Austria, Germany was the lesser of two evils, the Yugoslav government in fact preferred a successful *putsch* to an Italian occupation of Austria. As Vienna succeeded in re-establishing its control over the provinces, the problem of a foreign intervention subsided.

[1] A report from Austria submitted by the Head of the *Volksbund für das Deutschtum im Ausland* to the Foreign Ministry, 2 August 1934, GD, Ser. C, Vol. III, No. 143.

[2] Secret unsigned and undated report from Austria, GD, 6114/E454322; Selby to Simon, 28 July 1934, BrD, 2nd Ser., Vol. VI, No. 541.

[3] Erbach's report, 31 July 1934, GD, Ser. C, Vol. III, No. 137.

CHAPTER V

THE MAKING OF THE GERMAN–AUSTRIAN AGREEMENT, 1935–36

We should all have to choose between Austria and Abyssinia, if
Mussolini stuck to his mania for fame and sand.
Lord Vansittart, The Mist Procession

REPERCUSSIONS OF THE FAILURE OF THE *PUTSCH*

The abortive *putsch* of 25 July 1934 reveals the hollowness
on which Hitler's policy had been based hitherto. By or-
ganizing the German and Austrian parties as a unit and
labelling the party fight against the Austrian government as a
domestic issue, Hitler could not escape from the international
repercussions. Though he had disavowed Habicht's tactics he had
tolerated him as a person. Hitler discovered that he could not
pursue two different policies, one as head of the government and
the other as head of the party. The professionals of the Foreign
Office noted, not without a certain satisfaction, the ill success of a
policy conducted in disregard of their functions and advice. Muff,
the German Military Attaché in Vienna, wrote:[1]

The Party's struggle for Austria, while provoking ever sharper
counter-measures on the part of the government, led from constitutional to unconstitutional methods, from propaganda to terrorism, and
ended, inevitably, in an attempt at a forcible *putsch* and in incitement
to open revolt. As everyone possessing any insight had predicted,
the outcome of this policy was a complete débâcle, and, at the same
time, a defeat for the Reich, embroiled as it was in party politics.

Hitler had committed a blunder in foreign policy which
matched his unsuccessful November *putsch* in 1923 in the domestic sphere: but once again he showed a surprising ability to
adapt himself to a new situation. The failure of 25 July 1934 led to

[1] Muff's report, 30 August 1934, GD, Ser. C, Vol. III, No. 186; see also Muff's
report, 26 July 1934, ibid., No. 125.

a complete change of tactics; it closed the period of Austria's *Gleichschaltung* from within and the Austrian Nazi party had no longer the function of undermining the state. The *Gleichschaltung* was to be achieved by a change in the international situation and by pressure from outside.[1] The only task of the Austrian National Socialists was to provide the necessary instrument for taking over the state once the conditions were favourable. This necessitated a long-term policy. In the same manner in which the ill-success of the Munich *putsch* in 1923 had originated the policy of legality Hitler applied, eleven years later, the tactics of legality to his Austrian policy. Hess in his letter of 21 August 1934 to an Austrian Nazi interpreted the new course:[2]

As you know, after November 1923 the Führer took decisions which led to an entirely new and absolutely lawful policy being pursued by the NSDAP in Germany, decisions to which we adhered and which were later to prove justified and to achieve success.

But Hess made it perfectly clear that only the former tactics were being abandoned, not the goal itself:

Let me assure you that, despite everything the decisions now taken by the Führer in respect of National Socialism in Austria will one day, and that in a perfectly legal manner, enable all your wishes and ours regarding Austria to be fulfilled.

As a consequence of the new tactics Hitler ordered the immediate dissolution of the Austrian party bureau on 3 August. All members of the former *Landesleitung* were forbidden on pain of severest penalties to participate in illegal associations or activities.[3] The *Kampfring*[4] of the Austrians in Germany was to be reorganized so as to exclude in future any interference in Austria's internal affairs. For this purpose it was to be converted into a relief society concerned solely with the cultural, social, and economic care of its members.[5] Neither Party authorities nor anyone else were allowed to discuss, either in the press or on the wireless, questions concern-

---

[1] See 'Guiding Principles for German policy *vis-à-vis* Austria in the Immediate Future', approved by Hitler on 13 August 1934, GD, Ser. C, Vol. III, enclosure 2 in No. 167.
[2] Ibid., No. 173.
[3] Hüffer's memorandum, 7 August 1934, ibid., No. 149.
[4] The Austrian Nazis' organization in Germany.
[5] Hitler to Hess, 19 August 1934, ibid., No. 165.

ing German–Austrian policy, unless agreement had previously been reached between the Reich Propaganda Minister and the new minister in Vienna, Papen.[1] Furthermore, Hitler ordered the complete separation of the party organizations in Germany and Austria.[2] It was solely 'a matter for the Nazis in Austria to decide in what form they should build up a purely Austrian party'.[3]

As far as the disbanding of the Austrian Legion was concerned Hitler's new order was not enforced. Hitler himself assumed an ambiguous attitude between the Foreign Ministry pressing for its dissolution and the Austrian leaders trying to keep the Legion intact.[4] Hitler assured von Neurath that 'the dissolution of the Legion was in full swing but would take some time yet'.[5] As late as February 1935 the Austrian SA leader, Reschny, claimed that the Legion should continue to exist and its tasks consist of 'social work and military training'. Allegedly the order assigning national defence duties to the Legion stemmed from the Führer himself,[6] though Hitler dismissed Reschny's assertions as 'downright lies'.[7] Be that as it may, the total number of Austrian refugees in Germany never exceeded 35,000, of whom about one quarter were organized in semi-military formations.[8] The Austrian Legion was as a force, therefore, not significant enough to exercise any pressure on Austria or to carry any weight in political decisions.

The price Hitler had to pay for his new tactics was heavy. It meant the indefinite postponement of the *Gleichschaltung*, and the estrangement of his followers in Austria. Hitler's violent condemnation of the insurgents of 25 July – four years later he was to erect a monument in their honour – is evidence of how far he was

---

[1] Hitler to the Ministers Hess and Goebbels, Herr von Papen, and the office of the Secret State Police, 8 August 1934, GD, Ser. C, Vol. III, No. 151.

[2] 'Guiding Principles', ibid., enclosure 2 in No. 167.

[3] Hess to Frauenfeld, 26 August 1934, ibid., No. 173.

[4] Hüffer's note, 13 September 1934, ibid., No. 208.

[5] Neurath's marginal note, 21 November 1934, ibid., No. 337, note 7.

[6] Altenburg's memorandum, 27 February 1935, ibid., No. 510.

[7] Altenburg's memorandum, 8 March 1935, ibid., No. 522.

[8] Figures given in the Memorandum concerning the 1936 budget for the Austrian Hilfswerk, held on 13 and 14 October 1936, GD, Ser. D, Vol. I, No. 170, and Frick to Lammers, 12 October 1936, ibid., No. 168. – These figures are fairly accurate for the previous time, too, because with Hitler's new tactics and the lessening of tension in Austria the number of refugees coming to Germany decreased considerably.

willing to sacrifice the Austrian Nazi movement for his new policy. Hess reassured the party comrades:

The Führer and his collaborators find it very difficult to adopt this harsh attitude, but Germany's vital interests, and therefore indirectly also the interests of the German speaking peoples and not the least of the Austrian NSDAP itself, are at stake.[1]

In the international sphere Hitler acted swiftly to overcome the repercussions of the *putsch*. On 26 July, while the fighting in the Austrian provinces still continued, he appointed von Papen as new German Minister in Vienna. In his letter, which he immediately published, Hitler stressed that the 'attack on the Austrian Federal Chancellor, which the Reich Government most sharply condemn and regret, has aggravated through no fault of ours the already unstable political situation in Europe'.[2] From many aspects von Papen was a suitable choice. He had been instrumental in bringing Hitler to power in 1933, and was therefore the right man to persuade the Austrians that co-operation with the Nazis was feasible. As a devout Catholic, he meant to give the Austrians the necessary confidence. In the internal field Hitler got rid of an uneasy critic, who had barely escaped with his life from the purge of 30 June. But the Austrian government under Italian pressure still hesitated to accept von Papen as new German Minister in Vienna. It was not before the German Foreign Office disclosed that it would regard a refusal 'as a declaration of diplomatic war', that von Papen could assume his new post.[3]

Pursuing a strictly evolutionary method Hitler speculated on the co-operation of the nationalist-minded but anti-National-Socialist groups in Austria as means towards a *Gleichschaltung*, as he had done on his way to power in Germany. The appointment of Schuschnigg as the successor of Dollfuss facilitated such tactics. Dollfuss's death had left unchanged the political structure of Austria. The government still represented the dual role of Christian Socials and *Heimwehr*. In spite of its original intentions the Fatherland Front failed to eliminate the remaining parties in Austria. The *Heimwehr* continued to constitute a separate, militant force alongside it. As a result of the system of dualism,

---

[1] Hess's letter, 21 August 1934, GD, Ser. C, Vol. III, No. 173.
[2] Hitler to von Papen, 26 July, ibid., No. 123.
[3] Bülow's memorandum, 3 August 1934, ibid., No. 146.

Schuschnigg as representative of the Christian Socials, and Star-hemberg as leader of the *Heimwehr*, concluded a compromise, by which Schuschnigg became Chancellor and Starhemberg Vice-Chancellor, whereas Starhemberg assumed the leadership of the Fatherland Front with Schuschnigg as his second in command.

Zernatto, the general secretary of the Fatherland Front, commented on this settlement that 'a double government had been established, which could not last permanently'.[1] Right from the beginning Schuschnigg's aim was to find a way out of the dead-lock. Since the strength of the *Heimwehr* was based on its role as a counterpart to the National Socialists and on the financial support coming from Italy, Schuschnigg could only free himself from his dependence on it by coming to terms with the Nazis and by loosening the ties with Italy.

Such a course was enforced by the fact that Schuschnigg did not get along well with the Italians. Unlike Dollfuss he had a stiff, ascetic personality.[2] He was southern Tyrolese by birth and had been an Italian prisoner of war, circumstances which made him ill at ease with Mussolini. '*Ich kann nicht leugnen, dass mich ein gewisses Gefühl der Beklommenheit beherrschte*',[3] was his comment on his first meeting with the Italian dictator in August 1934, and his contemporaries reported that he suffered from a kind of Mussolini complex.[4]

In contrast to Dollfuss, Schuschnigg's conception was not only based on personal and tactical considerations but sprang from the deeper-rooted conviction that he had 'to embark on the course of appeasement in order to save Austrian independence'. This meant that 'everything had to be avoided which would give Germany a pretext for intervention and that everything had to be done to secure in some way Hitler's toleration of the status quo. It also meant finding a *modus vivendi* with the Nazis in Austria and those in Germany'.[5] Schuschnigg believed in a Pan-Germanism which objected to a 'Greater Germany dominated by Prussia' but was based on a belief, impossible to realize, in a Greater Germany modelled on the Holy Roman Empire. It was a mystical creed, as

---

[1] Zernatto, *Die Wahrheit über Österreich*, New York 1938, p. 151.

[2] Wiskemann, op. cit., p. 45; Fuchs, *Showdown in Vienna*, p. 18.

[3] Schuschnigg, *Requiem in Rot-Weiss-Rot*, p. 219. 'I cannot deny that I was governed by a certain feeling of anxiety.'

[4] See Smend's report, 20 September 1934, GD, 8048/E578534.

[5] Schuschnigg, *Austrian Requiem*, p. 5.

he once said to Prince Starhemberg.[1] However, this creed did not make Schuschnigg's task of projecting the image of an independent Austria easier.

Schuschnigg stressed Austria's German mission, which she had to fulfil as an independent state,[2] yet by emphasizing this mission he evaded the real issue, the absence of a true Austrian patriotism. Austria had known a dynastic, but not a national patriotism. Nationalism in Austria had always looked across the border to Germany. It was therefore logical that Schuschnigg tried to keep the past, dynastic form of patriotism alive. 'The monarchist movement,' he writes, 'was desirable from the point of view of strengthening the concept of Austrian independence', though he admitted that they 'could not risk an experiment in this direction'.[3]

Schuschnigg's attempt to end a struggle which he regarded as essentially fratricidal found immediate response in Austrian Nazi circles. The abortive *putsch* had weakened the radical wing of the party, whose members had either fled the country or been arrested, with the result that the more conciliatory part had gained the upper hand. Leading among them was Reinthaller, an agricultural engineer, who had belonged to the *Landbund*, until 1930, when in disappointment he had turned to the Nazis. He had become Gauleiter for Upper Austria, but the more radical Habicht had him removed from this post. Reinthaller had differed from Habicht in his assessment of the party's strength and its capacity for fighting the government illegally after the party had been outlawed. Nevertheless Reinthaller retained influence as a peasant leader and pursued his efforts at reconciliation. Already in autumn 1933 he had established contact with Schuschnigg, then Minister of Education, with whom he had served in the same regiment during the war.[4] But both being in inferior positions they could not realize their aims.

After the *putsch* of 25 July 1934 this former link took on new significance. Schuschnigg, as Chancellor, encouraged Reinthaller in his efforts to assemble the national groups in a new organiza-

[1] Starhemberg, op. cit., p. 176.
[2] Schuschnigg, *Farewell to Austria*, p. 8.
[3] Schuschnigg, *Austrian Requiem*, p. 195.
[4] Langoth, op. cit., p. 311; Erbach's report, 18 Oct. 1934, Ser. C, Vol. III, No. 257; Hüffer's memorandum, 20 August 1943, ibid., No. 166.

tion.[1] Reinthaller envisaged a national movement which would be independent from Germany, while adopting the Nazi programme as its basis. The former Pan-Germans and the *Landbund* would range themselves around the Nazi party as the hard core of the movement.[2]

Trying to win the confidence of the Austrian government, Reinthaller strongly objected to the contacts which were still maintained between the Austrian Nazis and their leaders in Germany. On 15 September he asked in a letter to Hess, who had approved of his action, that no more orders or instructions be sent to party comrades in Austria because he 'could not give any thought at all to further work until he had succeeded in convincing the Federal Chancellor that all contact between the Austrian NSDAP and authorities in Germany had completely ceased'.[3] Reinthaller finally managed to bring the different national groups together. A conference took place on 24 October, at which a programme for a meeting with Schuschnigg was worked out.[4]

Starhemberg was no more going to tolerate the contacts between Schuschnigg and the Nazis than he had the efforts of Dollfuss in the same direction. He watched with suspicion the advances which were made. He exercised strong pressure on Schuschnigg to ban the national movement which had been formed. Finally he succeeded in having a decree issued, in which the activities of the national movement were declared illegal.[5] Schuschnigg, however, refused to abandon his policy. The only way left to avoid Starhemberg's resistance was by dealing secretly with the groups represented by Reinthaller. Arrangements were made for a meeting and precautions taken to hold the conference without Starhemberg's knowledge.

On 27 October 1934 Schuschnigg received Reinthaller and other representatives of the national groups, among them Bardolff, Glaise-Horstenau, Seyss-Inquart, and Neubacher, in order to discuss possible co-operation. However, Starhemberg was warned by a collaborator, who telephoned him on the morning of the 27th and informed him of the impending meeting.

[1] Zernatto, op. cit., pp. 151, 152; Winkler, op. cit., pp. 203, 204; Seyss-Inquart's memorandum, Doc. 3254–PS, N.C.A., Vol. V, p. 963.
[2] Erbach's report, 18 October 1934, GD, Ser. C, Vol. III, No. 257.
[3] Reinthaller to Hess, enclosed in a report from Linz, GD, 8658/E606194–197.
[4] Eichstädt, *Von Dollfuss zu Hitler*, Wiesbaden, 1955, p. 74.
[5] Erbach's report, 18 October 1934, GD, Ser. C, Vol. III, No. 257.

Starhemberg immediately decided to intervene. Though not invited, and to Schuschnigg's complete surprise, he appeared at the conference. According to Starhemberg's account, Schuschnigg expressed in his speech his desire for appeasement and a compromise, which would end the struggle. The representatives of the national groups answered in the same vein. Starhemberg put a check on this kind of talk. He asked leave to speak and his speech was 'a blow aimed at all this atmosphere of appeasement'.[1] At Starhemberg's instigation the Italian Minister, Preziosi, likewise intervened and protested against the incipient reconciliation with the national movement.

After this failure Schuschnigg showed a much more cautious attitude. He was afraid of repeating the experience of being checked at the last minute by Starhemberg, though he did not discourage the efforts of the national groups to obtain representation in the government. Negotiations between Reinthaller, representing the National Socialists, Foppa of the Pan-German party, and Hueber of the *Heimatschutz* in Styria, led to the formulation of the programme of the 'National Front', which was put forward on 5 March 1935 in Linz. The National Front recognizing that it could not compete with the Fatherland Front as an independent group offered its co-operation within the framework of the Fatherland Front. It recognized the independence of Austria as the basis for future negotiations. On the other hand it demanded the right to form military formations from the former cadres of the SA and SS, as long as the government continued to tolerate the *Heimwehr*.[2]

This programme corresponded exactly with Papen's, Hitler's new ambassador in Vienna, idea of the right tactics. He wanted to put Austro–German relations on a basis satisfactory to both sides, which should gradually lead to an Anschluss. The first step in this direction was to give the Austrian government a feeling of security, and Papen hoped that the government would then make the desired concessions without regarding itself as being trapped. In his report of 17 May 1935 Papen therefore advised Hitler to recognize publicly Austria's independence. The Austrian Nazi Party should abandon its totalitarian intentions and compromise with those elements of the Christian Socials who favoured an

---

[1] Starhemberg, op. cit., p. 180.
[2] Langoth, op. cit., pp. 178–181.

agreement with Germany. Then the barrier between the two countries could be gradually removed and the institutions of the two countries become assimilated.[1]

Hitler agreed with Papen that the evolutionary method demanded the recognition of Austria's independence, at least for the time being. He took up Papen's suggestion and in his speech on 21 May 1935 he stated that 'Germany had neither the intention nor the wish to interfere in Austrian internal affairs or to force the annexation or incorporation of Austria into Germany'.[2] This conciliatory speech found an immediate echo in Vienna. A week later, on 29 May, Schuschnigg made a statement before parliament, in which he dismissed the allegation that Austria pursued a policy treacherous to the German cause. 'We have never ceased – and we shall never cease –,' he continued, 'to regard ourselves as a German state, and we consider the sympathy and respect of our friends abroad always as pro-Austrian, never as anti-German.'[3]

Papen now hoped that these two declarations would find their way into an official agreement between Germany and Austria and serve at the same time as a basis for Austrian concessions in the internal sphere. On 11 July 1935 he submitted to the Austrian government the draft of an agreement which reiterated the positions taken by the German and Austrian Chancellors.[4] For the rest Papen's draft envisaged a regulation for the press and radio activities, the permission to use German emblems in Austria, and the setting up of a committee which should deal with questions arising from the agreement.[5]

Papen's suggestion found no response. Opinions within the Austrian government continued to be divided. Whereas Schuschnigg obviously welcomed the initiative, Starhemberg and his supporters were opposed to the proposal. This split dictated dilatory tactics. On 9 September Papen referred to his suggestion and emphasized that 'he had spoken with Hitler and that he had been authorized now to negotiate about the draft on behalf of

---

[1] Papen to Hitler, 17 May 1935, Schmidt-prot., pp. 390–391; 27 April 1935, GD, 7826/E567831; Papen, *Memoirs*, p. 361.

[2] Quoted in Baynes, *Hitler's Speeches*, Vol. II, p. 1239.

[3] Quoted in *Documents on International Affairs, 1935*, Vol. I, p. 185.

[4] *Aktenvermerk (über den aktenmässigen Verlauf der Entspannungsbesprechungen)*, Vienna, 12 July 1936, Schmidt-prot. pp. 474 *seq.*

[5] See Papen's draft, Schmidt-prot., pp. 476–477; Papen, *Memoirs*, p. 363.

the German government'.[1] This move obliged the Austrian Foreign Minister Berger-Waldenegg to make a reply. It took him another three weeks before he finally, on 1 October 1935, handed Papen the Austrian counter-proposal, which accepted almost in its entirety Papen's original draft; with, however, the essential reservation that 'the government had not yet taken a position'.[2]

Papen's last hopes for an early success faded away when Italian troops invaded Abyssinia on 3 October, because Mussolini's decision for action against Abyssinia strengthened rather than weakened the pro-Italian *Heimwehr* wing in Schuschnigg's cabinet. The Abyssinian war with its subsequent split of the Stresa front with England and France on one hand and Italy on the other, forced Austria to make a choice between countries whose support was equally vital for her own defence. On 10 October during the debate at Geneva, Pfügl, the Austrian delegate to the League, intervened in favour of Italy. Together with Hungary, Austria refused to apply sanctions against Italy. For the time being Starhemberg's pro-Italian wing had won the upper hand. Yet Mussolini's Abyssinian adventure put Austria's friendship for Italy to a severe test. The anti-League policy found much criticism in Austrian government circles. In Geneva a principle was at stake, in which Austria herself had a strong interest. It was realized in Vienna that by estranging Britain and France and weakening the League, Austria might find herself in an isolated position, when she in turn might have to rely on the League for her protection.

Starhemberg, seeing these tendencies, and confident in an early Italian victory, determined to commit the Austrian government definitely to a pro-Italian course by strengthening his own position within the cabinet. At the same time he could fight out his personal feud with Fey. This time Starhemberg forestalled possible resistance by that part of the *Heimwehr* which was loyal to Fey. He arranged for the transport of several thousands of the *Heimwehr* from Lower Austria to Vienna. Under the threat of these formations Fey could not mobilize his own support and had to resign, together with Neustädter-Stürmer and State Secretary

---

[1] *Aktenvermerk*, Schmidt-prot., p. 474.
[2] Berger-Waldenegg to Papen, 1 October 1935, Schmidt-prot., p. 477; Hornbostel's testimony, ibid., p. 168; Berger-Waldenegg's testimony, ibid., p. 287.

Karminsky, on 17 October 1935. Thus Starhemberg gained considerable influence and he saw to it that officials who objected to the anti-League policy were dismissed.[1]

Papen knew that there was no chance of success for his proposal as long as Starhemberg's position was firmly established. He adapted his policy to the government reorganization of 17 October and held further negotiations for a compromise as useless. Yet he did not despair.

In spite of the Vice-Chancellor's clear victory [he commented to Hitler] the feeling of moving towards a completely uncertain development prevails among the Austrian public, even in the *Heimwehr* circles. . . . From our point of view the change of affairs is only too welcome. Every new weakening of the system is of advantage, even if at first it seems, in fact, to be directed against us.

Papen hoped to set Schuschnigg free from his dependence upon Starhemberg and reckoned that this would be brought about by influences coming from two directions. In the internal sphere, he advised,

. . . it will be a good thing to build up the increasingly excited public feeling against the Italian trend by clever and tactful handling via the Press without, however, giving the government justifiable cause for having recourse to the desperate measure of starting a new propaganda campaign against us.

For this purpose Papen advised that Goebbels 'was to put a few experienced journalists to work in this connexion'.[2]

Yet ultimately only a reversal of Mussolini's Austrian policy and his decision to abandon the *Heimwehr* as an instrument of Italian policy could give Schuschnigg full freedom of action. A change in Austria's domestic scene therefore depended upon a change in the international situation. In this respect Papen looked forward to the repercussions of the Abyssinian war.

We can confidently leave further developments to the near future; I am convinced that the shifting of powers on the European chessboard will permit us in the not too distant future to take up actively the question of influencing the south-eastern area.[3]

[1] Papen to Hitler, 18 October 1935, Schmidt-prot., pp. 394–395.
[2] Papen to Hitler, 18 October 1935, ibid., pp. 394–395, translation in IMT, Part 16, p. 349.
[3] Papen to Hitler, 18 October 1935, quoted in IMT, Part 16, p. 349.

MUSSOLINI'S WITHDRAWAL FROM AUSTRIA

In the international sphere the repercussions of July 1934 had been less far-reaching than may have been expected. Though moral indignation was considerable, no immediate changes occurred, and opinion in informed circles was divided as far as German complicity was concerned.[1] With the danger from the Nazi side averted, attention turned towards Italy. Léger, Secretary-General of the French Foreign Ministry, was apprehensive of an isolated Italian action and its probable reactions in Czechoslovakia and Yugoslavia. On 31 July 1934, he suggested to the British government the establishment of a standing committee with the task of watching events in Austria and consulting on common measures.[2] It should consist of the French and British ambassadors in Rome with an Italian representative as president. The body would, it was hoped, prevent Italy from acting independently and at the same time discourage Germany from interfering. Simon, however, opposed the idea arguing that this system 'would lend itself to misrepresentation'.[3]

The more active French policy in Austrian affairs was less a result of the Nazi *putsch* than a consequence of Barthou's policy based on his awareness of the threat from Germany. Already during his stay in Vienna on 19 June Barthou had given Dollfuss the assurance that 'all parties in France were determined to support him even though they could not be in agreement with the undemocratic side of his government'.[4] Compared with Paul-Boncour's statements of the previous year this was a big concession and the first step towards a Franco-Italian *rapprochement*.

During September 1934 discussions took place at Geneva on the fringe of the League, at which Aloisi, the Italian representative on the League Council, suggested a guarantee pact between France, Great Britain, and Italy. When turned down by the British Aloisi proposed that Italy should be given a mandate to act on behalf of the three powers in Austria. Being prepared to accept Italian predominance over Austria, if this was the only way

[1] Correspondence between Sir John Simon and Newton relating to the assassination of Dr. Dollfuss, Gainer to Newton, 27 July 1934 and 30 July 1934, BrD, 2nd Ser., Vol. VI, Appendix IV.
[2] Clerk to Simon, 31 July 1934, ibid., No. 548.
[3] Simon to Clerk, 3 August 1934, ibid., No. 560.
[4] Hadow to Simon, 21 June 1934, ibid., No. 467.

of keeping Germany out, Barthou favoured the Italian idea. This time, however, he met with the resistance of the Little Entente and especially Yugoslavia,[1] and unless he wanted to risk the complete estrangement of these countries, he had to renounce the idea. No agreement being reached, England, France, and Italy went back to their declaration of 17 February 1934, which was, as has been shown, empty of any force. They stated on 27 September 1934 that

the declaration of 17 February regarding the necessity of maintaining the independence and integrity of Austria in accordance with the Treaties in force retains its full effect and will continue to inspire their common policy.[2]

Trying to obtain a definitive renunciation from Germany Aloisi put forward the request that Germany should accede to the declaration of the three powers,[3] and he was supported by the German ambassador Hassel.[4] Berlin saw no reason for a reversal of its policy in this respect and again took a waiting attitude, because 'without Germany Austria would never be economically or politically sound again. Italy was not in a position to give aid by herself'.[5]

The failure of France to win British support, and of Italy to co-operate with Germany was the main reason for the final *rapprochement* between Rome and Paris. Barthou's assassination on 9 October 1934, a month before his visit to Rome, delayed but did not stop the development, which finally led to the agreements of 7 January 1935. These agreements ended the Franco-Italian post-war rivalry, which had ranged over south-east Europe, the Mediterranean, and Africa. With regard to south-east Europe Germany's relations with Austria were the core of the agreement. France and Italy invited Austria's neighbour states – Yugoslavia, Hungary, Czechoslovakia, and Germany – to conclude a pact of non-intervention, while it was left open to France, Poland, and Rumania to join the pact later. It should contain an undertaking to refrain from any interference in domestic affairs, and a further undertaking to permit no agitation, propaganda, or

[1] Köster's reports, 20 and 29 September 1934, GD, 5269/E324206–09.
[2] *Survey of International Affairs, 1934,* p. 485.
[3] Hassel's report, 11 October 1934, GD, Ser. C, Vol. III, No. 241.
[4] Hassel's report, 17 October 1934, GD, 7824/E443041–44.
[5] Köpke to Hassel, 23 October 1934, GD., Ser. C, Vol. III, No. 267.

attempts at intervention aimed at transforming, by force, the territorial integrity of any one of the other signatory states. The more important part of the agreement was, however, that Italy and France agreed on a consultative pact with the object of maintaining the integrity and independence of Austria. Both countries agreed to consult one another as to the measures to be taken. Since Italian influence in Vienna was already well established, France thereby recognized Italy's dominant role in Austrian affairs.

Although Great Britain agreed during the Franco-British negotiations in London on 1–3 February 1935 to consult France and Italy in the event of any threat to the independence of Austria, she left no doubt about her fundamental disinterest in central Europe. On 11 March 1935 Prime Minister MacDonald declared in the House of Commons that

. . . proposals for increasing the security in the Danube basin, with special reference to the integrity of Austria, involve no military commitments, direct or indirect, by this country.[1]

The British government was aiming at a settlement with Germany and tried therefore to avoid commitments directed against her. On 25 and 26 March Simon and Eden visited Hitler in Berlin hoping to find a basis for co-operation. Eden's main purpose was to bring Germany back into the League.[2] Hitler displayed a conciliatory attitude, but as soon as practical details were under discussion he showed the greatest reserve.[3] During the afternoon meeting, on 25 March, the discussion touched the Austrian question. They had no intention of threatening Austrian sovereignty, Hitler stressed, but 'Austrian security could best be achieved by leaving Austria completely alone'. This was conceded by Simon:

Britain had not the same interest in Austria as, for example, in Belgium. She had never interfered in Austrian affairs and was still confining herself to the hope that the problems there would be solved.[4]

---

[1] Ganterbein, *Documentary Background of World War II*, pp. 293–294.

[2] See Eden's account of the meeting in Lord Avon, *Facing the Dictators*, London, 1962, pp. 136, 137.

[3] Unsigned memorandum of the conversations on 25 and 26 March 1935, GD, Ser. C, Vol. III, No. 555: Schmidt, *Statist auf diplomatischer Bühne*, Bonn, 1949, pp. 293–303.

[4] Unsigned memorandum, 25 March 1935, GD, Ser. C, Vol. III, No. 555, p. 1059.

The subsequent Stresa conference from 11 to 14 April 1935 between France, Italy, and Great Britain did not alter the British position. The three powers met primarily to discuss German rearmament and to reassess the principles of Locarno. With regard to Austria they confirmed the declarations of 17 February and 27 September 1934 about the necessity of maintaining Austria's independence. But this was only an outward unity. No definitive commitments emerged from the conference. The famous Stresa Front closed a chapter rather than opened a new one. Six weeks after the condemnation of German unilateral rearmament at Stresa the British government concluded, without previous consultation with France and Italy, the Anglo-German naval treaty, which was essentially a unilateral abandonment of Versailles and strongly resented by the French.[1]

Moreover, the Italo-Abyssinian conflict was never officially discussed at Stresa though it dominated international meetings since the Wal-Wal incident in December 1934 and the Abyssinian appeals to the League in January and March 1935. It now seems certain that the French Prime Minister, Laval, had in fact, purchased Mussolini's co-operation during their negotiations in January 1935 by giving him a free hand in Abyssinia. Laval himself denied publicly the existence of an agreement between himself and Mussolini, but a secret publication of the Italian Foreign Office reveals that Laval gave verbal sanction to expand in East Africa and to settle, once and for all, every question with the government of Abyssinia.[2] However, no definite stand was taken and thus a problem which contained the cause of future disagreement had been patched up.

Mussolini's concentration on Abyssinia involved a strong interest in keeping the peace in south-east Europe. A non-intervention pact of the countries surrounding Austria as proposed by France and Italy in January 1935 would fulfil this purpose.[3] But the circumstances which had hitherto prevented a settlement

[1] Watt 'The Anglo-German Naval Agreement of 1935', *Journal of Modern History*, Vol. 28 (1956), p. 158.

[2] Francia: Situazione politica nel 1935, p. 16, quoted in Askew, 'The secret agreement between France and Italy on Ethiopia', in *Journal of Modern History*, Vol. 25 (1953), pp. 47, 48.

[3] Mussolini mentioned to Hassel that Austria as the only problem between Italy and Germany should be solved by the pact; Hassel's report, 14 May 1935, GD. 7826/E5667924.

between the Danubian countries still prevailed. Hungary could not but see in a Danubian pact a limitation of her revisionist aims. Yugoslavia continued to resent Italy's influence in Austria.[1] Moreover, the *rapprochement* between France and Italy immediately reduced the value which France had for Yugoslavia as a possible ally against Italy, and which Italy had as an ally for Hungary against the Little Entente. Both countries, therefore, resisted the pressure for a Danubian pact.[2]

Under these conditions Germany could afford a waiting position. But the Foreign Office recognized that a purely negative attitude would lead to an increase of international suspicion. Germany, preoccupied with her rearmament, had a strong interest in calming international tension. When Simon and Eden brought up the question of a Danubian pact during their visit to Berlin on 25 March 1935, Hitler and Neurath were therefore 'prepared to accept the idea in principle, but there were doubts about certain practical details concerning the meaning of "non-intervention" itself'.[3] Schmidt, Hitler's interpreter, later expressed his surprise at Hitler's mastery of the language of Geneva.[4] Hitler's conciliatory attitude did not mean that he had any intention of concluding a non-intervention pact. On 3 March Papen had recommended that a premise for a settlement of the Austo-German question should be the restoration of normal relations, by which he understood the admission of the German press as a whole, respect for the German national emblems, etc.[5] Hitler had approved of this condition. Since the pact proposed by France and Italy aimed on the other hand at the exclusion of any German influence, German adherence to the pact was out of the question. The attempts by Paris and Rome at securing the collaboration of the Danubian countries were therefore half-hearted and very soon ceased.

The failure to settle the Austrian problem with Germany did not divert Mussolini from his Abyssinian course.[6] The paradox,

[1] Bullit's report, 29 May 1935, US, 1935, Vol. I, p. 284.

[2] Heeren's report, 25 April 1935, GD, 7826/E567843–45; Hassel's report, 8 May 1935, ibid., E567893.

[3] Unsigned memorandum, 25 March 1935, GD, Ser. C, Vol. III, No. 555.

[4] Schmidt, op. cit., p. 303.

[5] Papen to Neurath, 3 March 1935, GD, Ser. C, Vol. III, No. 515.

[6] According to Grandi's account in the Italian paper *Oggi*, anno XV, n. 22, 28 May 1959, p. 16, Mussolini realized, during the Stresa conference in April 1935, that he had to give up his ambitions in Austria because of the Abyssinian crisis.

as it must have appeared to France and England, was that once they had become reconciled to Italy's tutelage over Austria, Mussolini would no longer be interested in such a concession. But his calculations were simple. Since Italian predominance had been established in Austria, Mussolini no longer considered the maintenance of Austria's independence as a purely Italian task. After the discussions of the Italo-Abyssinian dispute at Geneva in May 1935, where on 25 May the Council had left the settlement of the conflict in the hands of the two parties involved, Litvinov was convinced that 'Mussolini would evade arbitration and attack Abyssinia as soon as the rainy season was over about 1 September'.[1] Together with Eden and Laval, he recognized the dangers of such a development, and they urged Mussolini 'that he should not involve Italy deeply in Abyssinia as such involvement would make it impossible for Italy to intervene effectively in Austria'. For this Mussolini had a clear answer:

The independence of Austria was a European question and not one for Italy alone and he had no intention of opposing Germany in Austria unless he should receive full support from France and England.[2]

Mussolini now made the reaction to his Abyssinia policy the test-case for his future attitude towards other European countries.[3] On 25 May he told the Italian deputies that they had to consider international problems 'in relation to what may happen in East Africa and in relation to the attitudes which individual states may take up when the time comes for them to show us a real friendship, not a superficial one based on words alone'.[4] Only one problem compromised Italo-German relations, that of Austria, and Mussolini reminded England and France, whom he had just joined in the Stresa declaration, that he could easily come to terms with Germany by settling the Austrian problem with her.

It may therefore not be out of place to address a few words to those who would like to fossilize us on the Brenner to prevent us from moving in any other part of the world.[5]

[1] Litvinov to Bullit, Bullit's telegram, 29 May 1935, US, 1935, Vol. I, p. 283.
[2] Ibid., p. 284.
[3] Massimo Magistrati, La Germania e l'impresa italiana di Etiopia, *Rivista di Studi Politici Internazionali*, anno XVII, 1950, p. 585.
[4] *Scritti e discorsi*, Vol. IX, pp. 190–191; translation in *Documents on International Affairs*, *1935*, Vol. I, pp. 175–178.
[5] *Documents on International Affairs*, *1935*, Vol. I, p. 178.

I

Mussolini refused to let himself be dominated by the Austrian question. Rather than sacrifice his Abyssinian policy, he implied, he would abandon Austria.

Italy does not mean to limit her historic mission to a single political problem, or to a single military sector such as the defence of a frontier, even such an important one as the Brenner.

Hitler immediately understood the advantages to be gained from the Italo-Abyssinian conflict. At last the alliance with Italy had come within reach. Nothing could be more welcome than the diversion of Mussolini's attention from Austria, hitherto the biggest obstacle to such an alliance. Therefore complete neutrality had to be observed in Italy's conflict with Abyssinia. But this policy ran counter to a strong current of feeling among party circles, who had no sympathy for Mussolini's cause and the more adventurous of whom even contemplated fighting voluntarily for Abyssinia.[1] The press was hostile to Italy's Abyssinian campaign and in spring 1935 a film was exhibited which was favourable to the Negus and his rule.[2]

Hitler over-ruled such sentimentality. When the Emperor, Haile Selassie, expressed his wish to send a representative to Germany for the purchase of military equipment, including aircraft,[3] the German Minister in Addis Ababa was instructed to give an evasive reply.[4] On 16 January 1935 Hitler ordered that any press comment unsympathetic to Italy in the conflict with Abyssinia was to be avoided.[5] Mussolini noted this restraint with approval. On 26 May 1935, a day after his speech before the Chamber of Deputies, he mentioned to Plessen that the prohibition of deliveries of German arms to Abyssinia was evidence that 'Germany did not support Italy's enemies'.[6]

The only way left for the Western powers to prevent a drastic change in Mussolini's Austrian policy seemed a compromise with Italy over Abyssinia. Since Laval had already bargained that country away, this amounted to the question of whether or not

---

[1] Kordt, *Nicht aus den Akten*, Stuttgart, 1950, p. 403.
[2] Wiskemann, *The Rome–Berlin Axis*, Oxford University Press, 1949, p. 47.
[3] Schoen's telegram, 28 October 1934, GD, Ser. C, Vol. III, No. 280; Unverfehrt's telegram, 26 December 1934, ibid., No. 402.
[4] Telegram, 31 October 1934, GD, 8025/E577712.
[5] Neurath's memorandum, GD, 8033/E577840.
[6] Plessen's report, 26 May 1935, GD, 8069/E57906.

the British government was prepared to make a similar deal. Vansittart, willing to grant the necessary concessions to Italy if this meant the establishment of a common front against Germany, had always favoured such a course. In Sir Samuel Hoare he had at last found a Foreign Secretary who, 'from the first moment came under the influence of his singleness of purpose'[1] and was prepared to accept his advice.

Hoare's and Vansittart's problem was that in 1935 this policy did not correspond with a strong current in British opinion. The final results of the so-called peace ballot with eleven million votes underlining the confidence of the British public in the principles of the League became known in July 1935, when the crisis was driving to its climax. Hoare thought that – with a general election ahead – they could not defy this trend. On 18 August 1935 he wrote to Chamberlain that 'outside the Cabinet public opinion has been greatly hardening against Italy' and that 'the Government will lose heavily if we appear to be repudiating the Covenant'.[2]

By courting public opinion and in trying to strengthen the League, whose objective it was to grant Abyssinia protection against Italy, Hoare pursued a policy which was irreconcilable with his own aim of coming to terms with Mussolini. Hoare persuaded himself that he could follow 'a double line of approach' without sacrificing one policy to the other:

On the one hand, a most patient and cautious negotiation that would keep him on the Allied side; on the other, the creation of a united front in Geneva as a necessary deterrent against German aggression.[3]

Hoare was determined 'to keep in step with the French, and, whether now or at Geneva, to act with them'. He hoped to establish a common front with them at Geneva in the face of the Italian intentions, but this was a forelorn undertaking.

France had lost her confidence in the League, when British public opinion had swung in its favour. Moreover, for France the League was an instrument of European security. This meant she had no interest in using the League for the protection of Abyssinia, thereby turning Italy, one of its European members, into an enemy. 'Since the murder of Dollfuss,' Laval told Hoare,

---

[1] Viscount Templewood (Sir Samuel Hoare), *Nine Troubled Years*, London 1954, p. 138.
[2] Ibid., pp. 164–165. [3] Ibid., p. 168.

'Mussolini has turned to France.' They had 'to prevent Mussolini being driven into the German camp'. Since action against Italy implied the risk that Mussolini would abandon Austria, Laval was only willing to grant French support in return for a British guarantee of Austria's independence. On 8 September 1935 he wrote to London:

What would the reaction of England be, if the resort to sanctions, assuming that their eventual application had been recognized as possible and necessary in the case of Italy, caused an extension of the conflict to Europe, of which Germany could be tempted to take advantage for the realization of her Austrian ambitions? Would she feel obliged to give to the independence of Austria the guarantee which until now she has refused? I am not unaware of the reluctance of the government in London to commit themselves on a hypothetical basis, but the envisaged eventuality is so clearly connected with the actual crisis that we have the right to being precisely informed.[1]

Knowing that Hoare was unwilling to give such a guarantee, Laval tried to put the blame for his passive attitude on the British. But Hoare's refusal completed the vicious circle. Neither France nor England were going to take strong action without the other country and both were reluctant to take the lead. In this case the smaller countries refused to take a more determined position. Yugoslavia might have had the strongest motives for action against Italy, but she maintained her neutral position. On 20 September Prime Minister and Foreign Minister Stojadinović told Prince Paul:

I prefer their going to Abyssinia rather than to the Balkans. So long as France does not decide to which side she will go we have no reason to run out ahead of the great powers.[2]

The two-faced policy of the French and British governments resulted in an ambiguous attitude. On 12 September Hoare delivered his famous speech at Geneva expressing his confidence in the principles of the League. However, on 4 October, a day after the beginning of the Italian invasion, he tried to prevent Mussolini's estrangement by informing him in a personal message that 'England would not resort to military sanctions and that she

---

[1] Quoted by Heriot, *Jadis*, Vol. II, pp. 577–578 (my translation).
[2] Yugoslav Minute – quoted by Hoptner, 'Yugoslavia as a Neutralist 1937', *Journal of Central European Affairs*, Vol. XVI, 1956, p. 177. Hoptner's article is hereafter referred to as Hoptner.

would only reluctantly apply economic sanctions'.[1] On 7 December Hoare finally thought he could take his long postponed holiday in Switzerland, but made his fatal stop in Paris at the request of the French government.

Vansittart persuaded Hoare that 'the British government must understand the League powers today were not prepared to carry to its logical conclusion the policy of stopping aggression'.[2] The result of Hoare's two days discussions with Laval was the Hoare–Laval plan, which tried to buy off Mussolini with considerable concessions in Abyssinia.[3] An outcry of public opinion in England and a split within the British cabinet with Eden, as Minister for League of Nations Affairs supporting the League course, prevented the scheme. Hoare had to resign. Eden became his successor, but though less conciliatory towards Mussolini he was no more fortunate in enforcing a strong League policy.

In France, similarly, the failure of his plan brought down Laval. On 27 December 1935 there was a wave of hostility in the French chamber, with Leon Blum coming out strongly in favour of an alignment with England and Russia.[4] The Radicals blamed Laval for having failed to support the League when the British government had declared itself in its favour, and withdrew their support. Herriot resigned on 19 January, thus precipitating Laval's fall on 22 January 1936.[5] With the failure of Laval's tactics a French policy opposed to the Italian designs in Abyssinia was a foregone conclusion.

Having failed to achieve final success Mussolini's disappointment was the stronger when the Hoare–Laval plan did not materialize. Early in December 1935 at the Council of Ministers he was still of the opinion that if the present régime in Austria could not hold out 'Germany would, before long, not only be at the Italian, but at the Hungarian frontier as well. The route for Germany's expansion in the south-east would lie open'.[6] After

[1] Attolico to Neurath on the basis of Hoare's telegram transmitted to him from Rome, Neurath's memorandum, 4 October 1935, GD, 2784/D540426.
[2] Vansittart to Bingham, Bingham's report, 16 December 1935, US, 1935, Vol. I, p. 713.
[3] Grandi in his account of these events claims the authorship of the Hoare–Laval plan for himself and speaks actually of the Grandi–Vansittart plan, *Oggi*, anno XV, n. 22, 28 May 1959, p. 16.
[4] Herriot, *Jadis*, Vol. II, p. 630.
[5] Joll, 'The Making of the Popular Front', *St. Antony's Papers*, No. 5, p. 61.
[6] Hassel's report, 14 December 1935, GD, 8073/E579389.

the failure of the British and French attempts at reconciliation his attitude changed completely.

On 6 January 1936 Mussolini had a long discussion with the German ambassador. 'Austria had lost confidence in Italy's ability to protect her', the Duce told von Hassel. He feared that Austria would be driven into the arms of Czechoslovakia and ultimately France. To this he preferred an alignment of Austria with Germany. 'Because of Germany's benevolent neutrality,' Mussolini declared, 'it is possible to improve fundamentally the Italo-German relations and to remove the last bone of contention, the Austrian problem.'[1] In complete contrast to his reaction in July 1934, when he had mounted guard for Austria's independence, the Duce was now prepared to withdraw. 'Berlin and Vienna had to settle their relations on the basis of Austria's independence by concluding a treaty of friendship and non-aggression':

> This will practically bring Austria in the wake of Germany and have the result that Austria can conduct no other foreign policy than parallel to Germany's. I have no objections if Austria becomes – as a formally independent state – practically a satellite of Germany. I consider it a big advantage both for Germany and Italy that Germany gets a reliable satellite, while at the same time the German and Italian distrust will be eliminated and speculations for a Danubian pact be defeated.[2]

Hassel's report was the news Hitler had waited for. He summoned his ambassador from Rome, and on 20 January 1936, he held a special conference with Neurath and Hassel at the *Reichskanzlei*.[3] The Führer defined the German response to Mussolini's

[1] Hassel's report, 6 January 1936, GD, 6114/E454451–456; quoted also by Esmonde Robertson, 'Zur Wiederbesetzung des Rheinlandes 1936', Vierteljahreshefte für Zeitgeschichte, X (1962) Heft 2, pp. 188–190.

[2] Hassel's report, ibid. Wiskemann, op. cit., p. 56, dates the *rapprochement* between Germany and Italy later and thinks that it was mainly a result of the formation of the popular front with its effects upon Mussolini. Wiskemann's main evidence for the assumption that relations between Germany and Italy had not yet improved are von Neurath's remarks to Bullit, Bullit's memorandum, Doc. L – 150, NCA, Vol. XII, p. 890, that he 'could see no way to reconcile the conflicting interests of Germany and Italy in Austria'. It seems that the German documents now throw a different light on this conversation. Neurath tried to diminish the *rapprochement* between Italy and Germany in order not to arouse suspicions. He therefore misled Bullit deliberately.

[3] On the same day Attolico reaffirmed that Mussolini desired an agreement between Vienna and Berlin. Hassel's memorandum, 20 January 1936, GD, 6114/E454474–480.

new attitude towards Germany and the Austrian problem. Hitler admitted that it might have been a matter of some satisfaction to Germany – after Mussolini's demonstration on the Brenner in 1934 – if Italy did not emerge from the Abyssinian conflict too big and successful. But there was not time for sentimentalities. The events of 1934 had to be forgotten. There existed the much greater danger that Fascism, and as things stood, Italy, would be crushed in the contest, and a breakdown had to be avoided. Benevolent neutrality remained the guiding principle.

One should have no illusion that Germany is today to all intents and purposes isolated. . . . It is extremely undesirable that through the breakdown of Fascism in Italy this isolation becomes a moral isolation as well. We have to do everything so that the manifold opposition in the world against the authoritarian system of government does not concentrate on us as the only object.[1]

Yet, Hitler continued, Mussolini had to be told that he had to make good his words and conduct a policy in accordance with them. Mussolini had to leave no doubts that he wanted the agreement between Vienna and Berlin and that he objected to an alignment of Austria with Czechoslovakia.

Hitler did not press the Austrian issue further. After Laval's resignation on 22 January 1936 the Franco-Russian treaty was again under discussion and its ratification imminent. With it the possibility of a German retaliation arose and Hitler contemplated the occupation of the demilitarized zone of the Rhineland. For this purpose he had to secure Mussolini's neutrality, and he could not strike against Austria and occupy the Rhineland at the same time. Hassel, back in Rome, was directed to explore the Duce's probable reaction. Mussolini now faced the dilemma of how far he should commit himself and whether, after the early collapse of the Stresa front, he should abandon Locarno as well. His advisers were divided. Suvich continued to advocate an anti-German policy;[2] but Ciano, the Minister of Press and Propaganda, who had an eye on the Foreign Ministry, favoured a *rapprochement* with Germany, because 'France had betrayed Italy and one had to realize that Germany will last'.[3] On 22 February 1936 Mussolini met Hassel and though he was still cautious, he

---

[1] Hassel's memorandum, 20 January 1936, GD, 6114/454477.
[2] Hassel's report, 25 February 1936, GD, 6001/E443094.
[3] Memorandum, 13 February 1936, GD, 682440–443.

made it clear to Hassel that Italy would not side with France. They had not made a decision yet, because they were not directly interested.

Already now, however, I can declare, that we are not going to join in any counter-action, which might be caused by the German reaction to the ratification of the Franco-Russian Pact.[1]

With regard to Austria Mussolini stressed the importance of her independence, but added that he wanted relations between Germany and Austria to become normal. The attempts of Czechoslovakia, supported by France, to attract Austria had to be checked.

RIVAL NEGOTIATIONS OF SCHUSCHNIGG AND STARHEMBERG

Mussolini's fear that Austria would turn to the Little Entente as a consequence of his own inevitable detachment from Austria was not without foundation. Schuschnigg visited Prague on 16 and 17 January 1936 and discussed with President Beneš and Prime Minister Hodza the possibility of reinforcing the political and economic relations between the two countries. Hodza put forward a still more ambitious scheme and thought that because of Italy's preoccupation with Abyssinia the time for the realization of the old plans for a Danubian pact, with the exclusion of Italy, had come. On 22 and 23 February 1936 he visited Belgrade and on 9 and 10 March 1936 Vienna, sponsoring a Danubian economic pact as a precursor to a political agreement embracing the Little Entente, Austria, and Hungary.

How far the current rumours of an impending *rapprochement* between Austria and Czechoslovakia, on which Mussolini's suspicions were based, were justified is difficult to assess. Schuschnigg writes that during his conversation with Beneš in January 1936 at Prague he stressed the Austrian solidarity with Rome and Budapest and made it clear that 'Austria could not take part in any political group or alliance which was openly or potentially directed against Germany'.[2] Besides Schuschnigg's reluctance to commit himself too far, another obstacle to an alignment of Austria with the Little Entente was the danger of a restoration in

[1] Suvich's memorandum, 22 February 1936, GD, 6001/E443104–107.
[2] Schuschnigg, *Austrian Requiem*, p. 169.

Austria. Though Schuschnigg declared that the question of the restoration was not actual, he refused to renounce the possibility of a revival of the monarchy. It was for him 'a purely internal affair which would admit of no interference on the part of a third party'.[1]

But by emphasizing the domestic character of the Habsburg question Schuschnigg could not avert the repercussions which the propaganda of the Austrian Monarchists had on the Little Entente and especially on Yugoslavia. The possibility of a return of the Habsburgs was regarded in Belgrade as a threat to the nation's integrity. Already in August 1935 the Yugoslav Minister in Vienna, Nastasijevic, had proposed to Papen a secret military alliance for such an eventuality.[2] It seems that as a result Germany and Yugoslavia agreed to occupy Austria in the event of a decision to restore the monarchy.[3] Because of Schuschnigg's passive attitude and his refusal to renounce the idea of restoration, Hodza's attempts for a Danubian pact had no prospects and their failure was a foregone conclusion.

No doubt Hitler was right in declaring that the initiative lay with Mussolini, if he wanted to concede Germany a stronger influence in Austrian affairs. Since Mussolini had hitherto checked Schuschnigg's efforts at reconciliation with the Nazis by using the *Heimwehr*, only a withdrawal of his support from Starhemberg could alter the situation. The dual government in Austria had led to the paradox that Mussolini received his advice from two different representatives in Vienna:[4] Senator Salata, the President of the Italian Cultural Institute in Vienna, through whom he kept in touch with Schuschnigg, and the Italian Minister Preziosi who stood close to Starhemberg and the *Heimwehr* circles. Salata was a Triestino like his fellow-countryman Suvich, but in contrast to him he opposed the system of dualism and favoured an exclusive rule by Schuschnigg. He, rather than Suvich, now began to shape the Duce's opinion on Austrian affairs.

When Schuschnigg arrived in Rome in order to attend the

---

[1] Schuschnigg, *Farewell to Austria*, p. 229.
[2] Papen to Hitler, 21 August 1935, Schmidt-prot., pp. 393–394.
[3] Göring claimed that he himself had concluded such an agreement with the Yugoslavs. Tauschitz's report, 4 November 1936, Schmidt-prot., pp. 489–491: see Schuschnigg, *Austrian Requiem*, p. 195.
[4] Zernatto, op. cit., p. 156.

annual conference of the three countries of the Rome protocols from 21 to 23 March 1936, the atmosphere was completely changed from that at the meeting the year before. Whereas in 1935 Mussolini, together with Laval, had striven for a *rapprochement* of the Danubian countries, Schuschnigg found the Duce now preoccupied with the danger of too close an alignment of Austria with Czechoslovakia and annoyed about the initiative taken by Hodza. Mussolini therefore let Schuschnigg know that 'a further step should be made toward the internal pacification of Austria', and that the 'Austrian question, which stood in the way of a close alliance between Germany and Italy, had to be settled'.[1]

Telling Schuschnigg that he had to come to an agreement with Germany was virtually preaching to the converted. Yet Schuschnigg drew two conclusions from Mussolini's advice. He had no longer to fear Starhemberg's opposition to such a course, and secondly, it was high time to conclude such an agreement. Schuschnigg did not want Austria to be caught unawares by the Italo-German *rapprochement*. He reasoned that 'the first and foremost step was to assure ourselves of the support of our Italian friends, to the extent that their new friendship with Hitler Germany would not be cemented at the expense of Austria'.[2]

Mussolini's decision to throw his decisive weight on the side of Schuschnigg signified the end of dualism in Austria. Starhemberg's position, resting on Mussolini's friendship and financial support, was deprived of its very basis. After his return from Rome, on 24 March, Schuschnigg decided to deal the first blow against the *Heimwehr*. On 1 April 1936 the Austrian Assembly passed Schuschnigg's bill for the introduction of universal compulsory service. As the army was by then an integral part of the Fatherland Front this expansion of the public force strengthened Schuschnigg against the *Heimwehr*.[3]

Starhemberg was not slow in comprehending the new situation. He tried to forestall Schuschnigg's manoeuvres for a settlement with Germany by pursuing the same tactics to which he had resorted two years before, when threatened by Fey. He

---

[1] Zernatto, op. cit., pp. 153–156.
[2] Schuschnigg, *Austrian Requiem*, p. 122.
[3] Papen's reports, 21 April 1936, Schmidt-prot., p. 403; 29 April 1936, GD, 6114/E45681–685.

again made attempts at coming to terms with Germany before his opponent could do so. Already in his conversation with Papen in February 1936 Starhemberg had hinted at a common front of Germany, Austria, and Italy.[1] In his speech before the *Heimwehr* leaders of 25 April 1936 he put forward his ideas. The Western democracies could not offer adequate resistance to the Bolshevist invasion; consequently, it was necessary to set the idea of Fascism against Bolshevism and, above all, 'to bring the Fascist states into one front'.[2]

Starhemberg now took a further step in order to steal a march upon Schuschnigg. For his purpose he used the good offices of his friend Franz Hueber, the former Minister of Justice in the Vaugoin cabinet, who himself came from the *Heimwehr* but had declared himself for the National Socialists as the only force supporting an Anschluss.[3] Since Hueber was the brother-in-law of Göring, Starhemberg hoped to arrange through him a meeting with Göring himself.[4] Starhemberg met Hueber in the second half of April 1936. He told him that 'in order to conduct the common fight against Bolshevism and in order to know on which side Austria stood if a conflict in Europe broke out', he aimed at 'an agreement with Germany and for this purpose at a pacification within Austria'.[5]

Hitler having the option between Schuschnigg and Starhemberg decided to respond to their rival advances without committing

---

[1] Papen's report, 12 February 1936, Schmidt-prot., pp. 401–403; Köpke to Hassel, 6 April 1936, GD, 6114/E454650.

[2] Quoted by Gulick, op. cit., Vol. II, pp. 1710–1711; Papen's report, 13 May 1936, Schmidt-prot., pp. 404–405.

[3] Starhemberg, op. cit., pp. 226–227.

[4] Starhemberg's account, op. cit., pp. 226–229, and Hueber's account (see Renthe-Fink's memorandum, 6 May 1936, GD, 6114/E454690), differ considerably. Starhemberg writes that in fact Göring wanted to talk with him because 'Göring took a different attitude from Hitler over the Anschluss question and thought it made very little difference whether Austria belong to Germany or not.'
However, there seems little doubt that in the light of the unpublished German documents Starhemberg's version must be regarded as a self-justificatory falsification of the events. All the evidence points to Göring rather than Hitler as the pressing force in the Anschluss question. Hueber's account appears more trustworthy, because it was made at the time of the events and not destined for publication. Moreover, since Mussolini was going to drop him, Starhemberg had every reason to strike a bargain with the Nazis, as he had tried to do in 1934. Starhemberg himself writes that 'honesty and straight dealing were the hallmarks of Hueber's character', op. cit., p. 227.

[5] Renthe-Fink's memorandum, 6 May 1936, GD, 6114/E454690.

himself to either of the two parties, which were struggling for predominance.[1] But he did authorize Göring to accept Starhemberg's proposal for a meeting. Through Hueber as intermediary it was arranged that it should take place in May on Hungarian territory, and that a hunting party organized by the Hungarian Minister President Gömbös should serve as the necessary camouflage. Neither Schuschnigg nor Mussolini were to be informed until just before Starhemberg's departure.[2]

Hitler, seeing the negotiations materialize, now ordered that all acts of terrorism by Austrian Nazis had to be strictly avoided.[3] And on 11 May, in a conversation with Papen, he declared he was prepared to meet one of the leading Austrian personalities.[4] Such a meeting was rendered unnecessary by the rapid development of the internal struggle in Austria, which released Hitler from making a choice between Schuschnigg and Starhemberg. Starhemberg, driven into a corner, used the means of a desperate man. He decided to make a last bid for Mussolini's friendship by sending his telegram on 10 May on the Italian capture of Addis Ababa:

I congratulate your Excellency with my whole heart in the name of those who fight for Fascism in Austria and in my own name on the famous and magnificent victory of the Italian Fascist armies over barbarism; on the victory of the Fascist spirit over democratic dishonesty and hypocrisy; on the victory of Fascist sacrifice and disciplined courage over democratic falsehood.[5]

If his aim was to procure Mussolini's intervention on his behalf, the telegram was extremely ill-advised. Mussolini remained unmoved. On the other hand it caused lively protests in the Western capitals. Schuschnigg could not wish for a better opportunity to strike against his opponent and decided to exploit Starhemberg's blunder. On the day after the publication of the telegram, on 14 May, he excluded Starhemberg from the government, together with Foreign Minister Berger-Waldenegg, while he took over the Foreign Ministry himself. Starhemberg had to resign from the leadership of the Fatherland Front and had to

---

[1] Neurath's memorandum, 13 May 1936, GD, 6114/E454692.
[2] Renthe-Fink's memorandum, 6 May 1936, GD, 6114/E454690.
[3] Renthe-Fink's memorandum, 4 May 1936, GD, 6112/E453702.
[4] Neurath's memorandum, 13 May 1936, GD, 6114/E454692.
[5] Quoted in *Survey of International Affairs, 1936*, p. 430.

content himself – a truly Austrian solution – with his new post as supervisor of the mother's aid section of the Fatherland Front. The only measure Mussolini took was to send a telegram to Schuschnigg saying that he would be glad if 'Starhemberg would be, politically speaking, treated decently, i.e. that he will not be held to account'.[1]

Yet Starhemberg did not lose hope. On 15 May he left for Rome, where he was due to attend an Austro-Italian football match. He used the occasion to try and regain the Duce's support. Mussolini had only sympathy to offer. He strongly advised him to restrain himself.[2] According to Starhemberg the Duce told him that Schuschnigg should show what he could do alone, and if Schuschnigg failed he would be waiting in reserve.[3] But this was more consolation than real encouragement for the man he had just abandoned. When Starhemberg arrived in Vienna, on 20 May, Schuschnigg felt relief. 'There are no new resources available for a revival of the *Heimwehr*,' he told Papen:

> For weeks not the smallest wages have been paid. In order to take action, Starhemberg needs at least two million Schillings, and it is improbable that Mussolini has given him this money.[4]

The way for a settlement with Germany was free. The same day on which he had Starhemberg expelled, Schuschnigg approached Papen and declared that the moment for an agreement had come. But he wished that for the time being the scheme should still be kept secret in order not to cause unwanted resistance.[5] Moreover, before finally committing himself to the Germans, Schuschnigg wanted to arrange the details of the agreement with the Italians and for this purpose he worked together with Salata, whereas the Italian Minister Preziosi was completely ignorant of what was going on.[6]

Having made the necessary preparations Schuschnigg went to see the Duce himself. A meeting took place at Mussolini's country house at Rocca delle Caminate on 5 and 6 June 1936, where the

---

[1] Quoted in Schuschnigg, *Austrian Requiem*, p. 121.

[2] Mussolini to Hassel, Circular of the German Foreign Ministry, 26 May 1936, GD, 1744/402749–750.

[3] Starhemberg, op. cit., p. 238.

[4] Papen to Hitler, 20 May 1936, GD, 1744/402744–748.

[5] Papen to Hitler, 14 May 1936, GD, 1744/402742; Hornbostel to Tauschitz, 19 May 1936, Schmidt-prot., pp. 483–484.

[6] Anfuso, *Die beiden Gefreiten*, Munich, 1952, p. 21.

Austrian Chancellor expounded the principles of his future policy towards Germany and the agreement on which it should be based: participation of one or two nationalists in the Austrian government, amnesty for the Austrian Nazis, suppression of all propaganda on both sides, and a German recognition of Austria's independence.[1] The proposal permitted Mussolini to make concessions to Germany without abandoning the principle of Austria's independence. Austria, he told Schuschnigg, was, in the first place, a German country, and further it was too weak a country to pursue an anti-German policy.[2] Italy, on the other hand, was tied elsewhere and for the time being Austria had to stand on her own feet. He could help the Austrians more easily if Italy and they had good relations with Germany.[3]

The changes within the Italian government made by the Duce on 10 June confirmed the new Italian course. Being head of the government and Foreign Minister at the same time Mussolini had left the direction of Foreign Affairs mainly to Suvich, Secretary of State in the Foreign Ministry. He now dismissed Suvich and appointed Ciano as Foreign Minister. Ciano felt it was his task to give the Palazzo Chigi a new, fascist outlook.[4] He took pains to do the opposite of what Suvich had done, and told Heeren, the German Minister in Belgrade, that 'he was not like Suvich, who with the eyes of the Triestino could only look East; he felt he faced larger problems'.[5]

Having obtained Mussolini's consent Schuschnigg again contacted Papen. Once the final negotiations had started, they moved ahead rapidly. The drafting of the different proposals was, as far as the German side was concerned, Papen's work alone. Neither the German Foreign Office nor the party authorities played any part.[6] On the basis of Papen's proposal of the previous year Schuschnigg put forward a counter proposal on 19 June which fundamentally accepted Papen's ideas. Both of them agreed without difficulty on the principles of the agreement: Germany's

---

[1] Information given by Suvich to Hassel, Hassel's report, 6 June 1936, GD, 1744/402761.

[2] Mussolini to Frank, Ciano's Minute, 23 September 1936, *Ciano's Papers*, p. 45.

[3] Schuschnigg's testimony, Schmidt-prot., p. 432.

[4] Gilbert, 'Ciano and his Ambassadors', in *The Diplomats*, ed. by Craig and Gilbert, p. 514.

[5] Yugoslav Minute, quoted by Hoptner, op. cit., p. 169.

[6] Papen, *Memoirs*, pp. 362–364.

recognition of Austria's independence, a promise of non-intervention in her internal affairs, and an acknowledgement that Austria would conduct a foreign policy parallel to Germany's. On internal affairs Schuschnigg's most important concession was that the so-called national opposition was allowed representation in the Viennese government.[1] For this purpose Schuschnigg was at the same time engaged in negotiations with Glaise-Horstenau as representative of the national group. Papen demanded in addition that a restoration should only take place after previous consultation with Berlin. Schuschnigg, however, did not give in on this issue and rejected Papen's demand.[2]

France, England, and Russia realized the danger of Austria passing into the German orbit. The French and Russian ambassadors in Rome therefore suggested to the Italian government, early in June 1936, that the system of collective security should be re-established. They proposed a treaty between France, England, Italy, and the Soviet Union, in which Italy should undertake to defend the independence of Austria; in return the sanctions against Italy resulting from the Abyssinian war should be abandoned. But this was a rather illusory move. By then the sanctions were a spent force, and Suvich, who was still in office when the proposal was made, insisted on their unconditional abandonment.[3]

At the end of June Eden and the new French Foreign Minister Delbos, made a last attempt from Geneva to prevent the impending Austro-German *rapprochement*. They urgently invited Schuschnigg to meet them at the General Assembly of the League. And in Rome the French ambassador Chambrun warned Ciano against too close a *rapprochement* with Germany. 'Horizontal agreements bring peace,' he said, 'while vertical ones would inevitably lead to war.'[4] Mussolini, further alienated from France, since the Popular Front took office on 3 June, advised Schuschnigg against the visit to Geneva. Schuschnigg thereupon rejected the invitation, giving as his reason that 'the internal

---

[1] Hornbostel to Tauschitz, 20 June 1936, Schmidt-prot., pp. 484–485; Austrian Memorandum on the history of the negotiations, 12 July 1936, Schmidt-prot., pp. 474–475; *Entwurf eines Übereinkommens, Beilage C*, Schmidt-prot., pp. 478–479.

[2] Hornbostel to Tauschitz, 20 June 1936, Schmidt-prot., p. 484.

[3] Telegram to various German embassies, 4 June 1936, GD, 1486/368470.

[4] *Ciano's Papers*, 29 June 1936, p. 8.

and external position of Austria was of a clarity that left nothing to be desired'.[1]

Nevertheless Schuschnigg wanted to keep the active interest of the Western powers alive. He rightly feared that the anticipated agreement with Germany would have a detrimental effect.[2] In a circular to the Austrian embassies on 8 July 1936, he therefore stressed the importance of the agreement for Austria's independence, which rendered the concessions necessary.[3] Moreover, when Schuschnigg's negotiations with Papen were coming to a conclusion, Schuschnigg gave orders on 9 July 'to prepare and carry through quickly a campaign of propaganda to combat the strong opposition to this development which may be mobilized within the country or abroad'.[4] Meanwhile Papen, together with Glaise-Horstenau, went to Germany and submitted the details of the agreement to Hitler. Having obtained his consent they returned to Vienna where, on 11 July 1936, exactly one year after Papen's first proposal, Papen and Schuschnigg signed the so-called Gentlemen's Agreement.[5]

[1] Quoted by Gulick, op. cit., p. 1723.
[2] Schuschnigg, *Austrian Requiem*, p. 122.
[3] Telegram to various Austrian embassies, 8 July 1936, quoted in Fuchs, *Showdown in Vienna*, New York 1939, pp. 283–284.
[4] Official Report of the Conference of 9 July 1936, quoted in Fuchs, op. cit., pp. 277–282.
[5] German–Austrian Agreement of 11 July, 1936, GD, Ser. D, Vol. I, No. 152.

CHAPTER VI

THE WORKING OF THE GERMAN–AUSTRIAN AGREEMENT, 1937

Die Achse Berlin–Rom ist der Bratspiess, an dem Österreich
braun gebraten wurde.
Wandruszka, *Geschichte der Republik Österreich*[1]

SCHUSCHNIGG'S NEW POSITION BETWEEN BERLIN AND ROME

With the conclusion of the German–Austrian Agreement
the clash between the two fascisms in Austria came to
an end. Mussolini had left the field to Hitler. The
previous history of the Agreement, with Mussolini taking the
initiative, deciding the internal struggle in Austria, and participating in the negotiations himself, reveals that the Agreement
was in fact more of a settlement of the differences between
Germany and Italy than between Germany and Austria. 'The
event,' Mussolini told von Hassel on 11 July, 'will bring to an
end the unhappy situation of Austria as a football of foreign
interests and, above all, will finally remove the last and only
mortgage on German–Italian relations.'[2]

The deal which the two dictators had made was simple in its
terms: Hitler recognized the full sovereignty of Austria and renounced annexation;[3] Mussolini abandoned the instrument of
Italian policy in Austria, the *Heimwehr*, and consented to the
participation in political responsibility of the so-called 'National
Opposition in Austria'.[4] Both of them thought that the price
which they had paid was reasonable. Hitler had postponed the
Anschluss, which he could not achieve anyhow for the time
being, and gained Mussolini's friendship in return; Mussolini

---

[1] 'The Berlin–Rome axis was the spit on which Austria was roasted.'
[2] Hassel's report, 11 July 1936, GD, Ser. D, Vol. I, No. 155.
[3] German–Austrian Communiqué, 11 July 1936, ibid., No. 153.
[4] Clause IX of the Gentlemen's Agreement, ibid., No. 152.

K

had renounced a policy which he found impossible to continue and maintained Austria's independence at the same time.

As the Abyssinian war came to an end, Eden declared in the House of Commons on 18 June 1936 that 'sanctions did not realize the purpose for which they were imposed'. This first hint of a change in British policy seemed to reopen the possibilities of an understanding between Italy and the Western powers. Attempts by the Western countries to draw Mussolini to their side were, however, doomed to failure because of the Spanish civil war, the outbreak of which, on 17 July 1936, very nearly coincided with the Agreement. The Spanish war cemented the friendship between Hitler and Mussolini, which originated from Mussolini's estrangement over the attitude of England and France during the Abyssinian crisis.[1] On 6 August 1936 Ciano informed Hassel that Italy 'was opposed to the formation of blocs but that the Franco-Russian behaviour was driving Europe directly to a split between Communists and anti-Communists. . . . Closest co-operation between Germany and Italy was necessary in order to avert dangers that were arising. . . . As far as Italy was concerned, she was entirely available, if Germany should have any wishes in implementing her defence measures for any eventuality.'[2]

This was in fact a plea for German help disguised as an offer of assistance. Actively engaged in Spain, the Italian government did not want to run the risk of an intervention alone. Berlin had every reason to encourage the Italian policy. An Italian intervention in Spain would make Italy dependent upon Germany, intensify the estrangement from France and England, and tie up the Italian divisions in Spain instead of on the Brenner. Italian and German intervention, having led to a clash between the two dictators in Austria, had just the opposite result in Spain. The policies of Rome and Berlin moved along parallel lines for the very reason that in Spain Germany's interests were much less involved than in Austria. Hitler sent Frank to Rome, where he met the Duce on 23 September 1936, with the message that 'Germany's aid to the Spanish Nationalists was only motivated by ideological solidarity . . . she had neither interests nor aims in the Mediterranean. The Mediterranean was a purely Italian sea,

---

[1] See Alan Bullock, op. cit., pp. 318–320.
[2] Hassel's report, 6 August 1936, GD, Ser. D, Vol. III, No. 30.

where Italy had a right to positions of privilege and control. The interests of the Germans were turned towards the Baltic, which was their Mediterranean.' Moreover, Frank emphasized that the Austrian question was regarded as settled by the Agreement, 'to which Germany intended to adhere strictly'.[1]

Though Mussolini did not yet consider the moment appropriate to accept Hitler's invitation for a personal visit, he nevertheless sent his Foreign Minister to Germany to explore the situation. Ciano had talks with Neurath in Berlin on 21 October and with Hitler in Berchtesgaden on 23 October. The conversations between the two Foreign Ministers were substantiated in a protocol, which established co-operation on a number of issues, among them Spain, Austria, and the Danubian states.[2] Hitler, two days later, developed the broader lines of German policy. He reiterated that he had committed himself to the full in the Spanish question without any territorial or political aims. On the other hand he carefully avoided arousing Italian suspicions over Austria, a subject which he did not mention at all.[3] The only gesture he allowed himself was to show his guests Austria from the window of the Berghof remarking: 'So I am forced to look at Salzburg and my German fatherland through field-glasses'.[4]

Being aware of the influence which the Spanish war had on Italo-German relations, Eden proposed to Grandi, the Italian ambassador in London, to limit action regarding Spain to the three Mediterranean powers primarily interested: England, France, and Italy, leaving out Germany and Russia.[5] But Rome immediately informed Berlin of Eden's proposal, probably in order to keep the German interest alive. The German Foreign Ministry was not worried. They could not entirely understand what Eden was aiming at with his proposal, Attolico was told. 'At any rate, in a committee with England and France, Italy would be always in the minority.'[6] Ciano directed Grandi to

---

[1] Ciano's minute, 23 September 1936, *Ciano's Papers*, pp. 44–45. Wiskemann, op. cit., p. 65, writes that 'Mussolini quickly claimed the Austro-German Agreement as due to his own inspiration', but the unpublished German documents now reveal that the Agreement was in fact a result of the Duce's initiative.

[2] Ciano's minutes, 21 October, 1936, ibid. pp. 52–53.

[3] Ciano's minutes, 23 October, 1936, ibid. pp. 56–60.

[4] Anfuso, op. cit., p. 36.

[5] Hassel's report, 11 December 1936, GD, Ser. D, Vol. III, No. 149.

[6] Dieckhoff's marginal note, 12 December 1936, ibid.

decline the proposal on the ground that Italy considered Germany an essential element for maintaining European peace.

When Schuschnigg attended the funeral of General Gömbös in Budapest on 10 October 1936, he sensed the new atmosphere:

> Two large figures in resplendent uniforms: Italy and Germany who, out of the corners of their eyes, scrutinized each other from the spurs, past their daggers, up to the countless decorations.[1]

Göring and Schuschnigg arranged a meeting in Budapest, at which Göring employed a mixture of threats and persuasion. If Germany desired an Anschluss, he told the staggered Austrian Chancellor, it would have occurred long ago. That was a question which ultimately concerned only the nearest German divisional commander. Schuschnigg himself would surely not assume that Italy, in such an event, would hasten to the aid of Austria, if he stopped to think, that, after all, there were the British too, for whom nothing could be more opportune than that Mussolini should become involved in Austria in this manner. At any rate, he personally 'was convinced that in case of an Anschluss the Italians would not intervene with troops in favour of Austria'.[2]

Having put pressure upon Schuschnigg in this way Göring switched to a more conciliatory language:

> Listen, Herr *Bundeskanzler*, neither of us need these Italians. We shall straighten out such matters between ourselves. For us the only way is to do things from state to state without the interference of third parties.[3]

It was useless, Göring explained, to talk of an Anschluss: it would be preferable to choose the word *Zusammenschluss*, and he was thinking in particular of currency unification and a common tariff policy. Once these conditions had been fulfilled there were, according to Göring, no limits to a co-operation. He was prepared to build up the entire Austrian air force – gratis, in fact – and he offered to hand over to Austria as many as 600 aeroplanes and to

---

[1] Schuschnigg, *Austrian Requiem*, p. 102.
[2] Unsigned memorandum, 13 October 1936, GD, Ser. D, Vol. I, No. 169.
[3] Quoted by Schuschnigg, *Austrian Requiem*, p. 101.

accommodate the Austrian Air Force officers in German camps, even having their pay issued by Germany.[1]

Schuschnigg was neither intimidated by Göring's bluntness nor taken in by his proposals. He realized that he needed stronger backing in order to resist such pressure. He tried to revive Italy's interest in Austria and an occasion for doing so was provided by the conference of the Foreign Ministers of Italy, Hungary, and Austria from 11 to 12 November 1936. Schuschnigg told Ciano of Göring's flirtations, making the reservation that 'naturally these offers had been refused, but he had left himself open to accept certain supplies of arms'.[2] Schuschnigg urged Ciano that Italy should resume the supply of Italian military equipment. Ciano promised that Italy would do this, but Italy was no longer capable of supplying Austria with arms. From Rome came the message that because of the Spanish war and in view of the Italian needs even the restitution of Austria's old artillery stock, agreed upon earlier, had to be discontinued.[3]

Ciano for his part urged Schuschnigg to recognize the Spanish national government and to consider an abandonment of the League. Schuschnigg gave him to understand that he could not take these steps. Ciano was visibly annoyed by these reservations. He did not so much blame Schuschnigg for this refusal to toe the Italian line but the new State Secretary in the Austrian Foreign Ministry, Guido Schmidt, for whom he developed a strong personal dislike. To Ciano every day Schmidt 'showed himself to be more of a haggler, careerist, and fop', who thinks that 'he will find scope for his ambitions on the Geneva platform, and dreams of a League success à la Titulescu or à la Beneš'. Perhaps even more important for Italy's future attitude towards Austria was that the susceptible Ciano left Vienna shocked by the frigid attitude of its population. On no occasion did the citizens of Vienna make any gesture of friendship and sympathy towards Italy; they watched calmly, 'but never a salute, never any applause, never a shout'. Schuschnigg's policy of friendship towards Italy, Ciano concluded, was not at all popular.[4]

---

[1] Unsigned memorandum, 13 October 1936, GD, Ser. D. Vol. I, No. 169; Schuschnigg to Ciano, Ciano's minutes, 9–16 November 1936, *Ciano's Papers*, pp. 63–64.

[2] Ciano's minutes, 9–16 November 1936, *Ciano's Papers*, p. 64.

[3] Schuschnigg, *Austrian Requiem*, p. 123.

[4] Ciano's minutes, 1–16 Nov. 1936, *Ciano's Papers*, pp. 65–67.

No doubt Schmidt was in favour of co-operation with Germany, but in this respect he only reflected Schuschnigg's attitude. Papen and Glaise-Horstenau now suggested that Schmidt be invited to Berlin,[1] and Glaise-Horstenau advised that 'Schmidt be treated, both personally and politically, in such a manner that he was strengthened in the desire to work *with* the Reich, because he was said to be very ambitious and clever and to be working faithfully for a constructive application of the Agreement'.[2] Schmidt arrived in Berlin on 19 November 1936, where he first had a private conversation with Hitler, who treated him to one of his *tours d'horizon*, stressing his peaceful intentions towards Austria and Czechoslovakia. '*Ein Nebeneinander zwischen dem österreichischen und deutschen Wesen ist möglich,*' Hitler told his guest from Vienna.[3] After this Neurath, Tauschitz, Papen, and Meissner were called in, and the Führer extended his analysis of the situation, using Bolshevism as the chief bogy. The European states had to consolidate. This idea had created the understanding between Germany and Italy, and 'would help to remove any obstacles to an understanding in Central Europe'.[4]

Before Schmidt arrived in Berlin the draft of a confidential protocol had already been worked out between Papen and the Austrian government[5] and in their negotiations on 21 November 1936 Neurath gave it the final touches.[6] This protocol supplemented the Agreement of 11 July and regulated Austro-German relations in minute detail. Decorating inns in Austria by hoisting the German flag was permitted on special occasions, cultural exchanges were arranged; the Austrian government promised to examine the cases of 500 Austrian refugees, who, for economic reasons, requested permission to return to Austria; and the two governments agreed on the further expansion of commercial relations. All these were rather minor questions and only evidence of how much relations between the two states had normalized.

---

[1] Papen, *Memoirs*, p. 379.

[2] Megerle to Neurath, 29 August 1936, GD, Ser. D, Vol. I, No. 163.

[3] 'The Austrian and German cultures can live side by side.' Schmidt's testimony, Schmidt-prot., p. 35.

[4] Meissner's memorandum, 19 November 1936, GD, Ser. D, Vol. I, enclosure in No. 181.

[5] The German Foreign Ministry to the German legation in Austria, 12 November 1936, ibid., No. 177; Altenburg's memorandum, 13 November 1936, ibid., No. 178.

[6] Neurath's memorandum, 21 November 1936, ibid., No. 185.

But Austria made an important concession by declaring that 'she would not participate in new, more extensive economic coalitions in the Danube region without previous consultation'.[1] Though the same applied to Germany, it was obvious that the clause tied Austria economically to Germany and prevented her from joining a Danubian pact.

After Schmidt's return to Vienna he and Schuschnigg expressed relief. They had expected threats and instead the Austrian representative had been treated with respect and courtesy. Schmidt had apparently let himself be deceived by Hitler's peaceful assurances and remarked that 'in Rome they played with fire much more than in Berlin'. Schuschnigg was surprised that 'Berlin's demands were not after all so great as he had feared'.[2] Both of them came to the conclusion that it was, after all, possible to come to an arrangement with Germany.[3]

But Hitler's advisers were still at variance, as far as the tempo of Germany's Austrian policy was concerned. Göring was determined to quicken the pace. Whereas Hitler thought a recognition of Austria's independence indispensable in order to strengthen German—Italian co-operation, Göring urged that on the contrary Italy should acquiesce in an Anschluss for the sake of an understanding between Berlin and Rome: 'She should keep hands off Austria, so that even an Anschluss could be carried out if we so desired.'[4]

Foreign Minister von Neurath, seconded by the German Ambassador in Rome, advocated a much more cautious policy. When Göring arrived in Rome on 15 January 1937, von Hassel made vain attempts to restrain him. On the following day Göring told the Duce that it was necessary to clarify the Austrian problem 'if Italy wished to count on German support for Italy at critical moments, such as might arise from Italy's Mediterranean policy'.[5] But Mussolini was the wrong man to bully. He was unusually reserved, and even requested Göring to put his point of view in writing with the prospect of a reply on the day of Göring's return from his visit to Naples. He had no more success

[1] Text of the Protocol, 21 November 1936, GD, Ser. D, Vol. I, No. 182.
[2] Papen to Hitler, 24 November 1936, ibid., No. 185.
[3] Schuschnigg's and Schmidt's testimonies, Schmidt-prot., pp. 433–435, 31–49.
[4] Hassel's memorandum, 16 January 1937, GD, Ser. D. Vol. I, No. 199.
[5] Hassel's memorandum, 30 January 1937, ibid., No. 207; Berger-Waldenegg's report, 19 January 1937, Schmidt-prot., p. 515.

on his second visit. He had to force Mussolini to speak about Austria at all.[1]

In his blunt manner Göring had nevertheless stressed one of the weaknesses in Mussolini's policy. The Rome–Berlin axis, with Berlin at one end aiming at the absorption of Austria, was as irreconcilable with Mussolini's own objective of an independent Austria as Mussolini's policy in 1933 had been, when he had tried to combine his pro-German course and his attempts at drawing Austria into the Italian sphere of influence. A compromise finally emerged from the Göring–Mussolini conversations: Italy would not repeat her previous partnership with other powers, there would be no second 'watch on the Brenner'. Germany, on the other hand, would strictly pursue a policy along the lines of the Agreement; any German action on the Austrian question aiming at a change in the present situation was to take place only in consultation with Rome.[2]

In the Anschluss question the Duce was much more rigid than his new Foreign Minister, Ciano, who in a way was taken in by Göring's straightforward rudeness. When the Yugoslav representative at the League, Subotic, flattered him, Ciano replied:

That is why Göring and I understand each other so well. We analyse a situation, think a bit, and within five minutes our decision is made. And then we act.[3]

Ciano, more aware than the Duce of Italy's growing dependence upon Germany, sought a way to balance Germany's rising power in the south-east. That was why Germany's friends had to close their ranks: 'Germany is not only a dangerous adversary to her enemies but a difficult friend to her friends', he told Subotic, who was in Rome on 3 March 1937. 'Our 42 million and your 15 million will mean more together than separately':

Do not misunderstand me. I do not mean that we should turn against Germany, but we should – between us – organize our collaboration with her.

Ciano's attitude towards Germany was strongly influenced by the impending events in Austria. It was going to be just as impossible

[1] Ciano's minutes, 23 January 1937, *Ciano's Papers*, pp. 80–91. Hassel's memorandum, 30 January 1937, GD, Ser. D, Vol. I, No. 207.

[2] Hassel to Göring, 30 January 1937, GD, Ser. D, Vol. I, enclosure in No. 208; Ciano's minutes, 23 January 1937, *Ciano's Papers*, pp. 88–91.

[3] Subotic to Stojadinovic, 6 March 1937, Yugoslav minute, Hoptner, p. 160.

to prevent an Anschluss as to restore the Habsburgs. That, he insisted, 'must be kept in mind'. And Ciano's advice did not fall on deaf ears. When he went to Belgrade in order to continue the negotiations, he found the Yugoslav Premier and Foreign Minister, Stojadinovic, ready for an Italo-Yugoslav *rapprochement*. Stojadinovic told him that 'Austria had neither the moral nor the material conditions for living'.

> Once the Anschluss is an accomplished fact, all those countries who must oppose the German descent towards the Adriatic or along the Danube valley, will polarize around the Rome–Belgrade axis.[1]

Since the Italo-Yugoslav *rapprochement* had its origin in the desire to build a barrier against the German drive to the south-east, one might have expected that Hitler would oppose this understanding. But he did the opposite. He urged both Rome and Belgrade to conclude such an agreement, though his motives of course were different. Hitler calculated that by bringing Rome and Belgrade together Yugoslavia would have to break loose from the Little Entente. This would isolate Czechoslovakia, but did not mean that Hitler would have to abandon his aims in Austria; the impending Anschluss and its inevitability was the very thing which drew Italy and Yugoslavia together. In order to facilitate this *rapprochement*, Hitler worked upon the Hungarians to direct their irredentism against Czechoslovakia rather than Yugoslavia.[2] This would make it possible to entertain friendly relations with Hungary and Yugoslavia at the same time, while it was a further device to isolate Prague.

An alternative to this policy would have been a separate deal with Czechoslovakia. Ribbentrop's office explored, independently from the Foreign Office, the possibilities of such a course and conducted secret negotiations with Beneš in December 1936 and January 1937.[3] Haushofer, associated with the *Dienststelle* Ribbentrop, had several discussions with Beneš, and as a result he recommended to Hitler a treaty with Czechoslovakia, in order to strengthen German and weaken French influence in the

---

[1] Ciano's minutes, 26 March 1937, *Ciano's Papers*, p. 100.
[2] Ciano's minutes, 26 October 1936, ibid., pp. 58–59.
[3] For details of these negotiations see Weinberg, 'Secret Hitler–Beneš Negotiations in 1936–1937', *Journal of Central European Affairs*, Vol. XIX, 1960, pp. 366–374. Celovsky, *Das Münchener Abkommen 1938*, Stuttgart, 1958, pp. 88–90.

Danubian area. He argued in his report to Hitler that this policy would reduce the possibilities of a Soviet attack, Yugoslavia and Rumania could be included in the system, and though Hungary and Italy would be estranged because of the resulting increase of Germany's influence in the Danubian area, this treaty was the only chance to avoid a strengthening of Czech–Soviet and Czech–French relations. Beneš supported this initiative, but Hitler showed himself disinterested. He aimed at Prague's isolation and a treaty with her had no place in this scheme.

Hitler's policy showed the first signs of success when, in the autumn of 1936, France proposed to the countries of the Little Entente a military alliance as a defensive measure against possible German aggression. The Yugoslav Premier delayed an answer to the French proposal by all kinds of pretexts.[1] The forthcoming meeting of the Permanent Council of the Little Entente, due to open in Belgrade on 1 April 1937, would have forced Stojadinović into the open. But Ciano forestalled the meeting by travelling to Belgrade on 25 March, where he and Stojadinović concluded a treaty, in which the two countries pledged to respect their common frontiers and promised neutrality in case one of them should be attacked by a third country. Future relations of his country with Czechoslovakia, Stojadinović promised Ciano, 'will be reduced to an empty formality'.[2]

The new situation contrasted strikingly with the attitude which Rome and Belgrade had taken during the Nazi *putsch* of 25 July 1934. Then, threatened by a Nazi *putsch*, Italy as well as Yugoslavia had been ready to intervene, but their intervention would have been directed against each other. In the spring of 1937, in face of the much greater danger of an Anschluss, both countries resigned themselves to the loss of Austria and were bound together by the common fear of a German advance directed beyond. Austria found herself more isolated than ever. Three of the surrounding countries, Italy, Yugoslavia, and Hungary, were tied to Germany through friendly relations. No help could be expected from them. Common interest in not being attacked by Germany should have forced Czechoslovakia, as the fourth neighbour country, and Austria together. Yet Schuschnigg rejected this idea off-hand. The disparity of the two régimes made a

[1] Ciano's minutes, 26 March 1937, *Ciano's Papers*, p. 98.
[2] Ibid., p. 99.

rapprochement impossible.[1] 'No agreement of a political character is foreseen', Schuschnigg stated to Mussolini during his state visit to Italy on 22 April 1937:[2]

There is no possibility of authoritarian Austria's aligning herself with the ultra-democratic Paris–Prague axis. That would entail a change in internal policy which must be excluded.

During their meeting in Venice the Duce was at pains to destroy the impression that his policy towards Austria had changed. Austria had to understand, he explained to Schuschnigg, that Italy's intervention in Spain made considerable demands on the country, but Austria could count, in all circumstances, on the unchanged attitude in Rome.[3] Far from strengthening Vienna's position Mussolini's continued interest weakened it. Being incapable of rendering assistance himself his influence with Schuschnigg was still strong enough to restrain him from an anti-German policy. He strongly advised the Austrian Chancellor against such a course.

Though outwardly the reception in Italy had been as friendly as ever, Schuschnigg noticed that relations with Rome had distinctly cooled off. Contrary to all rules of courtesy the Duce left Venice before his guests.[4] When the Austrian Chancellor boarded the train for Vienna, he did not know that this was to be his last visit to Italy.

ATTEMPT TO PACIFY THE NAZI OPPOSITION

Schuschnigg was the third partner of the new arrangement who was content with the German–Austrian Agreement. His obvious gain was the exclusion of the *Heimwehr* from the political scene. With no rival in sight his internal position seemed unassailable. The dissolution of all para-military formations, decided upon in a night session of the cabinet from 9 to 10 October 1936, signified the formal end of the *Heimwehr*, whose fate had been decided after Mussolini had withdrawn his support. Yet, in retrospect, Zernatto, the General Secretary of the Fatherland Front, judged the blow directed against the *Heimwehr* as the worst mistake Schuschnigg

---

[1] See Schuschnigg, *Austrian Requiem*, pp. 123–124.
[2] *Ciano's Papers*, p. 109.
[3] Schuschnigg, *Austrian Requiem*, pp. 123–124; Ciano's minutes, 22 April 1937, *Ciano's Papers*, pp. 108–115.
[4] Schmidt's testimony, Schmidt-prot., p. 44.

made.[1] By eliminating his rival, Schuschnigg had deprived himself of the only militant instrument which supported his authoritarian rule. He could no longer count on it to counter-balance the Nazis. The strength of his régime was no longer based on *opposition* to the Nazis but on the compromise concluded with them.

The terms of this compromise were the following: Schuschnigg granted an amnesty on 23 July 1936, setting free 17,045 persons and quashing proceedings against 12,618 lesser participants, leaving only 213 persons who had not been pardoned,[2] and he promised the participation of the national opposition in political responsibility.[3] In return the Nazis were prepared to tolerate Schuschnigg's régime. Corresponding to this arrangement in the domestic sphere was a similar compromise in the international. Since Mussolini had come to terms with Germany, Schuschnigg depended upon Germany's non-interference in order to maintain Austrian independence. Hitler was willing to abstain from action, but received Schuschnigg's pledge 'to conduct his foreign policy in the light of the peaceful endeavours of the German government's foreign policy', and the latter had to agree that the 'two governments will from time to time enter into an exchange of views on the problems of foreign policy affecting both of them'.[4] As a result of the new *modus vivendi* Hitler could relax the pressure on Austria. He abandoned the levy of 1,000 Reichsmark on German tourists to Austria, which had been introduced early in 1933.[5] The press war between the two countries was stopped, and the distribution of a certain number of German newspapers in Austria and vice versa was permitted.

Though Schuschnigg and Hitler appeared equally satisfied by the Agreement, they looked at it from opposing viewpoints. For Schuschnigg it was the last concession. A basis for co-existence between the two countries had been found. By Hitler the Agreement was taken to mean that Schuschnigg had after all failed to stop the policy of *Gleichschaltung*; it was the decisive step in the evolutionary tactic which he pursued.

[1] Zernatto, op. cit., p. 168.
[2] Figures given in Papen's report, 23 July 1936, GD, Ser. D, Vol. I, No. 160.
[3] Clause IX (*b*) of the Gentlemen's Agreement.
[4] Clause VIII of the Gentlemen's Agreement.
[5] Clause VII of the Gentlemen's Agreement.

The most important lever for exercising pressure on the Austrian government was the clause of the Agreement which provided for the participation of representatives of the so-called 'National Opposition' in political responsibility. Schuschnigg was confronted with the dilemma of how he could fulfil this condition without risking his own position. He considered the appointment of a person from the national camp as Minister without Portfolio and proposed three candidates to his Vice-Chancellor and Minister of the Interior, Baar-Baarenfels. Two of these, the historians Professor von Srbik and Professor Menghin, were soon out of the running, because Baar-Baarenfels regarded the third candidate, Glaise-Horstenau, as the most acceptable because most harmless.[1]

The second appointment occasioned by the Agreement was that of Guido Schmidt as State Secretary to the Foreign Ministry. Schuschnigg had made up his mind about this beforehand and personal reasons determined his choice. He and Schmidt had gone to the same school belonging to the Jesuit order, were members of the same student organization, and after the death of Schuschnigg's first wife, their relationship had grown into a friendship. Schmidt's background had much to recommend him for the new post. He had worked as liaison between the Presidency and the Chancellery and his talents in mediation seemed useful in the era beginning with the Agreement.[2] Schmidt was a typical official and attached to none of the parties, though by temperament he inclined towards the Christian Socials. He has been regarded as an excessively treacherous person,[3] but his acquittal on a charge of high treason before an Austrian court, in June 1947, has helped to vindicate him. He was more instrument than initiator of Schuschnigg's policy.

Glaise-Horstenau did not remain content with his new post. He felt that his influence was limited and pressed for a post in the Ministry of the Interior which had been promised to him by Schuschnigg. Muff, the German Military Attaché, reported a

---

[1] Baar-Baarenfels's evidence, Schmidt-prot., pp. 318, 323; Schuschnigg's evidence, ibid., p. 583.

[2] Schuschnigg's evidence, ibid., pp. 431–434; Zernatto, op. cit., p. 163; Fuchs, op. cit., p. 26.

[3] Wiskemann, op. cit., p. 61. Wiskemann seems, however, to have ignored the material of Schmidt's trial. Extremely negative about Schmidt also is Fuchs, op. cit., pp. 26–29, 75–76.

conversation of 29 August 1936: 'He wonders whether there was any further use for him to remain in office. He will, however, not give up his position until he is expressly authorized or directed to do so by the Reich.' But Glaise-Horstenau added that 'he had to be supported by the Reich with every admissible pressure, especially in the economic field'.[1]

Glaise-Horstenau did not have to wait for very long. After the dissolution of all armed formations, on 10 October, Schuschnigg felt himself strong enough to proceed with the final reorganization of his government. On 3 November he dismissed the last representatives of the *Heimwehr* still in the cabinet, Baar-Baarenfels and Draxler, while he gave Glaise-Horstenau the portfolio of the Interior and appointed Neustädter-Stürmer as Minister of Security. Neustädter-Stürmer came from *Heimwehr* circles and had been a representative of the *Heimatblock*, the former party organization of the *Heimwehr*, but belonged to the wing with national inclinations.[2]

In his attempts to appease the national opposition, Schuschnigg had to over-ride resistance coming from his own quarters, the Christian Socials. They had not lent their support in order to relinquish their positions to the national opposition, which, according to Schuschnigg's intentions, was gradually to be called on to participate in the government.[3] Consequently Schuschnigg had to combine two tactics. He had to appease the Nazis and maintain the confidence of his own supporters at the same time. In order to counter-balance the impression of the cabinet reorganization and to reassure the officials of the Fatherland Front, he made a forceful speech on 26 November, in which he attempted to draw a line between National Socialism abroad and at home:

National Socialism in Austria stands opposed to us as an enemy. To settle with it is clearly and unequivocally an exclusively domestic affair, which nevertheless does not prevent us from welcoming gladly and with satisfaction any alleviation obtained or success scored by the leaders of the German Reich.[4]

[1] Altenburg's memorandum, 1 October 1936, GD, Ser. D, Vol. I, No. 166.
[2] Papen to Hitler, 4 November 1937, ibid., No. 171.
[3] Stein's memorandum, 30 November 1937, ibid., No. 190.
[4] Extract of Schuschnigg's speech before officials of the Fatherland Front at Klagenfurt on 26 November 1936, quoted in *Documents on International Affairs, 1936*, Vol. I, pp. 327–328.

Yet Schuschnigg could not escape from the consequences of his course. Neurath directed Papen to protest against this double line of approach and to question him as to whether he really believed that he could continue to take measures against National Socialism in Austria and at the same time follow with the Reich 'a common course in questions of the *Volkstum*'.[1] Schuschnigg immediately backed down from his firm stand. Nothing had been farther from his mind than to complicate relations with the Reich or put further obstacles in the way of the programme to effect a reconciliation with Austrian National Socialism, he told Papen:[2] 'I am well aware that the historical position of Vienna has come to an end and that the focal point of the German mission now lies in Berlin.'

The essential question now was in which form the reconciliation with the Nazis in Austria should take place. Paradoxically enough the least satisfied with the Agreement were the Austrian Nazis themselves. They had had no say in the previous negotiations, in which Papen had acted as the spokesman of their interests without their authorization. For them the Agreement was the second shock after the abortive *putsch* of July 1934. Not only had they failed to overturn the régime, but Schuschnigg's government was now firmly established, and partner in an official agreement with the German government. Therefore, some of them argued, as they had done in spring 1934, that Hitler pursued these tactics only for the sake of appearances; in reality he wanted them to pursue a radical fight.[3]

Hitler did not want to repeat the experience of an independent action on their part. He summoned two of their leaders, Rainer and Globocznigg,[4] to make his position clear. The two Austrian Nazis arrived at the Obersalzberg on 16 July 1936.[5] Rainer's account reveals their disappointment that they received no praise for their daily fight in the Führer's cause. On the contrary, Hitler

[1] Neurath to Papen, 28 November 1936, GD, Ser. D, Vol. I, No. 187.

[2] Papen to Hitler, ibid., No. 191.

[3] See Rainer's account in his speech at Klagenfurt, on 11 March 1942, before Nazi leaders concerning National Socialism in Austria from the July rebellion 1934 to the seizure of power on 11 March 1938 (hereafter quoted as Rainer's speech), Doc. 4005–PS, IMT, Vol. XXXIV, p. 16.

[4] There are various spellings of Globocznigg's name. This appears the most common one.

[5] Papen's account, *Memoirs*, p. 376, is inaccurate. Leopold did not see the Führer. He was at this time still in an Austrian concentration camp.

let fly at them, explaining in icy terms why he had concluded the Agreement. The burden of Austria was incompatible with his line of foreign policy. He had to cultivate friendly relations with Italy. The German army had to be rebuilt and its officer corps enlarged. This would take two more years; only then could he make policy. For that period the party in Austria had to maintain discipline and conduct a policy with the means made available to them. With a touch of the dramatic, the Führer, walking to the window, added: '*Ich bin ja der getreue Eckard Österreichs, hier stehe ich, und werde Euch nicht verlassen.*'[1]

After their return to Austria, Rainer and Globocznigg assembled the representatives of the different provinces at Anis near Salzburg on 17 July. They explained the Führer's directives for their policy, and it was decided that they should be strictly adhered to.[2]

Nevertheless differences within the party leadership – springing from tactical as well as from personal considerations, arose very soon. Schuschnigg's amnesty of 23 July reopened for Leopold, by seniority the leader of the party, the chance of further political activity. Since the *putsch* of July 1934 he had been almost continuously held in concentration camps. During his absence Klausner, the Gauleiter of Carinthia, had acted as deputy leader of the movement and he had entrusted Rainer with the organizational and Globocznigg with the political side of the party work. After Leopold's dismissal Klausner acknowledged his leadership, whereas Leopold confirmed the younger leaders such as Rainer and Globocznigg in their offices.[3]

But this state of affairs did not last for long. Leopold was the typical former Austrian non-commissioned officer. He never passed the examination that would have opened up a career as an officer; but on account of his long service and good conduct during the war he was given the honorary rank of captain. After the war he remained in the newly formed *Volkswehr* and joined the Social Democratic organization for Austrian regular soldiers.

---

[1] 'Yet I am the loyal Eckard of Austria; here I stand, and I shall never desert you.' Rainer's speech, loc. cit., p. 17.

[2] Rainer's report on the events in the NSDAP of Austria from the beginning of the last stage of the battle until the seizure of power on 11 March 1939 (hereafter quoted as Rainer's report), sent to Gauleiter Buerckel on 6 July 1939, Doc. 812–PS, NCA, Vol. III, pp. 587–596.

[3] Altenburg's memorandum, 22 September 1936, GD, Ser. D, Vol. I, No. 165.

In 1925 he joined the Nazi party, which caused his expulsion from the army.[1] Though Leopold had served from rank to rank until he had reached the top of the party, he showed a remarkable ability for making enemies. He displayed a strong dislike for the intellectuals and tacticians in the party and the predominance of the SA in Austria under his leadership caused the envy of the SS.

Right after the resumption of his leadership Leopold showed a greater independence from the tactical directives given by the Führer than the leaders in Carinthia, Klausner, Rainer, and Globocznigg. Though unwavering in his loyalty, he interpreted the Führer's order, that party offices in the Reich should observe non-interference in Austrian affairs, much more literally than was meant. Leopold concluded that questions of tactics had to be decided solely by the Austrian party itself. It was up to him to decide which form co-operation with the Schuschnigg government should take. In autumn 1936 Leopold stated that after the Olympic games in Berlin party members returned '. . . with all sorts of commissions, completely forgetting that Adolf Hitler has ordered strict non-interference, that such non-interference is a vital necessity for us and, after all, also a matter of honour, and that we absolutely do not need to go to the Reich for counsel and aid'.[2] He decreed that, under penalty of expulsion from the party, it was prohibited to communicate with party agencies in the Reich.[3]

Leopold disliked Papen's independent negotiations on the question of the national opposition and sought direct contact with Schuschnigg. He hoped to obtain the re-admission of the party in one form or another, even as a kind of 'cultural society'. The Carinthia party group under Klausner objected to such tactics. The attempt of a solution from inside was in their eyes heresy. Since the Führer had ordered that the time was not yet ripe to bring about a final solution through pressure from outside, they had reconciled themselves to a waiting attitude.[4] As a result of this divergence of opinion Leopold dismissed Rainer and

---

[1] Papen, op. cit., p. 384; Fuchs, op. cit., pp. 47–48; Zernatto, op. cit., p. 164.
[2] Bulletin No. 9 enclosed in Prof. Wehofsich's letter to Altenburg, 10 September 1936, GD, Ser. D, Vol. I, No. 164.
[3] With regard to Leopold's conception of the position of the Austrian party see his letter to Hitler, 22 August 1937, GD, 1291/344920–936.
[4] Rainer's speech, Doc. 4005–PS. loc. cit., pp. 7–8; Rainer's report, Doc. 812–PS, loc. cit., pp. 590–592.

L

Globocznigg from their positions. Instead he appointed Schattenfroh as his deputy, overruling party objections based on the fact that Schattenfroh had married a Jewess two years before.[1]

Schuschnigg received advice from two different sources that he should come to terms with the Nazi party under Leopold's leadership. Within his government Neustädter-Stürmer supported such a course, presumably in order to get some backing against the ecclesiastical block of the Fatherland Front.[2] In the German legation it was Counsellor Stein who told Schuschnigg that 'there was only one really large National Opposition movement in the country: the National Socialists behind Leopold. The rest of the National Opposition actually consisted only of generals – quite numerous, to be sure – without soldiers.'[3] Stein's policy was directly opposed to that of his superior, Papen. But it seems that he had the backing of the Foreign Office in Berlin, which resented Papen's position as ambassador on a special mission and his direct contacts with Hitler. The Foreign Office therefore encouraged Stein to send his reports independently of Papen.

Schuschnigg decided to follow the policy recommended to him by Neustädter-Stürmer and Stein. Consequently Neustädter-Stürmer envisaged, together with Leopold, the formation of an association which was to be called *Deutsch-sozialer Volksbund* and which was to unify all national forces with the Nazis as its core. They planned that after its establishment it should enter into negotiations with representatives of the Fatherland Front. Six hundred leading persons of Austria's public life thereupon signed a petition demanding the admission of the *Deutsch-sozialer Volksbund*, which was submitted to the Austrian Chancellor.

In order to gather all 'Nationals' in Austria and to form a representative body, which could make contact with Schuschnigg, a 'Committee of Seven' was founded with sub-committees for each of the states. The 'Committee of Seven' consisted of three National Socialists, all associates of Leopold: Jury, In der Maur, and Tavs; two contactmen of Minister Neustädter-

---

[1] Altenburg's memorandum, 22 September 1936, GD, Ser. D, Vol. I, No. 165.
[2] Seyss-Inquart, *The Austrian Question 1934–1938* (hereafter quoted as Seyss-Inquart's memorandum), NCA, Vol. V, p. 966.
[3] Stein's memorandum, 30 November 1936, GD, Ser. D, Vol. I, No. 190.

Stürmer, Ministerial Counsellor Wolfsegger and Vice-President Berghammer; one contactman of Minister Glaise-Horstenau, President Mannlicher; and finally Professor Menghin.[1] The 'Committee of Seven' worked out the statutes of the *Deutsch-sozialer Volksbund* and handed them to Minister Neustädter-Stürmer on 8 February 1937.[2]

Neustädter-Stürmer and Glaise-Horstenau thereupon informed the Austrian Chancellor of the preparatory work, which had been done, and Schuschnigg declared himself ready to start conversations with a small committee consisting of Jury, Mannlicher, and Menghin. In fact Schuschnigg had to hurry, because groups of the Fatherland Front had already issued statements against the formation of new political organizations. Opinion in the government camp with regard to the views on pacification remained divided. When, on 10 February 1937, members of the national opposition met under the chairmanship of Leopold, police suddenly arrived to arrest all those present. Leopold immediately protested and phoned Minister Neustädter-Stürmer, who ordered the police president to cancel his order, and after a little argument this was done.[3]

On 11 February Schuschnigg could now receive Jury, Mannlicher, and Menghin. Schuschnigg immediately realized that the National Socialists, represented by Jury, formed the true force behind the national opposition. He dismissed Mannlicher and Menghin after an introductory talk and continued the conversation with Jury alone. But even if Schuschnigg had wanted to make larger concessions, the opposition within his own camp tied his hands. He asked Jury not to insist on discussing the statutes of the *Deutsch-sozialer Volksbund*, but to accept that for formal reasons they would be withdrawn. In Schuschnigg's opinion it was essential to wait for a certain time before introducing them. But, the Chancellor declared, he was willing to do everything in his power short of official recognition to facilitate the activity of the national opposition. He offered to recognize the 'Committee of Seven' *de facto*, to remain in contact with it, and to see to it that its activity was not impeded. Moreover, Schuschnigg proposed

---

[1] Zernatto, op. cit., p. 174; Langoth, op. cit., p. 218.
[2] See for the full text of the memorandum of the 'Committee of Seven', GD, Ser. D, Vol. I, enclosure in No. 210.
[3] Papen to Hitler, 13 February 1937, ibid., No. 210.

that contactmen were to be appointed by the Fatherland Front
with the task of establishing liaison in national matters and to
make possible the collaboration of the Nationals within the
framework of the Fatherland Front. Persons in the administration particularly objectionable to the national opposition were to
be gradually removed.

Under the chairmanship of Leopold the Committee of Seven
considered Schuschnigg's compromise proposal on 12 February.
Leopold had not much choice left. If he insisted on the admission
of the *Deutsch-sozialer Volksbund*, he ran the risk of Schuschnigg
being driven back to less conciliatory groups and withdrawing
his proposals altogether. On the other hand, a *de facto* recognition
of the Nazi activities seemed sufficient as long as Schuschnigg
was in control of the police force and restrained them from taking
action against the Nazis. Leopold therefore decided to continue
the talks.

On the same day a conference took place at which Schuschnigg, on the proposal of Jury, met Leopold personally for the
first time. They rapidly agreed on a compromise based on
Schuschnigg's proposal to Jury. Leopold declared:

We take cognizance of the independence of Austria and shall act
in accordance with it. This statement applies also to the constitution
of 1934 and the law concerning the Fatherland Front, beyond which
we wish to form no additional political party.

For the time being he abandoned the formation of the *Deutsch-
sozialer Volksbund*. Schuschnigg in return promised to protect
from police action any offices in Vienna and the provinces 'that
might be established in furtherance of the pacification movement'. Finally he agreed to release 145 imprisoned National
Socialists.[1]

The relations between Schuschnigg and the Nazi opposition
were now apparently settled on a basis satisfactory to both sides.
Schuschnigg had saved his face and rejected an official recognition, Leopold had secured a free hand in his activities and hoped
obviously, after due pressure, for a freer one.

The Austrian Nazis immediately took advantage of their new
freedom of action. The Committee of Seven set up its office in

---

[1] GD, Ser. D, Vol. I, No. 210

the Teinfaltstrasse in Vienna and gradually this was turned into the Nazi headquarters under the direction of Tavs, the *Gauleiter* of Vienna.

But Leopold did not achieve his ultimate goal. Not one of his associates ever achieved office, nor did the prospects for an official recognition of the party increase. In the meantime the clerical circles of the Fatherland Front had mobilized their forces and put pressure upon Schuschnigg not to go any further in his concessions. As a result of this pressure Schuschnigg had to abandon his Minister Neustädter-Stürmer, as the initiator of the new policy, and on 20 March 1937 took over the Ministry of Public Security himself.

Neustädter-Stürmer's dismissal signified the end of the attempts by the Nazi party and the Austrian government to settle the dispute between themselves independently of Germany. Leopold's conception of the party's policy, which took the order of German non-interference literally and not as what it was meant to be – a purely tactical device given by Hitler – contained the cause of his failure. His vain attempts to obtain recognition for the party reveals that the Austrian Nazis could not achieve success without pressure from outside, and that they were too weak to force recognition from the Austrian government on their own account.

RIVALRY BETWEEN LEOPOLD AND SEYSS-INQUART

A combination of forces working against him caused Leopold's failure. First of all Papen had no place in his policy for a strong illegal party. Being a Catholic himself he hoped to convince Hitler that he had to give adequate assurances to the Roman Catholic church in Austria if he wanted the Anschluss. In his opinion the Austrian Catholics would only consent to a union if assured that they would not be exposed to the same persecution as Catholics in Germany.[1] This concession could only be obtained from Hitler by a governmental solution. The Austrian party leaders, Papen argued, must therefore recognize 'that bringing about a new political relationship between Austria and the Reich is not their responsibility'. Their only task was to win large sections of the population for a pro-German policy. They would thus be creating the 'medium within Austria which the Reich will utilize when

[1] Papen, *Memoirs*, p. 382.

its dynamic power is sufficiently developed to take up the problem'.[1] When Papen reported to Hitler in the *Reichskanzlei* on 13 March 1937 he stressed that 'the illegal party must be repeatedly convinced that the ultimate decision with regard to Austria lies outside of Austria, and that it therefore played only a passive role'.[2]

Leopold combated Papen's policy and resorted to the strongest measure at his disposal. In the May issue of the *Völkischer Beobachter*, the official organ of the Austrian Nazi party, he stated that

... the party has, in the immediate jurisdiction of Vienna, temporarily broken off social relations with the Metternichgasse. This measure applies to the person of the Ambassador, whose mission, in the opinion of the Austrian NSDAP, ended on July 11, 1936.[3]

Papen tried to bring about a retraction of this attack on his person, but to no avail; Leopold refused to see him. Thereupon he retaliated and ordered the members of the legation to break off relations with Leopold and his agents.

Papen's aim matched that of Zernatto, the General Secretary of the Fatherland Front, who appears to have been instrumental in the fall of Neustädter-Stürmer. Zernatto stood for the selection of individuals who would represent national interests in general, but remained firmly opposed to a deal with the Nazi party itself.[4] It was Zernatto who now proposed the appointment of Seyss-Inquart, an acquaintance of his, to Schuschnigg.[5]

Seyss-Inquart was a successful lawyer in Vienna. Apart from some early contacts with Dollfuss he had played no active part in Austrian politics. He had been a member of the Austrian–German *Volksbund*, which stood above party politics. But he finally became convinced that the old National politicians had lost their supporters to the Nazis, the only force which in his estimation could bring about the Anschluss. Typical of his careful and non-committal attitude, however, he did not become a member himself, because he did not yet wish to take such a binding allegiance upon himself.[6]

---

[1] Papen to Hitler, GD, 12 January 1937, Ser. D, Vol. I, No. 196.
[2] Papen to the German Foreign Ministry, 13 March 1937, ibid., No. 216.
[3] Papen's memorandum, 3 June 1937, ibid., enclosure in No. 229.
[4] Zernatto, op. cit., pp. 172–173.
[5] Seyss-Inquart's testimony, IMT, Part 16, p. 158.
[6] Seyss-Inquart's memorandum, Doc. 3254–PS, loc. cit., p. 962.

In April 1937 the first meeting took place between Seyss-Inquart and Schuschnigg in the latter's apartment. In his account Zernatto, who was also present, throws light on the unreal atmosphere surrounding the Austrian Chancellor and on Seyss-Inquart's approach to him. Seyss-Inquart had obviously prepared himself well for the meeting. After a long talk about music – the symphonies of Bruckner – the conversation turned to questions of *Weltanschauung* and politics. Seyss-Inquart thought the moment had come to explain his political creed. The beginning and end of it was the unification of all Germans in a *Volksreich*. In this *Reich* Austria would play an extremely important part. Though Seyss-Inquart could not say exactly what the final form of this *Reich* would be, he explained to Schuschnigg that he thought of a federal structure, possibly with a monarchical head.[1]

Schuschnigg, presented with some of his own pet ideas, was favourably impressed by his talk with Seyss-Inquart. He finally decided to abandon his contacts with the Committee of Seven and to follow Zernatto's advice. Seyss-Inquart seemed especially suited to act as the *confident* for his appeasement policy of the national circles. He therefore chose him as his representative for the policy of pacification and in a letter on 16 June he offered Seyss-Inquart the appointment to the Federal State Council under the condition that he would join the Fatherland Front.[2] To this Seyss-Inquart consented the following day.[3]

His appointment as representative of the national opposition had two aspects: the first one concerned his relationship with the Austrian Nazi party, the second one his position with the German government in Berlin. Seyss-Inquart hoped to associate himself with Leopold and for this purpose a conference took place on 23 June. Leopold was willing to co-operate, but on his own terms. He made it clear that he would only recognize Seyss-Inquart as representative of the interests of the party if he abstained from forming his own political group and subordinated himself to his, the party leader's, directives.[4]

To this Seyss-Inquart could not consent. He owed his appointment to the very fact that Schuschnigg had abandoned hope of

---

[1] Zernatto, op. cit., p. 179.
[2] Schuschnigg to Seyss-Inquart, 16 June 1937, GD, 1788/408158–159.
[3] Seyss-Inquart to Schuschnigg, 17 June 1937, GD, 1788/408160.
[4] Leopold to Hitler, 22 August 1937, GD, 1291/344920–936.

associating himself with the Nazi party. Though Seyss-Inquart did not say so openly to Leopold, it was obvious that there was no common platform for co-operation. Seyss-Inquart did exactly what Leopold had hoped to avoid. Trying to broaden his basis he took on the chairmanship of the defunct Austro-German *Volksbund*, and established contact with Leopold's rival group in the party, consisting of Klausner, Rainer, and Globocznigg. Moreover, he decided to go personally to Berlin in order to find out what support he could command for his policy.[1]

Seyss-Inquart made this journey early in July 1937. Schuschnigg, interested to facilitate the task of his representative for questions of the national opposition, gave his consent.[2] In Berlin Seyss-Inquart had two conversations with Hess and during the second, Hess, presumably after having discussed things with Hitler, showed himself much more interested and encouraged Seyss-Inquart to go ahead with his plans. Hess only regretted that Seyss-Inquart was not one of the old fighters, and Seyss-Inquart was left guessing whether this was meant as a compliment or a criticism. Seyss-Inquart had a further conversation with Göring, which according to Seyss-Inquart's account was only superficially impressive; Göring in fact favoured a much more rapid solution,[3] and for this reason seems to have backed Leopold.

As a first step in the gradual integration of the Nazi party and the Fatherland Front Seyss-Inquart initiated the fusion of the National Socialist peasantry with the Catholic Peasantry League. In Leopold's eyes this move constituted a direct threat to the integrity of the party and he opposed it violently. There was only one possibility left for him to wreck these attempts at reconciliation. He had to use the party organization, which he still controlled, and make a pacification impossible.

The Austrian Nazi party used the occasion of a meeting of Austrian and German ex-service men at Wels in the middle of July 1937; it was the first meeting permitted by the Austrian government in a number of years. In order to show the party's organized strength and to prove that a real settlement was impossible without its co-operation, the Austrian Nazis staged a big

---

[1] Seyss-Inquart's memorandum, Doc. 3254–PS, loc. cit., p. 968.
[2] Schuschnigg's testimony, Schmidt-prot., pp. 444–445.
[3] Seyss-Inquart's memorandum, Doc. 3254–PS, loc. cit., p. 968.

demonstration. The large crowd sang *Deutschland, Deutschland über alles* instead of the Austrian national anthem,[1] much to the embarrassment of the government officials – and Papen, who was supposed to make a speech of reconciliation. Papen therefore cut his speech as short as possible and left prematurely under some pretext. The Austrian police had to dispel the crowd by force. The Austrian Nazis were not slow in informing Hitler of the incident and for the moment they succeeded. Hitler was furious about the suppression of the Nazi demonstration.[2]

In a further attempt to normalize relations with Germany, Schuschnigg initiated a meeting of the commission, provided for in the Gentlemen's Agreement, for a discussion of the execution of the Agreement. Under Weizsäcker's direction the German delegation arrived in Vienna on 5 July 1937. Hitler especially appointed *SS-Gruppenführer* Keppler, the Chief of the Central Party Office for economic questions, to the delegation as the representative of party interests. The German delegation had various discussions with Schuschnigg, Schmidt, Zernatto, Glaise-Hortenau, and Seyss-Inquart, but the results were extremely meagre. The negotiations concentrated on minor details, such as whether the sale of Hitler's book *Mein Kampf* was to be permitted in Austria. When the German delegation left Vienna on 12 July no major problem had been solved. Weizsäcker observed that Schuschnigg was not refusing to make progress in the direction of the national opposition, but that 'he was plagued by the obvious fear of leaving his support behind him'.[3]

On 12 July Papen and Keppler called at Obersalzberg in order to report the results of the conference. Papen complained to Hitler that too many authorities in Germany were occupied with Austrian affairs. Hitler recognized this basic weakness and in order to enforce a stronger discipline gave Keppler basic authority to handle the relations of the party with Austria.[4] Keppler's appointment was a further blow to Leopold. Hitler had chosen a man who was already well experienced in the evolutionary method of getting to power. In 1932 he had used his connexions with leading economists in the negotiations with Papen which

[1] Papen's memorandum, Doc. 3300–PS, Schmidt-prot., p. 372.
[2] Papen, op. cit., pp. 397–398.
[3] Weizsäcker's memorandum, 10 July 1937, GD, Ser. D, Vol. I, No. 237.
[4] Weizsäcker's memorandum, 13 July 1937, ibid., No. 241.

finally resulted in the formation of Hitler's cabinet.[1] Moreover he had had close relations with Himmler, dating from the time when Himmler had taken over Keppler's 'circle of economists' and turned it into the *Freundeskreis* which financed Himmler's own private hobbies.[2] Leopold could not expect that Keppler would go out of his way to strengthen the Austrian party organization, which consisted mainly of SA formations.

Keppler tried to settle the dispute between Leopold and Seyss-Inquart and he organized a meeting with Leopold in Salzburg on 7 August. However, in their discussion, Leopold immediately turned against him:

> The fact that Hitler has appointed you [Leopold told Keppler] does not entitle you to give me orders as to my relationship to the party in Austria. After all, you cannot know what is of importance to us and what is not. You will have to leave this to me. I have been in the movement without interruption for 17 years. I have been *Ortsleiter*, *Kreisleiter*, and *Gauleiter*, and I am now *Landesleiter*.[3]

Leopold claimed that he too followed a policy along the lines of the July agreement, but only he was able to influence the Austrian Nazis to accept a long-term policy for three, four, or more years. He continued:

> What you demand of me here is impossible, it will lead to the same disaster as was formerly brought about by Habicht whom in the spring of 1933 I implored just as I am now imploring you.[4]

A further conference between Seyss-Inquart, Keppler, Leopold, and Tavs followed on 13 August, but it did not convince Leopold that he had to submit. On the contrary, Leopold destroyed all hope of a reconciliation. He issued instructions forbidding all party members to associate with Seyss-Inquart and Keppler. Reinthaller was dismissed from his official positions and Globocznigg expelled from the party.[5]

---

[1] Alan Bullock, op. cit., pp. 156, 220; see Keppler's letters to Baron von Schröder, 13 November 1932, *Nuremberg Military Tribunal*, Doc. Book No. 169, Doc. NJ–209; 28 November 1932, Doc. NJ–211.

[2] Keppler's Defence Documents, Doc. No. 59.

[3] Memorandum of Captain Leopold, 7 August 1937, Doc. NG–3282, IMT. 'The Ministries Case', Vol. XII, pp. 692–698.

[4] Ibid., p. 697.

[5] Leopold to Hitler, 22 August 1937, GD, 1291/344920–936.

Himmler took up the challenge; he refused to heed Glo-bocznigg's dismissal from the SS and personally ordered that he should stay.[1] Leopold appealed to Himmler to enforce the dismissal, but to no avail.[2]

Driven into a corner, Leopold now sought intervention from Hitler himself. In two long letters of 22 August and 9 September he pleaded for a decision in his favour, and asked for an order confirming that only he was competent to deal with matters concerning the Austrian Nazi party.[3] There is no evidence that these letters ever reached Hitler. Since they contained the whole story of the personal feud between Leopold on one side and Seyss-Inquart and Keppler on the other, they were probably never handed to the Führer. At the end of September 1937 Leopold decided to travel to Berlin personally to plead his case; but obstacles were put in his way. Seyss-Inquart in fact attempted to procure an order to prohibit him from crossing the border.[4] He did not succeed in this aim but Keppler, in Berlin, managed to prevent a meeting between the Führer and Leopold. On 1 October he wrote to the Führer's adjutant, that 'he did not consider it necessary that Leopold be received by the Führer'. He requested, however, in the event of an audience, to be able to participate in the conference.[5] Seyss-Inquart threatened to resign if Leopold gained any concessions.[6]

In fact Leopold had chosen a most unfortunate moment to go to Berlin. At about the same time, from 23 to 29 September, Mussolini paid his state visit to Germany. Hitler was not inclined to discuss the Austrian question for the moment. Driving for an alliance with Italy, he did everything to dispel the Duce's suspicions with regard to Austria. He gave Göring special instructions for his conversations with Mussolini, telling him that he did not approve of his previous Austrian policy which was too severe. No explosion of the Austrian question should be touched off in the foreseeable future; attempts to seek an evolutionary solution should be continued. For the same reason Hitler rejected

---

[1] Kaltenbrunner to Keppler, 3 September 1937, GD, 1291/344885–888.
[2] Leopold to Himmler, 8 October 1937, GD, 1291/345177–179.
[3] GD, 1291/344920–936 and 1291/344936–937.
[4] Zernatto, op. cit., p. 179.
[5] Doc. NG–3282, No. 3, IMT, 'The Ministries Case', Vol. XII, p. 698.
[6] Seyss-Inquart's letter to Glaise-Horstenau, 4 October 1937, GD, 1788/408115.

the idea of seeing Leopold. He was not pleased with Leopold, he declared; the strictest discipline should be demanded of him.[1]

Having been repudiated by the party offices, Leopold's last hope lay with governmental circles. He asked to be received by Foreign Minister Neurath, who, after a discussion with Keppler, refused to see him.[2] The only persons Leopold finally succeeded in seeing were Göring and Goebbels. The meeting with Göring took place on 8 October, but Keppler managed to be present, and after Hitler's recent rebuke, Göring could not come out as openly in Leopold's favour as he would have liked. After a lengthy dispute between Keppler and Leopold, Göring intervened and decided on a compromise. The leadership of the illegal NSDAP was to be in Leopold's hands, but the activities of Seyss-Inquart were not to be hindered in any way.[3] Leopold had to take the train back to Vienna without having obtained any backing for his policy.

Seyss-Inquart was not a man to leave matters to chance. A couple of days after Leopold's return he went to Berlin himself. He again met Hess and Göring, who this time showed themselves much more favourable towards his suggestions. Back in Vienna Seyss-Inquart reported to Schmidt and Zernatto about his contacts in Berlin.[4] In support of his personal feud with Leopold the Fatherland Front issued orders that a compromise with the Nazis was out of the question and that all contacts had to be avoided.[5]

Since the basis of the co-operation between Schuschnigg and Seyss-Inquart did not extend beyond their common struggle against the illegal party, differences were bound to become apparent after they had succeeded in isolating Leopold. When Seyss-Inquart discussed his visit to Berlin with the Austrians in Vienna, they showed understanding for the necessity of achieving a further *rapprochement* in the fields of economy, the armed forces, and the press. But these were delaying tactics. Foreign Minister von Neurath found no response from Schuschnigg for his pro-

---

[1] Keppler's memorandum, 1 October 1937, GD, Ser. D, Vol. I, No. 256.
[2] Altenburg's memorandum, 7 October 1937, ibid., No. 258.
[3] Keppler's memorandum, 8 October 1937, ibid., No. 260.
[4] Seyss-Inquart to Keppler, 25 October 1937, Doc. 3390–PS, NCA, Vol. VI, pp. 105–107.
[5] *Informationsdienst der Vaterländischen Front*, Vienna, 1 December 1937, GD, 1291/345138–146.

posal to resume the discussion regarding a customs union. He and Papen formed, independently of each other, the opinion 'that the will to carry out the Agreement was not present on the part of the Austrian government' and that 'with a continuation of the Schuschnigg methods we shall very soon be in an untenable position'.[1]

Finally, Seyss-Inquart himself reached the same conclusion; he reported on 13 December 1937 that 'proposals made for customs and currency union were politically impracticable and meant taking an utopian attitude towards the problems'.[2] Frustrated by his lack of success in obtaining any concessions he contemplated resigning from his post.[3] But Göring intervened and ordered that everything should be done to prevent his resignation. If it became necessary he should first report to Berlin.[4]

Göring in the meantime had pursued his own contacts with the Austrian government. They dated from the visit of the Austrian State Secretary Schmidt to Berlin in November 1936, when Göring and Schmidt had taken a certain liking to each other, though Göring with his bull-dozing manner and Schmidt, the Viennese intellectual, had little in common. They had corresponded at great length but their letters only rehearsed irreconcilable positions.[5] At Göring's invitation Schmidt came twice to Berlin, in September and November 1937, when Göring, independently of the Foreign Ministry, proposed a military alliance and a customs union. But his advances were rejected; consequently he refused Schmidt's invitation for a return visit to Vienna, because he was only willing to come 'if a positive result could be expected from his visit' and that was not the case.[6]

These endeavours found little interest on Hitler's part. At the famous conference with his generals and Foreign Minister Neurath at the *Reichskanzlei* on 5 November 1937, Hitler revealed for the first time that he considered a military solution of

---

[1] Neurath to Hitler, 10 August 1937, GD, Ser. D, Vol. I, Nos. 246 and 247. Papen to Neurath, 1 September 1937, ibid., No. 251.

[2] Seyss-Inquart's report, 13 December 1937, GD, 1788/408080.

[3] Altenburg's memorandum, 8 January 1937, GD, Ser. D, Vol. I, No. 276.

[4] Göring's telephone order to Keppler, 6 January 1937, Doc. 3473–PS, IMT, Vol. XXXII, p. 333.

[5] See Schmidt's and Göring's testimonies, Schmidt-prot., pp. 50–52, 300.

[6] Correspondence printed in Schmidt-prot., pp. 302–311.

the Czech and Austrian questions.[1] Four and a half years had elapsed since he had taken power. That was exactly the period he had demanded for the rebuilding of the armed forces at the conference of his ministers on 8 February 1933. During that period, he had predicted, no risk of an armed conflict could be run.[2] Hitler now made it clear that Germany need no longer fear the danger inherent in taking action: 'Germany's problem could only be solved by force and this was never without attendant risk.'

Hitler's central theme was Germany's need for space, and his other ideas were subordinated to it. As a first step he considered the incorporation of Czechoslovakia and Austria. But as far as the means to achieve this aim were concerned, Hitler revealed himself as a complete opportunist. He fixed 1943–45 as the latest moment when action should be taken. Before then action would depend entirely on a favourable situation, and in his opinion such a situation would arise when France found itself in a domestic crisis or engaged in a war with another state. He thought the 'latter possibility could emerge from the tensions in the Mediterranean', and was resolved 'to take advantage of it whenever it happened, even as early as 1938'. Hence he intended to keep Italy engaged in the Spanish war: 'A hundred per cent victory for France is not desirable, from the German point of view; rather we are interested in a continuance of the war and in the keeping up of the tension in the Mediterranean.'[3]

Generally the importance of this conference has been overstressed. Hitler wanted to convince his generals that the armament programme had to be expanded and he therefore exaggerated the possibilities of an armed conflict. As far as Austria was concerned, his aims were not original, though he had never before presented them in such crude terms. However, no plan for action against Austria emerged from the conference. It appears from Hossbach's memorandum that Hitler was much more preoccupied with Czechoslovakia than Austria. But even then Hitler made it

[1] For an account of the meeting see Alan Bullock, op. cit., pp. 336–339; see Wheeler-Bennett, *The Nemesis of Power*, pp. 359–362, as far as the reaction of the generals is concerned. A. J. P. Taylor, *The Origins of the Second World War*, London, 1961, pp. 131–134.

[2] Minutes of the Conference of Ministers, 8 February 1933, GD, Ser. C. Vol. I, No. 16.

[3] Hossbach's memorandum, 10 November 1937, GD, Ser. D, Vol. I, No. 19.

clear that he hoped circumstances would provide an opportunity for success in foreign policy without risking an armed conflict.[1]

Since Schuschnigg showed reluctance to continue with his policy along the lines of the Agreement, it became of major importance whether England, Italy, and France were prepared to take active measures on their own account should Schuschnigg's more independent course develop into a German–Austrian crisis. The signs were not encouraging.

There was no hope of Great Britain abandoning her reserved attitude towards Austria. Already on 14 April 1937 the Austrian government had informed London 'that recognition only in principle of Austrian independence by Great Britain and France prevented Austria from adapting its foreign policy to that of London and Paris'. It could consider a closer policy with these countries only if they 'were in a position to give effective guarantees for the political and territorial integrity of Austria'.[2] This move found no response.

Baldwin's replacement by Chamberlain in May 1937 gave a new impulse to the policy of appeasement. Chamberlain was convinced that it was possible to come to a settlement with Germany. A guarantee given to Austria could only irritate Berlin. On the contrary, when Lord Halifax visited Hitler at Berchtesgaden on 19 November 1937, he conceded that alterations in the European order 'might be destined to come about with the passage of time. Among these questions were Danzig, Austria, and Czechoslovakia. . . . But alterations should come through the course of peaceful evolution'.[3] This corresponded exactly with Chamberlain's opinion, who was prepared to give assurances that they would not use force to prevent the changes the Germans wanted in Austria and Czechoslovakia, if they could get them by peaceful means.[4]

In opening discussions with Hitler London had to take into account French suspicions of a separate deal between England and Germany. A conference was therefore arranged between

[1] See Taylor, op. cit., pp. 131–134.
[2] Austrian Foreign Ministry to Franckenstein, 14 April 1937, GD, Ser. D, Vol. I, enclosure 1, No. 220.
[3] Memorandum of Halifax's conversation with Hitler, 19 November 1937, GD, Ser. D, Vol. I, No. 31; Lord Avon, op. cit., p. 515.
[4] Quoted in Keith Feiling, *The Life of Neville Chamberlain*, London, 1947, pp. 332–333.

the Prime and Foreign Ministers of the two countries, from 28 to 30 November, in order to dispel the French fears. But Foreign Secretary Eden confided to the German and Italian ambassadors in London that he had left the French in no doubt that

the question of Austria was of much greater interest to Italy than to England. Furthermore, people in England realized that a closer connection between Germany and Austria would have to come about sometime. They wished, however, that a solution by force be avoided.[1]

Making Italy responsible for the protection of Austrian independence was a futile step. Mussolini's state visit to Germany in September 1937 had strengthened the Rome–Berlin axis. The formula, according to which Germany would do nothing without previous information, was reaffirmed.[2] But on the other hand Hitler received from Mussolini the assurance that, in case the Austrian question were exploded by another party, intervention on the part of Germany would be possible.

During his visit to Germany the Duce showed himself increasingly irritated about the Austrian attitude towards Italy. His annoyance served as self-justification for his inability to maintain Austria's independence. 'He was not pleased with Schuschnigg's policy in Austria,' he declared. 'He himself was alternately described as the arch-enemy of Austria, and asked for assistance.'[3] About a month later he told Ribbentrop, 'The fact that the Austrians had not modified their cold and negative attitude towards us has contributed to the decrease of Italian interest in Austria':

France knows that if a crisis should arise in Austria, Italy would do nothing. This was said to Schuschnigg, too, on the occasion of the Venice conversation. We cannot impose independence upon Austria which, by the very fact that it was imposed, would cease to be independence.[4]

The Duce's Foreign Minister drew the conclusions of this development. As a heritage of Mussolini's active policy in south-

---

[1] Ribbentrop's reports, 2 and 4 December 1937, GD, Ser. D, Vol. I, Nos. 50 and 59. Eden himself writes that he 'thought that our attitude on policy towards Austria should be prudent . . . while our military strength was still limited it was the best that we could do'. Lord Avon, op. cit., p. 503.

[2] Mussolini to Ribbentrop, Ciano's minute, 6 November 1937, *Ciano's Papers*, p. 146.

[3] Keppler's memorandum, 1 October 1937, GD, Ser. D, Vol. I, No. 256.

[4] Ciano's minute, 6 November 1937, *Ciano's Papers*, p. 146.

east Europe in 1934, Italy was still tied to Austria and Hungary by the Rome Protocols. Ciano concluded that these had by now been superseded.[1] The conference between the three countries in Budapest from 10 to 12 January 1938, ended in disagreement. The Hungarians objected to a statement proposed by Ciano and directed against the League. The Austrians on the other hand wanted a declaration about the independence of Austria, which out of consideration for Germany, Ciano felt he could not make.[2]

With the solidarity of England and Italy wanting, no action could be expected from France. In contrast to 1931, when France had checked the attempts to form an Austro-German customs union, France was too weak a country to lend force to her policy. Foreign Minister Delbos conceded in November 1937, that France 'had no essential objection to a further assimilation of certain of Austria's domestic institutions with Germany's, though she could naturally not declare her disinterestedness in territorial changes'.[3]

[1] *Ciano's Diary*, 18 December 1937, p. 60.
[2] Ibid., 10, 11 and 12 January 1937, pp. 63–64.
[3] Welczek's report, 27 November 1937, GD, Ser. D, Vol. I, No. 46. The German Foreign Ministry to various German diplomatic missions, 4 December 1937, ibid., No. 57.

M

CHAPTER VII

THE ANSCHLUSS, 1938

Everything had to be avoided which could give Germany a pretext for intervention and everything had to be done to secure in some way Hitler's toleration of the status quo.

Schuschnigg, *Austrian Requiem*

BERCHTESGADEN: THE CONFERENCE

The deadlock in the inter-governmental negotiations between Berlin and Vienna showed that previous methods for finding a solution had failed. On the other hand Vienna's international isolation made it imperative for the Austrian government to continue searching for a compromise with Germany. Von Papen with his instinct for the right moment sensed that the time was ripe for a personal meeting between Hitler and Schuschnigg. At the end of December 1937 he suggested to the Austrian Chancellor such a conference on Austro-German relations. But Schuschnigg and Schmidt were hesitant. The risks involved seemed considerable and they still regarded an exchange of notes sufficient to clarify the controversial issues.[1] Yet Papen did not lose hope. He made the same suggestion to Hitler who, attracted by the idea, declared himself ready to have a meeting with Schuschnigg, which could take place at the end of January 1938.[2]

Having obtained Hitler's consent Papen resubmitted his proposal to Schmidt on 7 January. Since Hitler himself authorized the approach the Austrians had to take Papen's move more seriously. Schmidt and Hornbostel did not regard the Austrian Chancellor as the right person for an encounter with Hitler.[3] Schuschnigg, however, reckoned that he could not risk a refusal. He thought Hitler would feel provoked and find a pretext to annex Austria. The better solution was in his opinion to have a

---

[1] Schmidt's and Hornbostel's evidence, Schmidt-prot., pp. 55, 180.
[2] *Amtserinnerung*, 8 January 1938, ibid., pp. 556–557.
[3] Hornbostel's and Schmidt's evidence, ibid., pp. 180, 448.

frank discussion and 'to take the bull by the horns'.[1] But he made three conditions: he demanded a formal invitation, safeguards against a subsequent cancellation of the conference, and the arrangement of a formal programme.

At the same time that Schuschnigg decided to meet Hitler he resolved upon decisive action against the Austrian Nazi party organization. It is not quite clear what his motives were for combining the two decisions. The activities of the Nazi headquarters in the Teinfaltstrasse were an open secret; the Austrian police thought it could control the movement better in its offices than by driving it underground.[2] Probably Schuschnigg hoped that by checking the illegal party he would strengthen his hand at the conference in Berchtesgaden. Be that as it may, having split the Nazi opposition and isolated Leopold's movement, he knew that he could safely strike without running the risk of counter-measures.

The immediate occasion for action was provided by an interview in which Tavs, the man in charge of the offices in the Teinfaltstrasse, had strongly criticized the Austrian government. The interview was first published by a Prague newspaper, on 22 January 1938, followed by the Viennese *Reichspost* on 25 January. The same evening the Austrian police arrested Tavs and made a search of his offices in the Teinfaltstrasse and his home. Having suffered no interference for a year the Austrian Nazis had abandoned all precaution and were taken by surprise. Tavs's memorandum on the present situation and his plan for action in 1938 fell into the hands of the police, and the Austrian government was shocked by the material disclosed.[3]

The Tavs plan revealed that the Austrian Nazis, inspired by their rivalry with Seyss-Inquart and feeling abandoned by the German authorities, contemplated extremely radical measures to regain the initiative. The course of action laid down in the plan was to find some pretext to provoke unrest among the Austrian Nazis and compel the government to use stringent measures against the party. This, Tavs thought, would force Germany's intervention. The German government, after informing Italy, would serve an ultimatum on Austria demanding the inclusion of

[1] Schuschnigg's evidence, ibid., pp. 437, 584, 602.
[2] Report by an informant, 29 January 1938, Doc. NG–3608, Case 11, 'The Ministries Case', Pros. Doc. Book No. 2.
[3] Papen's report, 27 January 1938, GD, Ser. D., Vol. I, No. 279.

Nazis in the cabinet and the withdrawal of government forces. In order to precipitate a German ultimatum, one of the detailed plans envisaged an attack on the German embassy in Vienna, by Austrian Nazis disguised as members of the Fatherland Front.[1]

It remains a matter for speculation whether party authorities in Germany had knowledge of the Tavs plan and whether they supported it. Zernatto in his account writes that some of the captured documents proved a connexion between Tavs and Rudolf Hess.[2] But it seems most improbable, in view of the rest of the documentary evidence, that Hitler knew about it or even approved of it.

Schuschnigg regarded the discovered material important enough to call an immediate conference of his ministers on the night of 25 January. After the report of Skubl, the police president of Vienna, it was decided to take further measures against the party, to which Seyss-Inquart and Glaise-Horstenau, both present at the conference, agreed.[3] The following morning the police closed the office in the Teinfaltstrasse and arrested Leopold. But no compromising material could be found against him and he was released on 27 January. The lack of publicity given to these events in Germany and Austria makes evident the implicit understanding which existed between Berlin and Vienna as far as measures against the Nazis under Leopold were concerned. The German press was directed to pass over the events in silence while the Schuschnigg government did not claim German complicity.[4]

On 26 January, the day after the successful raid against the Teinfaltstrasse, Schmidt proposed to Papen that perhaps the three most compromised Austrian Nazis, Tavs, Leopold, and In der Maur, could be transported to Germany should the forthcoming conference of the two heads of state show positive results. This would make it evident that the Reich authorities did not tolerate the methods which the Austrian Nazis had pursued.[5]

But the prospects for an early conference at the end of January

---

[1] The content of the Tavs plan can be found in Zernatto's account of these events, op. cit., pp. 182–185. Schuschnigg's account appears to be mainly based on Zernatto's book, Doc. 2995–PS, NCA, Vol. V, pp. 707–709.

[2] Op. cit., p. 185; Zernatto mistakenly dates the raid against the Teinfaltstrasse as taking place in November 1937, whereas it was definitely made on 25 January. Zernatto's error is repeated by Gulick, op. cit., pp. 1777–1778.

[3] Stein's report, 29 January 1938, GD, Ser, D, Vol. I, No. 280.

[4] Koerner, *So haben sie es damals gemacht*, Vienna, 1958, p. 69.

[5] Hoffinger's *Aktenvermerk*, 26 January 1938, Schmidt-prot., p. 557.

had faded away. During their talk Papen read a telegram to Schmidt which he had received from Neurath and which said that the Führer was now willing to receive Schuschnigg at Obersalzberg around 15 February. The time at which Papen got this instruction and the postponement of the meeting for a fortnight are significant. On 26 January Hitler dismissed Field-Marshal von Blomberg from his post. He was prepared to meet the Austrian Chancellor only after he had weathered the major internal crisis which he foresaw would follow this action. The way in which he did directly affected the situation in Austria.

On 31 January, the day on which Hitler received von Brauchitsch and von Rundstedt for a thorough discussion, Colonel Jodl, getting his information from Keitel, noted in his diary that the Führer had decided on the following line of action: 'He wants to divert attention from the army, and keep Europe in suspense. By re-distributing the posts he wants to avoid the impression of weakness, and rather to suggest a concentration of forces. Schuschnigg must not be allowed to gain courage, but must be made to tremble.'[1] Jodl's last note, almost added like an afterthought, suggests that Hitler was preoccupied with the fear that he would have to meet Schuschnigg at a moment when he was wanting in strength as a result of the internal German crisis. Such an impression had to be avoided.

The general purge on which Hitler had decided in Germany extended its arms to Vienna. On the evening of 4 February 1938, Papen received a telephone call from Berlin informing him that his mission had ended. No further reason was given and the voice on the line only added: 'I wanted to tell you this before you read about it in the newspapers.' Papen was naturally upset. He had seen Hitler only a week before in Berlin and Hitler had given no inkling of such an intention. Papen could only draw the conclusion that Hitler had lost faith in his policy.[2]

This concerned Papen the more because he believed himself on the verge of final success. After his return from Berlin on 31 January he had found an atmosphere in Vienna which seemed extremely favourable for the conversations contemplated with Schuschnigg. Seyss-Inquart and Glaise-Horstenau were already engaged in negotiations in which Schuschnigg showed himself

[1] Jodl's Diary, 31 January 1938, Doc. 1780–PS, IMT, Vol. XXVIII, p. 362.
[2] Papen, *Memoirs*, p. 406.

willing to comply with Seyss-Inquart's demands. The most important of these demands were:[1]

1. Release of all persons still held in jail in consequence of the *putsch* of July 1934.
2. Development of military, economic, and political relations with the Reich through the inclusion of persons from the ranks of the National Opposition. . . .
3. State Counsellor Seyss-Inquart to be granted control over the various Government committees. . . .

Moreover, Schuschnigg now urged Seyss-Inquart to accept a ministerial post in the cabinet. Seyss-Inquart discussed this with Papen, who advised him to abstain for the time being from making any promises. He argued that if the conference at Berchtesgaden could be arranged, they would raise a number of demands which would have to be agreed upon in advance.[2]

Now all this seemed to be at stake. Papen decided to see Hitler himself, and reached Berchtesgaden on 5 February. He found the Führer distrait and exhausted from the recent internal struggles. Apparently Hitler had forgotten that a meeting with Schuschnigg was planned. His attention was suddenly captured when he learned from Papen about the extent to which Schuschnigg was willing to make concessions. He was delighted; chance presented him with an opportunity to break the deadlock of the last few days by action. On the spur of the moment he sent Papen back to Vienna in order to arrange a meeting at Obersalzberg within the next few days.[3]

To everybody's surprise Papen reappeared in Vienna on 7 February. Schuschnigg had now even stronger reasons for visiting Hitler. Papen's dismissal seemed indeed to imply that Hitler was on the point of abandoning his evolutionary policy, which had permitted the Austrians to compromise with Germany. On the same evening Schuschnigg therefore notified Schmidt and Zernatto that he accepted Hitler's invitation and would visit him on 12 February.[4]

[1] This is only an extract of Seyss-Inquart's demands, which Schuschnigg was ready to consider; the full list is in Keppler's letter to Neurath, 2 February 1938, GD, Ser. D, Vol. I, No. 282. Keppler to Ribbentrop, 7 February 1938, ibid., No. 285.
[2] Papen to Hitler 4 February 1938, ibid., No. 284.
[3] Papen's memorandum, Schmidt-prot., p. 378; *Memoirs*, p. 407.
[4] Schmidt's and Schuschnigg's testimonies, Schmidt-prot., pp. 57, 584.

Schuschnigg now made a decision, which was most unfortunate as far as the subsequent development was concerned. He instructed Zernatto to continue the negotiations which he had begun with Seyss-Inquart, and to work out the basis for a co-operation between the national groups and the Fatherland Front. Seyss-Inquart was not to be informed of the forthcoming visit but Schuschnigg hoped that it would be possible to commit him to a programme. After having settled with the national opposition, he thought, he could then surprise Hitler with a *fait accompli* and forestall the pressure he expected.[1]

Zernatto and Seyss-Inquart entered into negotiations on 10 February. The fruits of their labours were the so-called *Punktationen mit Dr. Seyss-Inquart*. The core of Zernatto's draft was the concession that 'National Socialism not tied to a party undoubtedly contained basic conceptions which could become an organic part of the state ideology of the new Austria'.[2] The *Punktationen* envisaged the installation of Seyss-Inquart as arbiter in all matters concerning the Nazi opposition, a gradual amnesty of all Nazis still under arrest, a military co-operation between Germany and Austria after the necessary pre-conditions had been fulfilled, and the national opposition to be given posts in the different government and local offices. As a beginning the *Punktationen* envisaged the appointment of the well-known Nazis Jury, Langoth, and Professor Srbik, as State Counsellors; of Hueber, Göring's brother-in-law, as Sport leader; and of Reinthaller as economic counsellor.[3]

Zernatto's *Punktationen* formed the basis of a further conference between himself, Schuschnigg, and Seyss-Inquart during the afternoon of 11 February, shortly before the departure of the Austrian delegation to Berchtesgaden. Schuschnigg now conceded two appointments in principal: the Ministry of the Interior with Public Security to Seyss-Inquart and the Ministry of Finance. He only made the reservations that the recent acts of violence – organized in fact by Leopold and his followers who were watching these negotiations with hostility – made it impossible for him to proceed with the appointments for the time being; that would be yielding to mob pressure. He wanted to wait until 20 March in

[1] Zernatto, op. cit., p. 200.
[2] *Punktationen*, Schmidt-prot., p. 559.
[3] For the full text of the *Punktationen* see Schmidt-prot., pp. 557–559.

order to let things calm down sufficiently to make any action on his part acceptable to his own followers.[1]

Seyss-Inquart would not be put off any longer. Already, during a break in the afternoon negotiations of 11 February, he had summoned Mühlmann, one of the Austrian Nazi leaders, and had given him an outline of the progress so far made.[2] In the evening between 8 and 9 o'clock he met Rainer and other Nazis in his office and handed them the full details of the negotiations which he had just finished.[3] Seyss-Inquart demanded that Schuschnigg definitely commit himself, on the following day at Berchtesgaden, to make the ministerial appointments before 20 February. Moreover, Seyss-Inquart wished to settle accounts with the Nazis under Leopold and insisted that the old *Landesleitung* under Leopold be removed.

This information reached Berchtesgaden through two channels. Rainer immediately telephoned to Berlin in an attempt to catch Keppler, who had, however, already left for Berchtesgaden. Rainer's report was therefore communicated by teletype to Munich and there handed to Keppler, when passing through on his train.[4] Mühlmann, provided with similar instructions, left Vienna on the evening of 11 February on the same train as the Austrian delegation. While the Austrians had their coach taken off at Salzburg in order to spend the night there, Mühlmann went on to Berchtesgaden, where he arrived on the following morning ready to report to Hitler.[5]

Shortly before the departure for Germany, Schuschnigg handed a copy of Zernatto's *Punktationen* to State Secretary Schmidt and Hornbostel, the head of the political division in the Foreign Ministry. Both of them were taken aback by the extent of the concessions. They feared irreparable consequences should Hitler obtain advance knowledge of them, and had no doubt that it would be impossible to retreat, at Berchtesgaden, from a concession already made in Vienna.[6]

---

[1] Weesenmayer to Keppler, GD, Ser. D, Vol. I, No. 293; it follows from the content of the report that it was made on 11 February 1938, and it contains the message of the Austrian Nazis to Keppler.

[2] Mühlmann's testimony, Schmidt-prot., p. 249.

[3] Seyss-Inquart's evidence, ibid., p. 338; IMT, Part 16, p. 161.

[4] Rainer's speech, Doc. 4005–PS, loc. cit., p. 21.

[5] Mülhmann's evidence, Schmidt-prot., p. 248.

[6] Hornbostel's and Schmidt's evidence, ibid., pp. 169–173, 58, 198.

The history of the events leading up to the meeting throws a new light on the conference itself at Berchtesgaden. By negotiating with Seyss-Inquart for about a fortnight prior to his meeting with Hitler, Schuschnigg had given his trumps away before he even got to the conference table. On the morning of 12 February, immediately after the arrival of the Austrian delegation, the two Chancellors had a private discussion. Knowing how far Schuschnigg was willing to go, it was easy for Hitler to menace. For about two hours he unleashed a stream of threats. But when the conference was interrupted for lunch, Hitler had not yet put forward a single demand. As far as Hitler's intentions were concerned Schuschnigg was entirely in the dark, and so probably was Hitler himself.

The decisions were made during the afternoon. From two till four o'clock Schuschnigg and Schmidt were left to themselves talking with the generals, whom Hitler had ordered to Obersalzberg in order to demonstrate that the recent military crisis had left his position unaffected and that he was able to back his threats by force. Schuschnigg and Schmidt now learned to their surprise that one of the Austrian Nazi leaders, Mühlmann, was also present. Keppler and Mühlmann had in the meantime not remained idle. They had informed Ribbentrop of the negotiations in Vienna. While Schuschnigg was left waiting, Hitler – together with Ribbentrop – drafted, on the basis of Keppler's and Mühlmann's advice, the German demands. They were presented to Schuschnigg in the middle of the afternoon.[1]

When looking through the draft the terms laid down must have appeared familiar to Schuschnigg. The major part consisted of the same measures, which had been conceded in principle during the previous negotiations with Seyss-Inquart. In addition to these demands the Berchtesgaden draft requested, in the military sphere, the appointment of Glaise-Horstenau as Minister of the Armed Forces, a systematic exchange of officers, regular conferences between the General Staffs, and in the economic sphere the assimilation of the Austrian to the German economic system. Since Seyss-Inquart had urged from Vienna that the realization of the measures must be insured there was a time-limit

[1] Mühlmann's evidence, Schmidt-prot., pp. 248–250. Ribbentrop's testimony, IMT, Part 10, pp. 218–219.

attached to the demands: Schuschnigg had to carry out the measures by 18 February 1938.[1]

Schuschnigg was summoned to Hitler, who told him that he had to accept the terms immediately. Schuschnigg pointed out that he could not guarantee ratification. But Hitler no longer listened; he dismissed Schuschnigg and shouted for Keitel.[2] The mere presence of the head of the O.K.W. with Hitler for a few minutes was the only active part the generals played during the conference. This of course the Austrians could not know. Schuschnigg found himself under considerable pressure, but his claim that Hitler's demands were sprung as a complete surprise on him is self-justificatory and without foundation. He was presented with his own concessions; hence Hitler could safely threaten without having to fear that his bluff would be called.

Hitler seems not only to have deceived the Austrians but his own entourage as well, which made his performance still more convincing. His mood appeared incalculable and Papen rushed in to calm him down.[3] Finally Mühlmann was called, who, according to his testimony,[4] found Hitler irritated and pale. Hitler questioned him about the personality of Seyss-Inquart and whether he had enough backing in the national camp. But, Hitler added, he would rather march than make more concessions. Finally, Hitler declared that he would change his mind. Schuschnigg was again summoned and Hitler told him that he would give him until 15 February to send a definitely binding reply.

In the meantime Schmidt and Ribbentrop had bargained about the details of the agreement and Schmidt succeeded in obtaining a few alterations. Some formulations were modified, and the demands for an assimilation of the Austrian and German economic systems and the appointment of Glaise-Horstenau as Minister of the Armed Forces dropped.[5]

Back in Vienna Schuschnigg was under pressure from two fronts. Germany maintained the military threat. Hitler ordered that 'false but creditable news should be spread, which may lead

[1] Draft of the Protocol, GD, Ser. D, Vol. I, No. 294.
[2] Schuschnigg, *Austrian Requiem*, p. 24.
[3] Papen, *Memoirs*, pp. 418–419.
[4] Schmidt-prot., pp. 248–250.
[5] Protocol of the Conference of 12 February 1938, GD, Ser. D, Vol. I, No. 295.

to the conclusion of military preparations against Austria'.[1]
In Austria Schuschnigg found himself engaged in a contest with
the opponents of further appeasement in his own camp. The
decisive conference in Vienna took place during the afternoon
on 14 February. Federal President Miklas agreed to grant an
amnesty to those Austrian Nazis who were still in prison, but he
objected to the appointment of Seyss-Inquart as Minister of
Security. Schuschnigg now confronted Miklas with the alternative of accepting his resignation and appointing a Chancellor
who could pursue a different policy, or of keeping him at his post
and endorsing the result of Berchtesgaden.[2] With no other
candidate forthcoming to assume political responsibility at this
hour, the Austrian President had no choice but to give his consent.

BERCHTESGADEN: THE REPERCUSSIONS

Schuschnigg proceeded with the reorganization of his government on 15 February. Seyss-Inquart became Minister of the
Interior and Security. In order to neutralize this appointment and
to keep Seyss-Inquart in check, Schuschnigg retained State
Secretary Skubl, whom he could trust, in his post as Director of
Security and made him in addition Inspector-General for the
police. He kept General Zehner, whose removal had been de-
manded by the Germans, as State Secretary for National Defence.
Furthermore, in order to broaden the basis of his government and
give the impression of a general reshuffle, he made several new
appointments: Watzek, a former Social-Democratic official of the
Free Unions, became Secretary of Labour; Julius Raab, a Clerical,
Minister of Commerce; Adamovich, who inclined towards the
Christian Socials, Minister of Justice; Zernatto, Minister without
Portfolio; and Schmidt received the Ministry of Foreign Affairs.[3]

The first measure on which the new government decided was
the proclamation of a general amnesty, which covered all persons
who prior to 15 February had violated laws for political motives.
This included the imprisoned Austrian Socialists. Yet the main
beneficiaries were the Nazis and, as a result of the amnesty, not
only the participants of the *putsch* of July 1934, but also the
persons associated with the Tavs plans were released.

[1] This order was prepared by Keitel and approved by Hitler, Doc. 1775, NCA,
Vol. IV, p. 357.
[2] Schuschnigg, *Austrian Requiem*, p. 29.
[3] Stein's report, 17 February 1938, GD, Ser. D, Vol. I, No. 306.

Berchtesgaden did not gain its significance so much from these practical results as from the fact that the conference had finally stripped away the illusion that surrounded the reality of power in Austria. By surrendering after Hitler had imposed his will, Schuschnigg made it apparent that he could only hold Austria with Hitler's consent. Since he had been determined to make his concessions anyhow, he should have avoided the impression that they were solely a result of Hitler's pressure. After the formation of the new government he now tried to correct this belief. He decided to spread a harmless version of the meeting.[1] An instruction to the various Austrian embassies insisted that the Chancellor had succeeded in overcoming a difficult stage in Austro-German relations without any internal and external repercussions of a serious nature.[2]

Schuschnigg thus got the worst of both worlds. He could not prevent details of his meeting with Hitler from leaking out and confidentially admitted that he had been received with the utmost brutality.[3] But his official version made the task for Berlin much easier. When protests at Schuschnigg's treatment came in, it could be pointed out that according to Schuschnigg himself the Berchtesgaden agreement had settled the Austro-German differences. The British and French ambassadors made a protest on 17 and 18 February, but Ribbentrop remained adamant.[4] As the American ambassador in Paris commented, the protests were made 'mainly for the sake of the record out of a feeling that they could hardly afford to pass by recent events in complete silence'.[5]

As a result of the new situation several hitherto dormant forces tried to take the initiative. Starhemberg, in Davos, Switzerland, at this time, thought that he had found a chance to re-enter the political scene. When the first news of Berchtesgaden came out, on 13 February, he offered his co-operation to the Germans. He declared that he wanted above all a meeting with a leading personality from the Reich at a secret place. Starhemberg intimated that the *Heimwehr* had been dissolved only on paper

---

[1] Schuschnigg, *Austrian Requiem*, p. 30.
[2] Telegram to the various Austrian missions, 15 February 1938, Schmidt-prot., pp. 561–562 (translation in GD, Ser. D, Vol. I, enclosure in No. 322).
[3] Wiley's and Bullitt's reports, 15 February 1938, US, Vol. I, pp. 393–395.
[4] Ribbentrop's memoranda, 17 and 18 February 1938, GD, Ser. D, Vol. I, Nos. 308, 310.
[5] Bullitt's report, 17 February 1938, US. Vol. I, p. 402.

and continued to exist. He envisaged a solution which would allow
Austria to remain independent but in close association with
Berlin. Both armies should be placed under unitary leadership and
a *rapprochement* take place similar to the former Austro-Hungarian monarchy.[1] But his advance seems to have found no response from the German side. He was obviously regarded as a
spent force politically.

Otto of Habsburg, the pretender to the Austrian throne, in his
exile in Belgium, also thought he could stage a come-back. On
17 February he wrote a dramatic letter to Schuschnigg requesting
him to hand over the Chancellorship to him. Though even he
realized that a restoration was not feasible – 'at least for the decisive situation' – he thought that through his own Chancellorship
'the same advantages could be secured as through the formal
act of restoration'. He expounded his own programme for maintaining Austria's independence, adding that he was assuming full
responsibility for it 'as the legitimate Emperor of Austria'.[2] In his
reply on 2 March, Schuschnigg, though a Monarchist at heart, rejected the request. In his estimation, nothing was more likely to
provoke a German intervention than a restoration. Such a risk
had to be avoided at all cost.[3]

Schuschnigg realized that he had to counter-balance the effect
of Berchtesgaden and to restore confidence among his followers.
For this purpose he made a strong speech at an extraordinary
session of the Federal Diet on 24 February: 'We are here to
take decisions, to act, to rally the confidence of all who are prepared to take a positive stand,' he declared, and his speech
ended on a forceful note.[4]

But Schuschnigg's address to his officials does not reveal his
true frame of mind. In this respect his confidential letter to Otto
of Habsburg is much more expressive; there he pleaded with an
outsider in whose eyes he attempted to justify his policy. As often
in his career, his assessment of the actual situation was over-
shadowed by the image he had formed of Austria's mission:

[1] Stuck's report (from the secret files of the *Reichsführer-SS* Himmler), 13
February 1938, GD, 1291/345133–135.
[2] Otto of Habsburg to Schuschnigg, 24 February 1938, text in Fuchs, op. cit.,
Appendix VI, pp. 295–300.
[3] Schuschnigg to Otto of Habsburg, 2 March 1938, ibid., pp. 300–303.
[4] Schuschnigg's speech quoted in *Documents on International Affairs, Vol. 2*, pp.
53–62.

'Austria is unable to remain true to her task,' he wrote, 'in the moment when she, in order to safeguard her existence, is compelled to bring about an international war.' Schuschnigg was a prophet resigned to his own forecasts, rather than a politician. Anticipating that Austria would have to bow to force, he advised the Crown Prince 'that this should also take place without the dynasty also being drawn in with it'.[1]

With Schuschnigg reluctant to take the initiative everything depended upon whether Austria's independence would be maintained from outside. Only an immediate revival of the Stresa Front could save the Austrian position. In the face of Hitler's advance, for the first time achieved by a military threat, the three powers of Stresa continued to pass on the responsibility to each other. Paris tried to initiate a common protest with London but this proposal was turned down.[2]

London waited for Rome to take action. During the debate on Austria in the House of Commons on 16 February, Eden found himself under strong pressure because of his refusal to commit himself to any active policy. It was true that the British government stood by the declaration of Stresa, he stated, but 'this was a declaration of three governments and Italy had not, as yet, consulted His Majesty's Government on the matter'.[3] Behind the scenes Eden tried to bring this consultation about and asked the Italian ambassador repeatedly to call upon him. Yet Grandi preferred to stay away, pretending to play golf, which he disliked, rather than 'allow Eden to escape the position of obvious embarrassment in which he has found himself in the Commons'. A talk with Eden, Grandi felt, 'would cast a shadow on the Rome–Berlin Axis'.[4]

Ciano was aware of this. Nevertheless he was convinced that the impending Anschluss made it necessary to exploit the British hope of an Italian intervention on behalf of Austria as long as this illusion could be maintained. He therefore directed Grandi to take up negotiations with the British government: 'We find ourselves in the interval between the fourth and fifth act of the Austrian

---

[1] Schuschnigg to Otto of Habsburg, 2 March 1938, loc. cit., p. 301.
[2] Vollgruber's and Franckenstein's reports, 22 and 23 February 1938, Schmidt-prot., pp. 530, 541, 542; see also Heeren's report, 22 February 1938, GD, Ser. D, Vol. I, No. 321.
[3] *Hansard*, 16 February 1938, cols. 1864–65.
[4] Grandi to Ciano, 19 February 1938, *Ciano's Papers*, p. 165.

affair,' he wrote, 'this interval alone can be used for the negotiations in London. . . . We cannot always hold all the cards between us.'[1]

Grandi now asked to meet the British Prime Minister, though
Eden still thought that he should see Grandi alone in the first
instance.[2] This failed to convince Chamberlain, who disapproved
of the cautious and reserved approach of his Foreign Secretary.
He did not want Eden to be present but Eden insisted, Grandi
having avoided him for some days.[3] When Grandi, Chamberlain,
and Eden finally met at 10 Downing Street on 18 February their
discussion developed along lines entirely different from those
originally planned by Eden. The Italian Ambassador refused
outright to discuss Austria, making it clear that Italy no longer
felt herself bound by the Stresa declaration.[4] When Chamberlain
suggested that all was not yet lost in Austria Grandi answered,
almost in the words of his Foreign Minister, 'that possibly they
were only at the end of the third act of four. . . . In the view of
Italy, however, Germany was now at the Brenner.'[5] At the same
time he stressed that it would soon be too late for an understanding between London and Rome. How, he asked Chamberlain,
could Mussolini be expected to move troops to the Brenner, as he
did before, if he felt that Great Britain was a potential enemy?[6]

The British Prime Minister was determined to take the chance
of a settlement with Italy. It was this issue which finally caused
the split between him and his Foreign Secretary. Just as Eden had
rejected a compromise with Italy over Abyssinia in 1936, he now
refused to agree to a settlement as long as Italy did not make
a substantial withdrawal of troops from Spain. Rather than
abandon a policy which brought him into office after the failure
of the Hoare–Laval plan, Eden resigned.[7] The Austrian question,
on the other hand, played no part in this dispute. Eden, as much
as Chamberlain, had accepted the German advance in Austria.
The British attitude to events in Austria, Grandi informed Rome,

[1] Ciano to Grandi, 16 February 1938, ibid., p. 161.
[2] Lord Avon, op. cit., p. 578.
[3] Eden's diary note, quoted in Lord Avon, op. cit., p. 582.
[4] Grandi to Ciano, 19 February 1938, *Ciano's Papers*, pp. 164–185.
[5] Eden to Perth (Rome), 18 February 1938, quoted in Lord Avon, op. cit.,
Appendix C, pp. 616–618.
[6] Quoted in Feith, op. cit., p. 338.
[7] Lord Avon, op. cit., pp. 577–583.

'has been and will remain an attitude of indignant resignation'.[1]
'What in fact could we do?' wrote Ciano on 23 February. 'Start
a war with Germany? At the first shot we fired, every Austrian,
without exception, would fall in behind the Germans against us.'[2]
The Italians had lost the conviction that the Austrians themselves
wanted to maintain their independence.

The least content with the arrangements made at Berchtesgaden were the Austrian Nazis under Leopold. After the Agreement of 1936 this was the second deal between Berlin and Vienna
in which they had not participated and whose advantages they
did not share. Seyss-Inquart's key position in Austria's internal
affairs made them dependent upon the opponent of their previous
policy and limited the scope of their opposition. In a handbill
the Austrian Nazi party commented on Seyss-Inquart's appointment that the reorganization of the government 'did not deserve
the fanfare with which it was heralded in the press'.

Schuschnigg has again called into his government only those men
upon whom he relies. This clear fact can not be obscured by using the
press, free of charge, to call one or the other of the Ministers 'the
representative of the national opposition'. The national opposition
and its leaders have sent no man possessing their confidence into the
cabinet.[3]

But the Austrian Nazis could not openly fight Seyss-Inquart,
who was sanctioned in his new position by Hitler. They decided
instead to provoke him into further arrests and then brand him as
a traitor to the National cause. Tavs, released under the amnesty,
allegedly issued orders for the breaking of the window of the
German legation, and Rüdiger, another of Leopold's associates,
was said to have gone so far as to declare that 'even the Führer
had no right to meddle in Austrian affairs'.[4]

Hitler, though he was usually inclined to tolerate rivalries
among his followers because he could exploit them for his own
purpose, now turned against Leopold for two reasons: first,
Leopold and his followers defied his policy openly; secondly, he
no longer needed the pressure which Leopold had exerted upon
the Austrian Chancellor. After Schuschnigg had been tempted

---

[1] *Ciano's Papers*, p. 183.   [2] *Ciano's Diary*, p. 79.
[3] Copy of handbill, Doc. 3576–PS, NCA, Vol. VI, pp. 273–274.
[4] Veesenmayer's report on the Austrian Situation up to 18 February 1938,
GD, Ser. D, Vol. I, No. 313.

to grant major concessions to Seyss-Inquart, Hitler could safely rid himself of Leopold. In Hitler's opinion the Berchtesgaden agreement was so far-reaching that if completely carried out the Austrian problem would be automatically solved.[1]

Both Seyss-Inquart and Leopold travelled to Berlin in order to argue their case. But Seyss-Inquart made sure that he arrived first. On 17 February, he had his first discussion with the Führer at the *Reichskanzlei* and demanded the removal of Leopold and his associates to Germany. This, he insisted, was a precondition for his policy in Austria.[2]   When Leopold appeared before the Führer on 21 February, it was only to learn that he had been replaced by Klausner, the representative of the party group in Carinthia. Leopold tried to complain that he had not been informed in advance about the meeting at Obersalzberg. Hitler would not tolerate any opposition; he reprimanded Leopold severely and especially reproached him for his activity after that conference. Finally Klausner himself was called in and told that he was to replace Leopold. Hitler then explained to them that Seyss-Inquart had assumed a very difficult task. He had to be supported by the party in every way. In particular 'the radical party elements had to be curbed in order not to render Seyss-Inquart's position impossible, who now and then would have to lock up Nazis too'.[3]

Leopold was charged with fetching Tavs, Rüdiger, In der Maur, and Schattenfroh from Austria and these Austrian Nazi leaders were received by Hitler on 26 February. They were ordered to stay in Germany. But Hitler explained that though he had had to change his tactics, they should not interpret their removal as discriminatory. With regard to his future tactics Hitler decided that the Austrian question could never be solved by a revolution: 'There remained only two possibilities: force, or evolutionary means, and he wanted the evolutionary course to be taken, whether or not the possibility of success could today be foreseen.'[4]

Hitler's tactics did not prevent the acceleration of events in

---

[1] Keppler's memorandum, 28 February 1938, GD, Ser. D, Vol. I, No. 328.
[2] Seyss-Inquart's memorandum, Doc. 3425–PS, NCA, Vol. VI, p. 127; Seyss-Inquart had made this demand once before through Papen; Papen to Hitler, 14 February 1938, GD, Ser. D, Vol. I, No. 297.
[3] Keppler's memorandum, 22 February 1938, ibid., No. 318.
[4] Keppler's memorandum, 28 February 1938, ibid., No. 328.

Austria. As a result of the loss of confidence in Austria's position a heavy flight of capital from Vienna led to a considerable drop in Austrian securities in foreign countries. The Austrian Nazis made full use of their newly gained liberties, though party leaders had instructions to prevent demonstrations as far as possible.[1] After Hitler's speech in the *Reichstag* on 20 February, which was broadcast in Austria, the Austrian Nazis demonstrated in the streets of Vienna, and in Graz they virtually took possession of the city.

The situation threatened to get out of hand. On 21 February the Austrian government therefore banned all demonstrations and processions that were not organized by the Fatherland Front. Seyss-Inquart, as Minister of the Interior and Security, supported this measure in a broadcast on 22 February. In his appeal he asked the Austrian Nazis that 'they must realize that the sovereign emblems of the Reich and its national anthem must not be used for demonstrations, or misused . . . There must be no illegal activity beyond the existing laws'.[2] He managed to persuade the local leaders in Graz to cancel a demonstration planned for 27 February. This did not mean that the ultimate aim had been abandoned. Keppler commented:

> At present we are inclined to apply the brakes to the movement, in order to wring more and more concessions from Schuschnigg. It seems the prime necessity, for the time being, to secure for the future further possibilities of organizing legally and for that reason to forego a parade or two.[3]

For the time being Hitler was content with the results he had obtained.

THE ANNEXATION

Schuschnigg was well aware that the German government had only compromised in order to consolidate its position. Its aims remained the same. He decided to force a decision and challenge the National Socialists openly rather than let the reins slip gradually from his hands. There was only one way left: a direct appeal to the Austrian people. Their declaration in favour of an independent state would forestall the evolutionary method of the Nazis

---

[1] Weesenmayer's report on the situation up to 18 February, 1938, GD, Ser. D, Vol. I, No. 313.

[2] Quoted in *Survey of International Affairs, 1938, Vol. I*, p. 198.

[3] Memorandum of his trip to Vienna, 3 to 6 March 1938, GD, Ser. D, Vol. I, No. 335.

and increase the risk of German armed intervention. Hitler,
Schuschnigg hoped, would not dare to act counter to the declared will of the population if it decided against an Anschluss.[1]

On Friday afternoon, 4 March, Schuschnigg held a conference
with Schmitz, the Mayor of Vienna, and the Ministers Zernatto,
Ferntner, and Stockinger, and informed them of his intention to
hold a plebiscite on the Anschluss question. Schmitz was charged
with preparing a memorandum concerning the necessary pre-
liminaries by Tuesday, 8 March.[2]

Only by taking the Nazis by surprise and by shortening the
period in which they could resort to counter-measures and
counter-propaganda, did a favourable result seem assured. Precautions were taken to keep the knowledge of the plan confined
to the persons immediately concerned. On 6 March Schuschnigg
obtained the consent of the President,[3] and on the evening of 8
March he finally told Seyss-Inquart about it. But he asked him
for his word of honour to keep the information secret until he had
announced the plebiscite on the following day.[4]

Schuschnigg's decision created a new situation for the Socialists.
The Chancellor needed their votes, in order to defy the Nazis.
For the first time since the suppression of the Socialists in
February 1934 he had to rely on their support. This necessitated
a belated attempt to rally them around the régime. Already, on 3
March, a conference had taken place between the Austrian Chancellor and a committee of workers' representatives under the
chairmanship of Hillegeist.[5] Though Schuschnigg did not mention the plan of a plebiscite, closer co-operation in face of the
threat from the National Socialists was discussed. The Socialists
promised their support, but made it dependent upon the fulfilment
of four conditions:

1. The same freedom in political activity as granted to the
National Socialists.
2. Free elections in the trade union movement.
3. Concession of one daily newspaper of their own.
4. Guarantees for a 'social course'.

[1] Schuschnigg, *Austrian Requiem*, pp. 35–36.
[2] Muff's memorandum, 8 March 1938, GD, Ser. D, Vol. I, No. 338.
[3] Miklas's evidence, Schmidt-prot., p. 260.
[4] Affidavit by Schuschnigg, Doc. 2996–PS, NCA, Vol. V, p. 713.
[5] Hillegeist's evidence, Schmidt-prot., p. 269.

Schuschnigg had no objections in principle to these demands, and details of the co-operation were left subject to later negotiations.[1]

Schuschnigg hoped to obtain the support of the two countries of the Rome Protocols, Italy and Hungary. The Hungarian Foreign Minister, Kanya, received a detailed account of the situation while he was on a short visit to Vienna, and according to Schuschnigg Kanya was confident that Hitler was only bluffing.[2] The Duce was less optimistic. Schuschnigg sent Liebitzky, the Austrian Military Attaché in Rome, to find out what he could about Mussolini's opinion. Questioned about his attitude towards the plebiscite, Mussolini retorted: 'This piece of ordnance will explode in your hands.'[3] If the plebiscite was in favour of Schuschnigg, it would be branded as a fake, if it went in favour of an Anschluss it would make the position of the government untenable. But Mussolini did not expect that the Germans would invade Austria openly.[4]

The Duce's message reached Schuschnigg on 9 March, when he was already in Innsbruck and when everything had been prepared for the announcement of the plebiscite. 'Now I can no longer go back,' Schuschnigg replied,[5] but it is doubtful whether he really wanted to reverse his decision, after he had made up his mind. The same evening he publicly announced the holding of a plebiscite on the coming Sunday, 13 March. The delivery of his speech was immediately followed by the broadcasting of the formula, on which the population should vote:

For a free and German, independent and social, for a Christian and united Austria! For peace and work and the equality of all who acknowledge their faith in our people and Fatherland![6]

No doubt Schuschnigg was right when he anticipated a strong reaction from the Nazis. They were especially annoyed, because Schuschnigg seemed to be trying to defeat them with their own

---

[1] Josef Buttinger, *Am Beispiel Österreich*, Köln 1953, p. 510, gives an excellent account of these negotiations.

[2] Schuschnigg, *Austrian Requiem*, p. 38.

[3] Extracts from Mussolini's broadcast, 16 March 1938, *Documents on International Affairs, 1938, Vol. I*, p. 236; *Ciano's Diary*, 10 March 1938, p. 87.

[4] Liebitzky's evidence, Schmidt-prot., p. 223.

[5] Hornbostel's and Liebitzky's evidence, Schmidt-prot., pp. 172, 223.

[6] Quoted in *Survey of International Affairs, 1938, Vol. I*, p. 203.

methods. As the British Ambassaor in Berlin commented, 'both in the wording of the question and in the manner in which the plebiscite was to be carried through, Schuschnigg seemed to have taken a leaf out of the Nazi book'.[1] The arrangements indeed left room for considerable doubt on the impartiality of the plebiscite. The voting age of twenty-four excluded those who for the most part formed the rank and file of the Nazi movement. No party elections had been held in Austria since 1930. A register of Austrians entitled to vote did not therefore exist, nor was it possible to prepare one within four days. The plebiscite slogan allowed for no alternative. And finally the election committees were formed only of representatives of the Fatherland Front.

Seyss-Inquart was uncertain what to do once Schuschnigg had informed him about the plebiscite. On the morning of 9 March, he decided to contact the Nazi leaders. But this step was unnecessary. The night before the news of the plebiscite had leaked out through Zernatto's secretary, who was a National Socialist. When Seyss-Inquart received the Nazi leaders Klausner, Globocznigg, Rainer, and Jury, they had full knowledge of the scheme. 'Is it true . . . ?' they asked, when they arrived in Seyss-Inquart's office. 'I am bound not to speak by my word of honour,' Seyss-Inquart replied, 'but we want to act as if it is true.'[2]

In their discussions the Austrian Nazis came to the conclusion that they could do nothing without Hitler's instructions. They resolved therefore upon two measures: to inform the Führer immediately, and to protest in a letter to Zernatto against the planned plebiscite, leaving the details of counter-measures subject to the Führer's decision. When Rainer telephoned to Berlin he got Keppler on the line, who immediately rushed to the *Reichskanzlei* and informed the Führer of the events in Austria. Schuschnigg's sudden change from the timid person whom Hitler had himself handled at Berchtesgaden to a man determined on action appeared so incredible to Hitler that he refused to believe the news. He went to the door, called his pilot, told him to get an aircraft, and sent Keppler right away to Vienna, where he should inform himself personally:[3] should the news be true Keppler was to try and prevent the plebiscite; if this proved impossible, he was to

---

[1] Henderson to Halifax, 10 March 1938, BrD, 3rd Ser., Vol. I, No. 4.
[2] Rainer's speech, Doc. 4005–PS, IMT, 'The Ministries Case', Vol. XII, p. 674.
[3] Keppler's evidence, ibid., p. 768.

insist on the addition to the plebiscite of a question on the Anschluss.[1]

Shortly after Keppler's plane had taken off, Globocznigg arrived from Vienna with full details of the situation. But no further decisions were taken on 9 May. Hitler waited for the result of Keppler's mission. Glaise-Horstenau was at this time in Germany, and after he heard Schuschnigg's announcement over the radio in the evening had immediately betaken himself to Berlin. During the night of 9 March he had a discussion of two and a half hours with Hitler, in which Hitler rambled on in his usual fashion without committing himself to any plan.[2]

Next morning, 10 March, at about 10 o'clock, Keppler arrived back at the *Reichskanzlei*. He had nothing new to tell. However, after Hitler had listened to his report, he called for Keitel and other generals and declared that he was not going to tolerate the plebiscite. Keitel informed the Führer of the existence of an operational order, which had been prepared for the eventuality of a German retaliation against a return of Otto of Habsburg to Austria. This directive was now adopted for the present situation as *Sonderfall Otto*.[3]

While the army improvised details for an immediate invasion of Austria, Hitler gave two orders: one directed to the Austrian Nazi leaders, the other to Seyss-Inquart. During the afternoon of 10 March, he sent Globocznigg back to Vienna with the announcement that he gave the Austrian Nazis freedom of action and would back them in everything they did.[4] In the evening he dictated a letter to Seyss-Inquart ordering him to demand from Schuschnigg the postponement of the plebiscite and new arrangements which would make a National Socialist vote possible.[5] The second order supplemented the first. By giving the party freedom of action Hitler hoped to exert the necessary pressure on Schuschnigg to obtain a plebiscite on his own terms. However, the main threat was contained in the letter to Seyss-Inquart. Hitler let it be clearly understood that he would take

[1] Weizsäcker to Ribbentrop, 9 March 1938, GD, Ser. D, Vol. I, No. 339; Keppler's affidavit, Doc. 3248–PS, IMT, Case 11. 'The Ministries Case', Doc. Book, No. 2, p. 116.

[2] Glaise-Horstenau's evidence, IMT, Part 16, p. 178.

[3] Doc. C–175, NCA, Vol. VI, p. 1010.

[4] Rainer's report, Doc. 812–PS, NCA, Vol. III, p. 594.

[5] Seyss-Inquart's memorandum, 3254–PS, NCA, Vol. V, p. 981.

military action if Schuschnigg did not comply with his demand. He enclosed the necessary pretext for an intervention; the draft of a telegram to be sent by Seyss-Inquart asking for German intervention. Finally there was a time-limit attached to the demands: Schuschnigg had to reach a decision by noon on 11 March.[1]

Next morning, 11 March, Seyss-Inquart went to the Vienna airport, where he received Hitler's letter from a courier, and Glaise-Horstenau, who brought the latest news from Berlin. Seyss-Inquart and Glaise-Horstenau read Hitler's message in the car while driving to Schuschnigg, to whom they presented Hitler's demands. Their discussion dragged on until 11.30 a.m. Seyss-Inquart therefore extended the time-limit on his own initiative until 2 o'clock in the afternoon.[2]

The next step Seyss-Inquart and Gleise-Horstenau took was to inform Klausner and the other Austrian Nazi leaders of their conversation. The Austrian Nazis thereupon realized that they would be deprived of any initiative if Schuschnigg's probable concessions appeared to result solely from the German threat. In a vain attempt to assert themselves they sent Schuschnigg an ultimatum of their own, which in its contents simply repeated Hitler's terms.

Confronted with this ultimatum from two sources Schuschnigg decided to cancel the plebiscite. He consulted some of his ministers, among them Zernatto and Schmidt, and the Federal President, and then informed Seyss-Inquart and Glaise-Horstenau at 2 o'clock that the plebiscite had been called off.[3]

In Berlin the Führer had in the meantime waited for a reply to his ultimatum. He was ignorant of the extension of the ultimatum by Seyss-Inquart and that is probably the reason why he signed, at 1 o'clock, directive No. 1 for the operation *Otto*. But even then Hitler had not finally decided upon action. His order stated that he intended to 'invade Austria with armed forces to establish constitutional conditions and to prevent further outrages against the pro-German population'. But wavering as always he retracted at the end of the phrase. This order was only

---

[1] Seyss-Inquart's affidavit, Doc. 3254–PS, NCA, Vol. V, p. 981.
[2] See Mackensen to Ribbentrop, 11 March 1938, GD, Ser. D, Vol. I, No. 342; Seyss-Inquart's testimony, IMT, Part 16, pp. 164–166.
[3] Seyss-Inquart's affidavit, Doc. 2996–PS, NCA, Vol. V, p. 713.

to be enforced, 'if other measures prove unsuccessful'.[1] He added that the forces detailed 'must be ready for action on 12 March at the latest from 12.00 hours'. Another order by Hitler gave a direction for policy if Czechoslovakian or Italian troops were encountered on Austrian territory: Czechoslovak military units were to be regarded as enemies, Italians as friends.[2]

When Göring rang up Seyss-Inquart at 2.45 p.m. to find out how things stood, Seyss-Inquart told him that Schuschnigg had given in and called off the plebiscite.[3] This should have made further pressure unnecessary but Göring, at this moment, had 'the instinctive feeling that the situation had become mobile and that now, finally, the possibility was there of bringing about a total solution'.[4] The measures taken by Schuschnigg were in no way satisfactory, he told Seyss-Inquart, and though he 'could not commit himself officially he would take a clear stand very shortly'.

The reason why Göring hesitated was that he had first to converse with Hitler on the situation created by Schuschnigg's compliance. When he returned to the telephone after twenty minutes, a new line of action had been decided upon. Schuschnigg's last concession served as a springboard for the next demand: Schuschnigg's resignation. And as a matter of course, Göring added, 'an immediate commission by the Federal President for Seyss-Inquart to form a new cabinet would have to follow Schuschnigg's resignation'. Seyss-Inquart was told to send the telegram which had been enclosed in Hitler's letter. And in order to leave nothing to chance, Keppler was now sent to Vienna with a list of the ministers who had to be included in Seyss-Inquart's future cabinet.

Faced with this new ultimatum Vienna made a last minute attempt to obtain foreign help. During the afternoon of 11 March the British, French, and Italian Ministers asked their governments, what the Austrian Chancellor should do.[5] At 4.30 p.m.

---

[1] Doc. C–102, NCA, Vol. VI, pp. 911–912; Jodl's diary, 11 March 1938, Doc. 1780–PS, NCA, Vol. IV, p. 362.

[2] Doc. C–103, NCA, Vol. VI, p. 913.

[3] Transcripts of telephone conversation prepared by Göring's *Forschungsamt*, Doc. 2949–PS (hereafter quoted as 'telephone transcripts'), NCA, Vol. V, p. 629.

[4] Göring's testimony, IMT, Part 9, pp. 103–104.

[5] Palairet to Halifax, 11 March 1938, BrD, 3rd Ser., Vol. I, No. 19.

Lord Halifax's reply arrived, saying that the British government 'cannot take responsibility of advising the Chancellor to take any course of action which might expose his country to dangers to which His Majesty's Government are unable to guarantee protection'.[1] Mussolini likewise refused to commit himself in any way.

Paris was paralysed by a governmental crisis, but nevertheless tried to take the initiative. Knowing that London refused to cooperate unless Rome participated, Paris approached the Italian government. The French Chargé d'Affaires asked Ciano by phone for an interview in order to discuss the Austrian appeal. Ciano made it clear that there was no point in talking: 'If he had nothing else to say, he need not come at all.'[2]

These appeals from Vienna were made against Schuschnigg's better judgement. He did not think it necessary to wait for their results. 'Help from outside seemed to him completely undesirable. Bloodshed and civil strife was just what he wanted to avoid.' He would not 'call for help and shoulder the responsibility for a war'. Moreover, he felt that military resistance would be hopeless: 'Two days later the masses in Vienna would have shouted their gratitude to the Führer just as though we had not resisted.'[3] When, therefore, Seyss-Inquart submitted Göring's ultimatum he handed in his resignation, which was accepted by the President at 3.30 p.m. Schuschnigg promised, however, to continue in office provisionally until a new Chancellor had been appointed.[4]

After Schuschnigg's resignation Göring concentrated on the second part of his demand: the appointment of Seyss-Inquart as Chancellor. But to this came unexpected resistance from the President. Miklas refused to have Seyss-Inquart forced upon him. Rather than accept German dictation, he wanted to let force take its course and, for the moment, anyhow, he believed Göring was still bluffing.[5] But he found the appointment of a suitable successor to Schuschnigg impossible. Skubl, Ender, and finally General von Schilhawsky, the Inspector of the Army, were approached, but they all refused the task. This failure did not alter

[1] Halifax to Palairet, 11 March 1938, BrD, 3rd Ser., Vol. I, No. 25.
[2] *Ciano's Diary*, 11 March 1938, p. 87.
[3] *Austrian Requiem*, pp. 48, 201.
[4] Schuschnigg's affidavit, Doc. 2996–PS, NCA, Vol. V, p. 715; Seyss-Inquart's testimony, IMT, Part 16, p. 76.
[5] Miklas's evidence, Schmidt-prot., p. 261.

Miklas's determination to reject the appointment of Seyss-Inquart. Consequently Austria was left without a government for the next hours.

Miklas's obstinacy threatened to disturb the German plans. Aware of the importance of public opinion and the necessity of a legal façade, Hitler, in contrast to Göring, refused to install Seyss-Inquart by military means. Miklas's determination to strip away this façade was a serious obstacle to Hitler's policy. When therefore during the afternoon of 11 March, the message came from Vienna that Seyss-Inquart had been appointed, Hitler expressed relief. At 6 p.m. he withdrew the orders to the troops. Austria was not to be invaded after all.[1]

But he triumphed too soon. An hour later it turned out that the news had been false. President Miklas continued in his resistance to Seyss-Inquart's appointment. Göring again telephoned to Vienna and instructed Seyss-Inquart:

Please, do inform us immediately about Miklas's position. Tell him, there is no time now for any joke. . . . The invasion will be stopped and the troops will be held at the border only if we are informed by 7.30 that Miklas has entrusted you with the Federal Chancellorship.[2]

This new time-limit was now approaching. Miklas did not change his position. Hitler, however, still wavered on what he should do.

The evidence suggests that Hitler continued to hope he could repeat his *coup* of Berchtesgaden and obtain Austria's *Gleichschaltung* without using direct force. The question foremost on his mind was what Mussolini's reaction to the changes in Austria would be. During the course of 11 March he therefore decided to send Philip of Hesse with a personal letter to the Duce. The main purpose of this letter was to plead for Mussolini's understanding, so that Hitler could have his way in Austria without losing the Duce's friendship. Mussolini had to comprehend, Hitler wrote, 'his determination to restore law and order in his homeland, and enable the people to decide their fate according to their judgement in an unmistakable, clear, and open manner'.[3]

Together with Göring, Hess, Bormann, von Neurath, von Papen, and other high officials Hitler sat in the smoking-room

---

[1] Johl's diary, 11 March 1938, loc. cit., p. 362. Papen, *Memoirs*, p. 429; Affidavit of Altenburg, IMT, 'The Ministries Case', Vol. XII, p. 781.

[2] Telephone Transcript, loc. cit., p.. 535–536.

[3] GD, Ser. D, Vol. I, No. 352.

of the *Reichskanzlei* during the afternoon of 11 March. They waited for Mussolini's answer to Hitler's letter and the high tension in the room was increased by the fact that the telephone apparatus had broken down in the smoking room, so that for every conversation with Vienna Hitler and Göring had to go to the switchboard, some distance away. Major-General von Grolmann, one of the eye-witnesses, relates:[1]

When it was already dark Hitler was called to the telephone booth and I saw Göring push in with him. When they came out again Göring was talking excitedly to Hitler and while they were on their way back to the sitting room Hitler, who had previously been listening thoughtfully to Göring, suddenly slapped his thigh, threw his head back and said: 'Now for it.' At once Göring rushed off and called Bodenschatz about bringing the Luftwaffe into action and from then on the orders followed thick and fast.

Hitler had changed his mind once again and overcome his fears as far as Mussolini was concerned. Jodl noted in his diary: '20.30 hours: Briefing received ... that the situation has changed once more. The occupation will take place.'[2] At 20.45 Hitler's order went out that the entry of the German armed forces into Austria should commence at daybreak on 12 March.[3]

In Vienna, in the meantime, the Austrian Nazis did not hesitate to use the threat of German armed intervention to bring themselves to power, yet they were dismayed to learn that the entry of German troops might become a reality. Quite rightly they anticipated that their own rule would not outlive the presence of German troops on Austrian territory. This necessitated a two-faced policy. They had to produce the impression that the military pressure was genuine and to prevent the execution of the threat at the same time. Göring's pressure for a radical solution was therefore most unwelcome to them.

At 5 p.m. on 11 March, Rainer and Globocznigg went to the German legation and spoke with Göring on the phone. Globocznigg made it clear that 'the independence of Austria should be maintained, but that everything else should be ruled on a National Socialist basis'. Moreover, he requested that the Austrian Legion

---

[1] Affidavit of Wilhelm von Grolmann, Case 11, Doc. Book 3 Keppler, Doc. No. 77, pp. 41–43.
[2] Doc. 1780–PS, NCA, Vol. IV, p. 363.
[3] Doc. C–182, NCA, Vol. VI, p. 1017.

would not be sent from Germany immediately, but only later, after a plebiscite had been arranged.[1]

The fact that Göring ignored these demands made the Austrian Nazi leaders still more suspicious. In the evening hours of 11 March they came to the conclusion that they could only forestall the entry of German troops by taking over power on their own account. At 7.30 p.m. Göring's ultimatum expired without German troops crossing the border. It was high time for them to act, if they wanted to exploit the threat of invasion. Rainer therefore declared: 'We must use the moment when the government believes that the march is on for action. I will give the order for the seizure of power.'[2]

This decision led to a clash with Keppler, who was there in Vienna to represent the interests of Berlin. In his opinion the party had to confine itself to the task of creating a pretext for an invasion, everything else had to be left to the Führer. But Rainer overruled Keppler. An estimate of their strength by the Austrian Nazi leaders showed that they could mobilize 6,000 SA-men and 500 SS-men. They issued the first order at about 8 p.m.; fifty SS-men, many of whom had already taken part in the *putsch* of 25 July 1934, received the task of occupying the Chancellery.

Though orders had been already issued by Hitler, he still insisted that the entry into Austria had to take place on the basis of a request by the Austrian government. Since Miklas refused to make Seyss-Inquart Chancellor, no government which could send such an appeal existed. Göring found a solution. Though the government had abdicated, he declared on the phone to Muff in Vienna, Seyss-Inquart himself remained. He should stay in office, and carry out necessary measures in the name of the government. Half an hour later, at 8.48 p.m., Göring instructed Keppler on the kind of measure that was expected from Seyss-Inquart. He dictated to Keppler the draft of a telegraphic appeal which requested the German government 'to send troops as soon as possible'. Göring added almost as an afterthought: 'Well, he does not even have to send the telegram – all he needs to do, is to say: agreed.'[3]

But Seyss-Inquart had already refused to send the telegram

---

[1] Telephone Transcript, loc. cit., pp. 630–633.
[2] Rainer's speech, IMT, 'The Ministries Case', Vol. XII, p. 676.
[3] Telephone Transcript, loc. cit., pp. 638–641.

which had been enclosed as a draft in Hitler's letter. He had not changed his position in the meantime.[1] While Göring went to a ball at the *Haus der Flieger* his adjutants continued the efforts to obtain Seyss-Inquart's appeal. Finally General Bodenschatz telephoned to Keppler in Vienna and told him that Göring needed the telegram urgently. Keppler saw no way out. Without having obtained Seyss-Inquart's consent Keppler gave the cue: 'Tell the General Field-Marshal that Seyss-Inquart agrees.'

When Göring could tell Hitler that the Austrian government had made the request, it was not the only load taken off Hitler's shoulders. In Rome Philip of Hesse had found at 9 p.m. a chance to talk with the Duce, who told him that 'Italy is following events with absolute calm'.[2] Coming from the Palazzo Venezia Philip of Hesse immediately telephoned the Führer at 10.25 p.m. Hitler could hardly control his enthusiasm:

Tell Mussolini I will never forget this. . . . Never, never, never, whatever happens. . . . If he should ever need any help or be in any danger, he can be convinced that I shall stick to him, whatever may happen, even if the whole world be against him.

Mussolini's disinterest meant that no precautions were needed. New orders went out. The march into Austria was to take place not with warlike equipment but in a peaceful manner.

Meanwhile in Vienna the Austrian Nazis were engaged in the actual job of taking over power. They had surrounded the Chancellery and forty SS-men had found access to the Chancellery itself. Finally, at about midnight, President Miklas gave in. He consented to the appointment of Seyss-Inquart to the Chancellorship and signed the new list of ministers. Having taken over power the Austrian Nazis no longer needed the threat of an invasion, and even less the invasion itself. At 2 o'clock in the morning, therefore, Seyss-Inquart made an attempt to stop the march of German troops. At his request Muff rang up Berlin demanding that 'the alerted troops should remain on, but not cross the border. If this had occurred at any point, they should be withdrawn'. Weizsäcker had Hitler woken up; but Hitler replied that it was too late to cancel the military orders.[3] Knowing that he could act without risk he saw no need to change his decision.

[1] Seyss-Inquart's memorandum, Doc. 3254–PS, NCA, Vol. V, p. 984.
[2] *Ciano's Diary*, 12 March 1938, p. 87.
[3] Weizsäcker, *Memoirs*, p. 122.

On the morning of 12 March German troops rolled over the border into Austria. They were welcomed by an enthusiastic population. Hitler crossed the border – as a symbolic gesture – near Braunau am Inn, his birthplace, at 3.50 p.m. From there he drove to Linz and was received by Seyss-Inquart, the new Austrian Chancellor. Hitler had originally intended to keep Austria independent and only to establish through his person a union in the direction of the most important acts of government between Austria and Germany. He later claimed that the overwhelming reception of the Austrian population had convinced him that the Austrian people would be disappointed if he did not immediately carry through the Anschluss.[1]

But the feelings of the Austrians were only of importance to Hitler as long as they served his purpose. His real motives were far less emotional. When he realized to his surprise that he could get Austria without firing a shot, he took his chance and decided upon the annexation. In a conversation with Austrian Nazi leaders during lunch in Linz, on 13 March, Hitler revealed his motives.[2] At about 3 p.m. he suddenly took out his watch and declared: 'At this moment an important law is being issued. Article one reads "Austria is a province of the German Reich"!' When asked how Europe would react, Hitler replied:

England has sent me a protest. I would have understood a declaration of war; to a protest I shall not even reply. France is completely preoccupied with her internal affairs and cannot act alone . . . For Italy this is a serious political change. But Italy is our friend and Mussolini a statesman of great stature who knows and comprehends that there can be no other development.[3]

The law concerning the union of Austria with Germany provided for a plebiscite on the union. When the votes were cast, 99·08 per cent voted in its favour. Twenty years had elapsed since the break-up of the Austro-Hungarian Empire had brought the Austrian state into existence – very much against its own will. Whereas in 1919 the Austrian constitution had foreseen that 'German-Austria should be a constituent part of the German

[1] Affidavit of Generalfeldmarschall Milch, IMT, Case 11, 'The Ministries Case', Book 3 Keppler, No. 96, pp. 27–30.

[2] Langoth's memorandum of the conversation, printed in Langoth, op. cit., pp. 239–242.

[3] Memorandum by Langoth of the conversation, Langoth, op. cit., pp. 239–242.

Reich,[1] this law was dictated by Hitler in 1938. The right of self-determination was only applied after the annexation. One may question whether history between the two World Wars would have taken a different course, if conciliation had prevailed and Austria and Germany had been united twenty years earlier. No answer exists to this speculation. However, one is left regretting that the Austrian people's desire for an Anschluss was never considered in its own right, but was simply used in the game of power politics.

The paradox remains that whereas the Anschluss had been a principal aim of German policy, Hitler achieved it almost against his own will. Wishing to pursue a policy of legality, as he had done in the domestic sphere on his way to power in Germany, Hitler had adjusted himself to a long-term policy in Austria. He insisted again and again on elections and the participation of the Austrian Nazis in the government. Since he knew the relative strength of the Nazi movement, he had no need to fear democratic methods. The annexation of March 1938 was forced upon him by events. Schuschnigg's desperate decision to stem the tide by a plebiscite on his own terms provoked a crisis in which Hitler, till the last moment, hoped to avoid military methods. And only when he found – to his own surprise – no resistance, he let himself be persuaded by Göring into the annexation. The success certainly left its mark on Hitler. He had become aware that his previous evolutionary methods could be speeded up by threats, and ultimately by force, without being challenged.

[1] *Staatsgesetzblatt für die Republik Österreich*, 1919, No. 174, p. 399.

BIBLIOGRAPHY

I. Documentary Material

A. *Unpublished Documents*

1. German Documents of the *Auswärtiges Amt*, Public Record Office, London:[1]

	Serial Numbers
Politische Beziehungen Frankreich-Tschecheslowakei	K16
Österreich: Ein- Aus- und Durchfuhr	K47
Die österreichisch-tschechoslowakische Zollunion	K48
Deutsch-österreichische Zollunion	K48
Deutsch-österreichische Zollunion: Dokumente (Abschriften) zur Vorgeschichte, Einleitung und Ausführung sowie zum Abbruch der Aktion.	K49
Briefwechsel des Staatssekretärs von Bülow mit Regendanz	K50
Material für den Besuch des Herrn Reichsministers in Wien	K51
Deutsch-österreichische Aktion	K52
Allgemeine auswärtige Politik	K53
Politische Beziehungen Österreich-Deutschland einschliesslich der Anschlussfrage	K54
Die deutsch-österreichische Arbeitsgemeinschaft in München und die österreichisch-deutsche Arbeitsgemeinschaft in Wien	K55
Politische Beziehungen Österreich-Tschechoslowakei	K60
Deutsch-österreichische Zollunion	K1148
Italien: Allgemeine auswärtige Politik	1486
Reichskanzlei: Österreich	1549
Österreich: Politische Beziehungen zwischen Österreich und Deutschland	1744
England	2368
Frankreich	2406
Italien	2784
Österreich	3086
Abessinien	3088

[1] Photostats of German Foreign Office documents filmed as numbered serials will be cited by serial and frame numbers only.

	Serial Numbers
Akten der Botschaft Wien	4938
Politische Beziehungen Deutschland-Frankreich	5881
Politische Beziehungen Frankreich-Österreich	5975
Politische Beziehungen Italiens zu Deutschland	6001
Politische Beziehungen zwischen Italien und Ungarn (1927– 1935)	6057
Jugoslawien: Handelsvertragsverhältnisse zu Deutschland	6063
Die Sanierung der österreichischen Kreditanstalt	6075
Handelsvertragsverhältnis Österreichs zu Deutschland	6076
Österreich: Innere Politik, Oktober 1927–Mai 1936	6079
Berichte Papens an den Führer, 1934–April 1936	6081
Nationalsozialismus in Österreich	6111
Nationalsozialistische Terrorakte	6112
Intervention Englands, Frankreichs und Italiens	6113
Österreich; Nationalsozialistische Verhandlungen für ein Abkommen, 1933–Mai 1936	6114
Österreichische Legion	6115
Zwischenstaatliche Beziehungen: Kleine Entente	6192
Donaupakt, April 1935–März 1936	7826
Italien, 1.2.34–31.12.35 (Neue Reichskanzlei)	8035
Italien und Jugoslawien, 30.3.30–25.3.36	8047
Italien-Österreich, 8.8.30–25.5.36	8048
Die italienisch-ungarischen Besprechungen in Rom im März 1934	8051
Italienische Aussenpolitik; Allgemein	8073
Politische Beziehungen zwischen Österreich und Deutschland (1932–1936)	8643

2. Documents of 'The Ministries Case', No. 11 (von Weizsäcker and 20 others), before U.S. Military Tribunal at Nuremberg, November 1947–April 1949.

B. *Published Documents*

Beiträge zur Vorgeschichte und Geschichte der Julirevolte. Herausgegeben auf Grund amtlicher Quellen, Vienna, 1934.

Ciano's Diplomatic Papers, edit. by Malcolm Muggeridge, London, 1948.

Der Hochverratsprozess gegen Guido Schmidt vor dem Wiener Volksgerichtshof. Die gerichtlichen Protokolle mit den Zeugenaussagen, unveröffentlichten Dokumenten, sämtlichen Geheimbriefen und Geheimakten, Vienna, 1947.

o

Die Deutsche Nationalversammlung im Jahre 1919. Herausgageben von Prof. Heilfron, 1–8, Band, Berlin.

Documentary Background of World War II, 1931–1941. Compiled and edited by James W. Gantenbein, New York, 1949.

Documents of British Foreign Policy, 1919–1939. First Series, Vol. I; Second Series, Vol. I–VI; Third Series, Vol. I. H.M.S.O., London, 1946–57.

Documents on German Foreign Policy, 1918–1945. Series C, Vol. I–III; Series D, Vol. I–V. H.M.S.O., 1949–59.

Documents on International Affairs, 1931–1938, Oxford University Press, for R.I.I.A., 1932–41.

Foreign Relations of the United States, Diplomatic Papers, 1931–1938. Washington, 1946–55.

Great Britain. *Parliamentary Debates.* Official Report, House of Commons.

I Documenti Diplomatici Italiani 1921–1935, Settima Serie, Vol. III, Rome, 1959.

Journal Officiel de la République Française. Débats Parlementaires. Année 1930 et 1931.

League of Nations: *The Restoration of Austria.* Agreements arranged by the League of Nations and Signed at Geneva on 4 October 1922, with the Relevant Documents and Statements. Geneva, 1922.

Treaty Series, Vol. XII, No. 334. *Restoration of Austria.* Protocol No. I, II, III. Geneva, 1922.

The economic situation of Austria. Reports presented to the Council of the League of Nations by W. T. Layton, C.H., and Charles Rist. Geneva, 19 August 1925.

The Financial Reconstruction of Austria. Geneva, November 1926.

Official Journal. 12th Year, No. 7. Minutes of the 63rd Session of the Council. 18–23 May 1931. Geneva.

Documents relating to the Organization of a System of European Federal Union. Geneva, 15 September 1930.

Les Deliberations du Conseil des Quatre (24 Mars–28 Juin 1919), Notes de l'Officier Interprête Paul Mantoux, Vol. I–II, Paris, 1955.

Nazi Conspiracy and Aggression, 8 volumes and 2 supplementary volumes, A and B. Washington, 1946–48.

The Death of Dollfuss. An official history of the revolt of July 1934, in Austria. Translated by J. Messinger, London, 1935.

The Speeches of Adolf Hitler, 1922–1939, edited by Norman H. Baynes, Vols. I and II. Oxford University Press, 1942.

The Treaty of St. Germain. A Documentary History of its Territorial and Political Clauses. Hoover War Library Publications.

The Trial of German Major War Criminals, Parts 9–22, London, 1946–1950.

Trial of the Major War Criminals before the International Military Tribunal; Documents in Evidence, Volumes XXIV–XLII; Nuremberg, 1947–49.

Trials of War Criminals before the Nuremberg Military Tribunals, Case 11, Volume XII, 'The Ministries Case', Nuremberg, October 1946–April 1949.

C. *Newspapers*

The references to *The Times* are taken from my direct consultation of its files. The other newspapers I have seen in the form of quotations in the German Embassy reports or in the form of cuttings in the files of the German Foreign Office, unless otherwise indicated.

II. Memoirs and Diaries

Lord D'Abernon, *An Ambassador of Peace*, London, 1929.

Filippo Anfuso, *Die beiden Gefreiten*, Munich, 1952.

Count Ciano, *Ciano's Diary, 1937–1938*, London, 1952.

Robert Coulondre, *De Staline à Hitler*, Berlin 1936–40, Paris, 1950.

Julius Curtius, *Bemühung um Österreich*, Heidelberg, 1947.

    Sechs Jahre Minister der deutschen Republik, Heidelberg, 1948.

Hugh Dalton, *Call Back Yesterday*, London, 1953.

Herbert von Dirksen, *Moskau, Tokio, London*, Stuttgart, 1949.

André François-Poncet, *De Versailles à Potzdam*, Paris, 1948.

    Souvenir d'une ambassade à Berlin, Paris, 1946.

G. E. R. Gedye, *Fallen Bastions*, London, 1939.

Sir Nevile Henderson, *Failure of a Mission*, London, 1940.

Edouard Herriot, *Jadis*, Paris, 1952.

Herbert Hoover, *The Great Depression*, London, 1953.

Erich Kordt, *Wahn und Wirklichkeit*, Stuttgart, 1947.

    Nicht aus den Akten, Stuttgart, 1950.

Franz Langoth, *Kampf um Österreich*, Wels, 1951.

Robert Lansing, *The Peace Negotiations*, London, 1921.

Otto Meissner, *Staatssekretär unter Ebert, Hindenburg, Hitler*, Hamburg, 1950.

Franz von Papen, *Memoirs*, London, 1952.

Karl Renner, *Österreich von der ersten zur zweiten Republik*, Vienna, 1953.

Anton Rintelen, *Erinnerungen an Österreichs Weg*, Munich, 1941.

Paul Schmidt, *Als Statist auf der diplomatischen Bühne*, Bonn, 1949.

Kurt von Schuschnigg, *Ein Requiem in Rot-Weiss-Rot*, Zurich, 1946.

    Austrian Requiem, New York, 1946.

    Farewell Austria, London, 1939.

Prince Starhemberg, *Between Hitler and Mussolini*, London, 1942.
Edgar Stern-Rubarth, *Drei Manner suchen Europa*, Munich, 1947.
Gustav Stresemann, *Vermächtnis*, Berlin, 1932.
André Tardieu, *La Paix*, Paris, 1922.
Viscount Templewood, *Nine Troubled Years*, London, 1954.
Lord Vansittart, *The Mist Procession*, London, 1958.
Ernst von Weizsäcker, *Memoirs*, London, 1951.
Franz Winkler, *Die Diktatur in Österreich*, Zürich, 1935.
Guido Zernatto, *Die Wahrheit über Österreich*, New York, 1938.

III. Secondary Works

Earl of Avon, *The Eden Memoirs: Facing the Dictators*, London, 1962.
Margaret Ball, *Post-War German–Austrian Relations*, London, 1937.
Antonin Basch, *The Danube Basin and the German Economic Sphere*, London, 1944.
E. D. Baumgärtner, *Die österreichische Presse in ihrer Stellungnahme zur Anschlussfrage*, Dissertation, Vienna, 1950.
Edward W. Bennett, *Germany and the Diplomacy of the Financial Crisis, 1931*, Harvard University Press, Cambridge, U.S.A. 1962.
Karl Bracher, *Die Auflösung der Weimarer Republik*, Stuttgart, 1957.
Heinrich Benediktaus (Hergeber), *Geschichte der Republik Österreich*, Munich, 1954.
Julius Braunthal, *The Tragedy of Austria*, London, 1948.
Gordon Brook-Shepherd, *Dollfuss*, London, 1961.
  Anschluss: The Rape of Austria, London, 1963.
Alan Bullock, *Hitler, A Study in Tyranny*, London, 1955.
Joseph Buttinger, *Am Beispiel Österreichs*, Cologne, 1953.
Boris Celovsky, *Das Münchener Abkommen von 1938*, Stuttgart, 1958.
R. T. Clark, *The Fall of the German Republic*, London, 1935.
N. Clough, *Beiträge zur Beurteilung der österreichischen Anschlussfrage in öffentlichen Meinung der Vereinigten Staaten Nordamerikas*, Dissertation, Heidelberg, 1933.
Muriel Currey, *Italian Foreign Policy, 1918–1932*, London, 1932.
Gordon A. Craig and Felix Gilbert (eds.), *The Diplomats, 1919–1939*, New York, 1953.
Hugh Dalton, *Towards the Peace of Nations*, London, 1928.
S. Davis, *The British Labour Party and British Foreign Policy, 1933–39*, Ph.D. thesis, London, 1950.
Oswald Dutch, *Thus Died Austria*, London, 1938.
Ulrich Eichstädt, *Von Dollfuss zu Hitler*, Wiesbaden, 1955.
Erich Eyck, *Geschichte der Weimarer Republik*, Zürich, 1956.
Keith Feiling, *The Life of Neville Chamberlain*, London, 1946.

Robert Ferrel, *American Diplomacy in the Great Depression*, London, 1957.

Martin Fuchs, *Showdown in Vienna*, New York, 1939.

Franz Gartner, *Der Plan einer deutsch-österreichischen Zollunion und die Wiener Presse*, Dissertation, Vienna, 1949.

G. M. Gathorne-Hardy, *A Short History of International Affairs, 1920–1939*, London, 1950.

Charles A. Gulick, *Austria: From Habsburg to Hitler*, Berkeley, University of California Press, 1948.

James Joll (ed.), *The Decline of the Third Republic*, London, 1959.

Fr. Kleinwaechter und H. v. Paller (Herausgeber), *Die Anschlussfrage in ihrer kulturellen, politischen und wirtschaftlichen Bedeutung*, Vienna, 1930.

Ralf Koerner, *So haben sie es damals gemacht, Die Propagandavorbereitungen zum Österreichanschluss durch das Hitlerregime*, Vienna, 1958.

Jan Krulis-Randa, *Das deutsch-österreichische Zollunionsprojekt von 1931*, Zürich, 1955.

Mary Macdonald, *The Republic of Austria*, Oxford University Press, 1946.

Robert Machray, *The Struggle for the Danube and the Little Entente*, London, 1938.

Roger Manvell and Heinrich Fraenkel, *Hermann Göring*, London, 1962.

Henry Cord Mayer, *Mitteleuropa in the German Thought and Action*, The Hague, 1955.

Gerhard Meinck, *Hitler und die deutsche Aufrüstung*, Wiesbaden, 1959.

Friedrich Meinecke, *Die deutsche Katastrophe*, Wiesbaden, 1946.

L. B. Namier, *Diplomatic Prelude*, London, 1948.
Europe in Defeat, London, 1950.
In the Nazi Era, London, 1952.

H. Rönnefarth, *Deutschland und England; ihre diplomatischen Beziehungen vor und während der Sudetenkrise, November 1937–September 1938*, Dissertation, Göttingen, 1951.

Massimo Magistrati, *L'Italia a Berlino, 1937–1939*, Rome, 1956.

Gaetano Salvemini, *Prelude to World War II*, London, 1953.
Mussolini Diplomatico, Bari, 1951.

Rudolf Schlesinger, *Central European Democracy and its Background*, London, 1953.

A. J. P. Taylor, *The Origins of the Second World War*, London, 1961.

A. Tautscher (Herausgeber), *So Sprach der Kanzler, Dollfuss Vermächtnis*, Vienna, 1935.

Arnold J. Toynbee (ed.), *Survey of International Affairs, 1930–1938*, Oxford University Press for R.I.I.A., 1933–41.

Otto Wedel, *Die deutsch-österreichische Zollunion im Spiegel der reichsdeutschen Presse*, Dissertation, Heidelberg, 1937.

J. W. Wheeler-Bennett, *Information on the Problem of Security*, London, 1927.

Disarmament and Security since Locarno, London, 1932.

Munich, Prologue to Tragedy, London, 1948.

The Nemesis of Power, London, 1956.

Luigi Villari, *Italian Foreign Policy under Mussolini*, New York, 1956.

Elizabeth Wiskemann, *The Rome–Berlin Axis*, Oxford University Press, 1949.

Ludwig Zimmermann, *Deutsche Aussenpolitik in der Ära der Weimarer Republik*, Göttingen, 1958.

IV. Articles

E. Anchieri, 'Les rapports italo-allemands pendant l'ère nazi-fasciste', *Revue d'Histoire de la Deuxième Guerre Mondiale, Septième Année*, No. 26, Janvier, 1957.

W. C. Askew, 'The Secret Agreement between France and Italy on Ethiopia, January 1935', *The Journal of Modern History*, Vol. XXV, March, 1953.

Karl-Dietrich Bracher, 'Das Anfangsstadium der Hitlerschen Aussenpolitik', *Vierteljahreshefte für Zeitgeschichte*, 5, 1957.

Alfred Diamant, 'The Group Basis of Austrian Politics', *Journal of Central European Affairs*, Vol. XVIII, July, 1958.

Ernst Geigenmüller, 'Botschafter von Hoesch und der deutsche Zollunionsplan', *Historische Zeitschrift*, Vol. 195, 1962.

S. W. Gould, 'Austrian Attitudes toward Anschluss, October 1918–September 1919', *The Journal of Modern History*, Vol. XXII, September, 1950.

Herbert Gross, 'Industriewirtschaftliche Auswirkungen einer deutsch-österreichischen Zollunion', *Schriften des Weltwirtschaftsarchiv Kiel*, Vol. 34, 1931.

Oswald Hauser, 'Der Plan einer deutsch-österreichischen Zollunion und die Europaische Föderation', *Historische Zeitschrift*, Vol. 179, 1955.

J. B. Hoptner, 'Yugoslavia as Neutralist: 1937', *Journal of Central European Affairs*, Vol. XVI, July, 1956.

Arthur G. Kogan, 'Germany and the Germans of the Hapsburg Monarchy on the Eve of the Armistice 1918: Genesis of the Anschluss Problem', *Journal of Central European Affairs*, Vol. XX, April, 1960.

Massimo Magistrati, 'La Germania e l'impresa italiana di Etiopia', *Rivista di Studi Politici Internazionali*, a. XVII, 1950.

Walter Pese, 'Hitler und Italien 1920–1926', *Vierteljahreshefte für Zeitgeschichte'*, 3, 1955.

F. G. Stambrook, 'The German–Austrian Customs Union Project of 1931. A Study of German Methods and Motives', *Journal of Central European Affairs*, Vol. XXI, April, 1961.

Gustav Stolper, 'Die deutsche Zollunion', *Der Deutsche Volkswirt*, No. 26, 27, 28, 1931.

Paul R. Sweet, 'Democracy and Counter-revolution in Austria', *The Journal of Modern History*, Vol. XXII, March, 1950.

Thilo Vogelsang, 'Neue Dokumente zur Geschichte der Reichswehr', *Vierteljahreshefte für Zeitgeschichte*, 2, 1954.

D. C. Watt, 'The Anglo-German Naval Agreement of 1935; An Interim Judgement', *The Journal of Modern History*, Vol. XXVIII, June, 1956,

Gerhard L. Weinberg, 'Secret Hitler–Benes Negotiations in 1936–1937', *Journal of Central European Affairs*, Vol. XIX, January, 1960.

Henry Winkler, 'The Emergence of a Labour Foreign Policy in Great Britain, 1918–1929', *The Journal of Modern History*, Vol. XXVIII, September, 1956.

INDEX